# Google Workspace User Guide

A practical guide to using Google Workspace apps efficiently while integrating them with your data

**Balaji Iyer**

BIRMINGHAM—MUMBAI

# Google Workspace User Guide



**Associate Group Product Manager**: Alok Dhuri
**Publishing Product Manager**: Aaron Tanna
**Senior Editor**: Mark D'Souza
**Content Development Editor**: Rakhi Patel
**Technical Editor**: Simran Udasi
**Copy Editor**: Safis Editing
**Project Coordinator**: Rashika Shetty
**Proofreader**: Safis Editing
**Indexer**: Tejal Soni
**Production Designer**: Shankar Kalbhor
**Marketing Coordinater**: Anamika Singh

First published: March 2022

Production reference: 1180222

Published by Packt Publishing Ltd.
Livery Place
35 Livery Street
Birmingham
B3 2PB, UK.

ISBN 978-1-80107-300-4

`www.packt.com`

*'Om shree guruve namah' – A Sanskrit mantra*

*I bow to all my masters who sculpted me.*

*Dedicated to my parents and in-laws for their sacrifices. To my wife, Sri, for sharing her life with me and juggling work/life to enable me to complete this book. And to my son, Adrith, who always keeps me young at heart.*

# Foreword

I have known Balaji Iyer for more than a decade now. From acquaintances to friends to conquering marathons to co-founding a company together, I have had the opportunity to get to know him personally and professionally. It gives me great pleasure in writing this foreword for yet another challenging undertaking from him.

Balaji is a big proponent for investing time and resources in the core competencies of a company, and leverage third party solutions for everything else. Google Workspace is one such great solution for small and big businesses. Being a technical evangelist and also having a strong background in cloud technologies, Identity management and security, Data Management, and implementing enterprise-wide technology solutions makes him the ideal person to author this book.

Tradelytics is powered by Google Workspace, and I have been a beneficiary of all the fantastic features Google Workspace brings to the market. Workspace is a boon for small and medium businesses. Its low cost of entry and user-based subscription model enables us to ramp up or ramp down licenses as needed and not have to worry about breaking the bank.

Whether you are new to Google Workspace or you are a power user, this book has you covered. This book is a comprehensive, in-depth work, laid out in a very easy to understand approach. He not only explains the different concepts and "how-to" of Google Workspace, but he has also covered the practical applications with case studies. With the exposure of AppScript and custom development, he helps the user address the gaps and use Workspace effectively. I strongly believe that this book would be a great companion to users looking to implement Google Workspace in their organization.

*Abhi Jeevaganambi*

*CEO, Tradelytics*

# Contributors

## About the author

**Balaji Iyer** is a technologist with a long career in designing and building applications, from the client-server era to the modern cloud era. He has built and expanded several applications at a global scale and currently leads engineering teams that build performant, reliable, and user-friendly products in the cloud. He is a certified Google Cloud Architect professional. He cares about connecting passion to purpose and is maniacal about simplifying technology so that it can reach the masses. Outside of technology, Balaji is fond of long-distance running and has a few full marathons under his belt. He also continues to play cricket and tennis on weekends and goes on long hikes with his son when time permits.

# About the reviewer

**Rancho Iyer** (she/her) is a customer engineering specialist at Google, helping customers plan their productivity and collaboration rollouts with immersive demonstrations of Google Cloud Identity and Google Workspace. She has worked at Google for 2+ years and brings 8+ years of Google deployment experience from across medium and large enterprises and organizations. She leads a chapter within Women@Google. Outside of work, she is an avid hiker and has taken up long-distance running.

*I would like to thank Packt for giving me the opportunity to review this book. I extend my gratitude to my family and mentors who have made me a better person.*

# Table of Contents


## Preface

## Part 1: Getting Started – Google Workspace

### 1
### Introducing Google Workspace

The evolution of Google Workspace 4
- Gmail 5
- Google Docs and Google Drive 5
- Google Apps for Business 6
- G Suite to Google Workspace 7
- Carbon-neutral data centers 8

Google Workspace – what's included? 9
- Additional Google services in Google Workspace 12

Google Workspace licensing models 12
- Google Workspace Education editions 12
- Google Workspace Business editions 15
- Google Workspace Enterprise editions 16

Choosing the right edition 19

Domain host versus Google Workspace 20
- What is a domain? 20
- What is the DNS? 21
- Secondary domains versus domain aliases 24

Summary 26

### 2
### Configuring Users and Apps

Google Cloud Identity and admin roles 28
- Cloud Identity features 29
- Cloud Identity editions 31

Configuring OUs in Cloud Identity 31

Configuring users in Cloud Identity 33

Adding users to Cloud Identity 34
Deleting users 36

Using Google Cloud Directory Sync (GCDS) 40
GCDS configurations 43

Managing licenses 45
How to enable automatic license assignment? 46
How to manually assign licenses to users? 47

Configuring applications in Workspace 47
Google Workspace core services 49
Google additional services 50
Enabling Gmail 51

Sharing resources via Calendar 53
Summary 54

# Part 2: Data Security

## 3
## Application Security

Context-Aware Access using Cloud Identity 58
Configuring Context-Aware Access 59

End-user security 60
Password monitoring 61
2-step verification 62

Single sign-on 63
Password vaulted apps 64
Secure LDAP 66

Google apps security 67
Gmail 68
Google Drive 72
Calendar 77
Google Chat 81
Google Meet 82
Sites 84
Vault 85
Other services 87
Marketplace apps 88

Summary 91

## 4
## Automated Security Auditing

Google Workspace security center 94
Security Health 95
Security dashboard 98
Security investigation tool 101

Data loss prevention 107
Creating a rule from a template 110
Alert center 112

Segregation of data by regions 116
Endpoint management 117

Mobile management 118

Automated device management 121

Reports 123

Summary 126

# Part 3: Data Integrations

## 5
## Beyond Workspace

Google Classroom 130
- Enabling Google Classroom 131
- Managing Google Classroom settings 132
- Grades and rosters 136
- Student unenrollment 136

Google Workspace Marketplace apps 137
- Managing Marketplace apps 140
- Add-ons for Google Workspace services 141
- Access control for third-party applications 145

Google Assistant for Google Workspace 152
- Nest Hub 153
- Enabling the Search and Assistant service 154

Using third-party clients 155
- Enabling access for mail clients 156
- Using Google Workspace Sync for Microsoft Outlook (GWSMO) 158

Accessibility for users 158

Summary 159

## 6
## Designing Custom Applications

Apps Script 162
- Hello World! 163
- Code editor 165
- Macros 166
- Creating a custom menu item 168
- Interactions with the Gmail and Sheets APIs 173
- Using Google Forms with Apps Script 177
- Adding Apps Script for Google Docs 180
- Creating a web application using Apps Script 182
- Apps Script security and best practices 185

AppSheet 186
- Enabling AppSheet 187
- Build an app using AppSheet 188

Summary 193

# Part 4: Migrating Data

## 7

## Data Migration

Data transfers within Google Workspace 198
User life cycle changes 198
Suspending users 199
Archiving users 201
Transferring user data 203
Transferring Google Drive content 203
Google Takeout 204
Data migration from external sources 210
Data migration service 211
Migrating a large amount of user data 219
Preparing the Workspace domain 220
Google Workspace Migration for Microsoft Exchange 220
Google Workspace Migrate (Beta) 224
Summary 225

## Business Case Studies

Case study #1 227
Case study #2 230

## Index

## Other Books You May Enjoy

# Preface

Picking a productivity suite for a company has become a multi-horse race recently, and the horse named Google Workspace is seemingly running faster and catching a lot of attention. A productivity suite has to get several areas right for it to be successful, including ease of collaboration, communication, user satisfaction, the ability to enable a remote/hybrid work culture, and the ability to access content from a variety of devices. Google Workspace seems to be to doing well in these areas and its user adoption has grown at a rapid pace in the last few years.

I'm always fascinated by technology and how Google builds products at a global scale. This book is an attempt to condense and highlight useful features in the vast universe of Google Workspace. This book also takes a peek under the hood of several features and demystifies how they operate in the real world.

I do hope you enjoy reading this book as much as I enjoyed writing it.

## Who this book is for

This book is for admins, as well as home users, business users, and power users looking to improve their efficiency while using Google Workspace. Basic knowledge of using Google Workspace services is assumed.

## What this book covers

*Chapter 1, Introducing Google Workspace*, gives an overview of Google Workspace, its history, and how it evolved over the years. This chapter also will introduce you to core services, the different Workspace editions and their capabilities, and how they help different types of businesses and educational institutions.

*Chapter 2, Configuring Users and Apps*, takes a detailed look at Google Cloud Identity and admin roles, how to get started with Workspace and set up an organization, and how to configure users in the organization. This chapter also talks about configuring applications and tie users and applications together.

*Chapter 3, Application Security*, showcases how to configure security to keep users and data safe in Google Workspace. It takes an in-depth look at the features available for end-user security, such as password monitoring and 2-step verification. It also examines the security features that are available for core services such as Gmail and Google Drive.

*Chapter 4, Automated Security Auditing*, talks about how Google Workspace enables enterprises to maintain a good compliance posture and tackle complex requirements for compliance standards such as **Peripheral Component Interconnect** (**PCI**) and the **General Data Protection Regulation** (**GDPR**). A detailed overview of the security center, along with a practical guide on how to use features like data protection and security rule configuration will be helpful for enterprise users that are looking to derive maximum utility from Google Workspace.

*Chapter 5, Beyond Workspace*, highlights non-core services in Workspace that can be beneficial for educational institutions and throws light on extending the capabilities of Workspace via Marketplace apps, how to integrate Google Assistant, and how to leverage accessibility features to make Workspace inclusive for everyone.

*Chapter 6, Designing Custom Applications*, walks through the automation capabilities that exist in Workspace. It introduces Apps Script, a development environment and scripting language that helps extend the functionality of Google Workspace services. It then moves on to introduce AppSheet, a low-code environment, and showcases how to build applications using AppSheet.

*Chapter 7, Data Migration*, illustrates pragmatic scenarios for data transfers triggered from within Google Workspace services. It lays out a blueprint for how to handle user life cycle changes and migrate data from other platforms to Google Workspace. This chapter also looks at the Google Takeout service, which allows users to import all of their data from over 50 Google services.

To tie together everything that we have learned in this book, we close with two business case studies attached as annexes to enable readers to synthesize the technology and business cases and learn how to make a pitch for moving to Google Workspace.

# To get the most out of this book

Google Workspace has several editions and some of the features discussed in this book are specific to certain editions as indicated where relevant in the book. Kindly ensure you are subscribed to the appropriate edition to take full advantage of the features and topics discussed here. This book also assumes that you are familiar with web applications and have used popular services such as Gmail. Also, while discussing the design of custom applications, a little familiarity with programming concepts and in particular introductory-level knowledge of JavaScript is assumed.

Since Google Workspace is **Software-as-a-Service** (**SaaS**), you can access all features via an internet browser. There is no need to install any software on your computer unless you are working on migrating data to Google Workspace from other platforms.

| Software/hardware covered in the book | Operating system requirements |
|---|---|
| Apps Script | Windows, macOS, or Linux |
| AppSheet | |
| Google Workspace Migration for Microsoft Exchange | |

**If you are using the digital version of this book, we advise you to type the code yourself or access the code from the book's GitHub repository (a link is available in the next section). Doing so will help you avoid any potential errors related to the copying and pasting of code.**

# Download the color images

We also provide a PDF file that has color images of the screenshots and diagrams used in this book. You can download it here: `https://static.packt-cdn.com/downloads/9781801073004_ColorImages.pdf`.

# Conventions used

There are a number of text conventions used throughout this book.

`Code in text`: Indicates code words in text, database table names, folder names, filenames, file extensions, pathnames, dummy URLs, user input, and Twitter handles. Here is an example: "The Apps Script code editor will launch in a new window with a default file named `code.gs`, prepopulated with a `myFunction()` function."

A block of code is set as follows:

```
function myFunction() {
 Browser.msgBox("Hello World")
}
```

**Bold**: Indicates a new term, an important word, or words that you see onscreen. For instance, words in menus or dialog boxes appear in **bold**. Here is an example: "Once happy with the options selected, users can then hit the **Create** button to generate a downloadable version of their data."

> **Tips or important notes**
> Appear like this.

# Get in touch

Feedback from our readers is always welcome.

**General feedback**: If you have questions about any aspect of this book, email us at `customercare@packtpub.com` and mention the book title in the subject of your message.

**Errata**: Although we have taken every care to ensure the accuracy of our content, mistakes do happen. If you have found a mistake in this book, we would be grateful if you would report this to us. Please visit `www.packtpub.com/support/errata` and fill in the form.

**Piracy**: If you come across any illegal copies of our works in any form on the internet, we would be grateful if you would provide us with the location address or website name. Please contact us at `copyright@packt.com` with a link to the material.

**If you are interested in becoming an author**: If there is a topic that you have expertise in and you are interested in either writing or contributing to a book, please visit `authors.packtpub.com`.

# Share Your Thoughts

Once you've read *Google Workspace User Guide*, we'd love to hear your thoughts! Scan the QR code below to go straight to the Amazon review page for this book and share your feedback.

`https://packt.link/r/1801073007`

Your review is important to us and the tech community and will help us make sure we're delivering excellent quality content.

# Part 1: Getting Started – Google Workspace

The objective of this part is to familiarize readers with Google Workspace and its services. This section will provide a high-level overview of the different products and services and will also give a brief introduction to its capabilities.

This part comprises the following chapters:

- *Chapter 1, Introducing Google Workspace*
- *Chapter 2, Configuring Users and Apps*

# 1
# Introducing Google Workspace

When running any business, whether it's a small start-up or a large enterprise with hundreds of thousands of employees, communication tools can allow effective collaboration and ensure the success of the company. Because the recent COVID-19 pandemic has accelerated the transition from in-person to remote work, there is more need than ever for a highly available, secure, and agile productivity suite. This new work environment has created a demand for an ecosystem of tools that team members can leverage to streamline their communication and collaboration. This book is about one of the most popular web-based productivity suites available today: **Google Workspace**.

Google Workspace is a collection of **software as a service** (**SaaS**)-based productivity and collaboration tools developed and marketed by Google.

In this chapter, we will give a brief overview of Google Workspace and how it came into being. This chapter will also introduce you to core services that exist in the Google Workspace portfolio. We will also learn about different Google Workspace editions and the differences between their offerings.

We will cover the following main topics:

- The evolution of Google Workspace
- Google Workspace editions
- Google Workspace licensing models
- Domain host versus Google Workspace

# The evolution of Google Workspace

As you may know, a **productivity suite** is a set of applications that includes apps for content management, writing documentation, processing voluminous data, communicating with your team members, and more. Traditionally, these applications were only available on desktops. However, several are now available as web applications that will let you connect from any device, anywhere. This model of distributing software – where a cloud provider hosts applications and makes them available to end users over the internet – is known as SaaS.

The market for SaaS-based productivity suites has grown steadily over the years, with big tech leading the way. After desktop-based productivity suites dominated the market for over two decades, companies started to understand their limitations for an evolving workforce. Desktop-based applications restrict users to specific computers, offering limited capabilities in terms of file sharing and real-time collaboration functionality. Overall, these may limit your work environment, and employees may feel siloed and frustrated.

In the not-so-distant past, imagine how a document may have been shared using one of these common ways:

- The document could have been saved and sent as an email attachment.
- The document could have been copied to a shared directory on the corporate network file system.
- The document could have been copied to a portable drive and physically handed to another user who required it.

Today, with business happening at the speed of light, all of these options are not scalable. For example, emails would frequently fail when email servers rejected attachments for being too large. Files had to be compressed before they could be sent, only for the recipient to receive a corrupted version on the other end.

Thankfully, those days are well behind us due to the power of the internet and the proliferation of cloud technologies.

Google is a pioneer and an internet-first company that started building scalable platforms that pushed people out of the comfort of their desktops. By the early 2000s, Google had established itself as the most popular search engine, and the breakthrough moment for collaboration tools can be traced back to April 1, 2004. If a product was launched on April 1 these days, people would rub it off as an April fools' joke. However, this product garnered enough attention and adoption that it spawned a whole new generation of ecosystems around SaaS-based applications.

## Gmail

**Gmail** revolutionized how people used email. With its intuitive inbox powered by Google search technology, 500x more storage than its competitors, and its quirky features (such as 1 GB mail storage to begin with, labels instead of conventional folders, and a search embedded inbox), Gmail blew away its competition. Gmail also focused on reliability and security, which began to make users comfortable with the SaaS model.

Gmail had several features that were light-years ahead of the competition that also spawned a new generation of web technologies. For instance, email conversations were not always sorted by time; instead, they were grouped by conversations, which made navigating them very intuitive for users. The way Gmail was able to achieve this was through the liberal use of **JavaScript** and also using the asynchronous loading of web pages. This technology increased in popularity and became known as **Ajax**, and it enabled Gmail to provide a very intuitive conversation-style inbox, which was fundamentally different from how other email providers operated. **Microsoft Hotmail**, for instance, was entirely built on HTML and required the user to reload the entire page before an action could be performed.

## Google Docs and Google Drive

Buoyed by the success of Gmail, Google started building several SaaS applications that mimicked and replaced several desktop applications. The journey has not been easy, and true to its trial-and-error style, Google experimented with different product launches and had to sunset several products rapidly that did not meet its business standards.

Through a series of acquisitions, Google pulled together the **Google Docs** platform around 2007. Google Docs allows users to create and edit documents online while collaborating with other users in real time. This marked the beginning of SaaS-based office productivity tools coming together.

As content creation and management exploded over the years, the need for storing huge amounts of data and making it shareable became ubiquitous. As a natural step in the evolution of Google Docs, Google launched **Google Drive** in 2012. Google Drive is a personal cloud storage service that allows users to create content and upload and share multimedia and documents across a range of devices.

## Google Apps for Business

While Google enjoyed tremendous success with individuals, these products were also very attractive to businesses. Businesses typically prefer to have their own branding in their domains and not have to rely on the free and generic domains that Google offers. Google has been testing offering businesses their own domains since 2006. Originally dubbed **Google Apps for Your Domain**, Google allowed the hosting of Gmail accounts with custom domain names and provided admin tools to manage them. This experiment was a success, and Google immediately followed it by releasing **Google Apps Premier Edition**, which offered more storage, API integration, phone compatibility, and better reliability. This was swiftly adopted by some of the top companies in the S&P 500.

For larger organizations that demanded a more robust support and compliance model, Google released **Google Apps for Business** in 2011. The Google Apps for Business bundle offered a rich feature set that included **Sync for Microsoft Outlook** and access to a third-party marketplace. Google Apps for Business was very mature for its time, and due to its secure data handling and processing, it was the first web-based application suite to receive **Federal Information Security Management Act** (**FISMA**) certification and accreditation.

While enjoying success, Google Apps for Business was renamed **Google for Work** and then later morphed to **G Suite** in 2016. In the same year, Google released **Jamboard** – a cloud-connected digital whiteboard that came with a 55-inch screen. With Jamboard, users can sketch out ideas, draw synchronously, and use it for creative problem-solving.

## G Suite to Google Workspace

After almost 4 years, in 2020, Google rebranded G Suite as Google Workspace. However, Google Workspace is not just a name change – it also reflects the evolution of work and life in the last few years. In the Google Workspace launch blog post (`https://cloud.google.com/blog/products/workspace/introducing-google-workspace`), Google introduced three major developments in Google Workspace:

- A bundle of enhanced services was included, catering to various sizes of customer organizations.
- Instead of a suite of services, it is now a well-integrated product, offering a fluid user experience across each app.
- The blog post reiterated how work tools are organized within the product.

Google Workspace provides apps for boosting productivity and collaboration for businesses of all sizes. Employee satisfaction and retention are important for a company's culture, and Google Workspace aims to allow open collaboration as part of this. This product enhancement brings a unified user experience, allowing users to stay focused, with the ability to access and share information quickly. As of 2021, Google Workspace has about 6 million businesses signed up and using its services.

One of the most obvious impacts of COVID-19 has been the sharp increase in employees working remotely, and this is likely to continue for some time, even after the pandemic is declared over. Surveys from consulting companies indicate that 20-25% of workforces in advanced economies would work from home three to five days a week. This is 4-5x more remote work than prior to the pandemic (`https://www.apollotechnical.com/statistics-on-remote-workers/`). Several companies are already planning to utilize flexible workspaces, and with supporting technologies such as Google Workspace, the move to bring people back into the office will be a slow one.

Several traditional industries, such as airlines, hospitality, aerospace, airports, retail, and food services, have suffered a great deal during the pandemic. On the other hand, propped up by productivity suites such as Google Workspace, telemedicine, online banking, and streaming entertainment have taken off.

## Carbon-neutral data centers

Google Workspace, as part of the **Google Cloud** infrastructure, comes with the commitment of giving its users a highly secure, reliable, and resilient cloud-based productivity suite that is powered through their carbon-neutral data centers. Having been in the business of cloud technology for more than a decade, Google has invested in its infrastructure to make it sustainable, along with a commitment toward operating on 100% carbon-free energy by 2030.

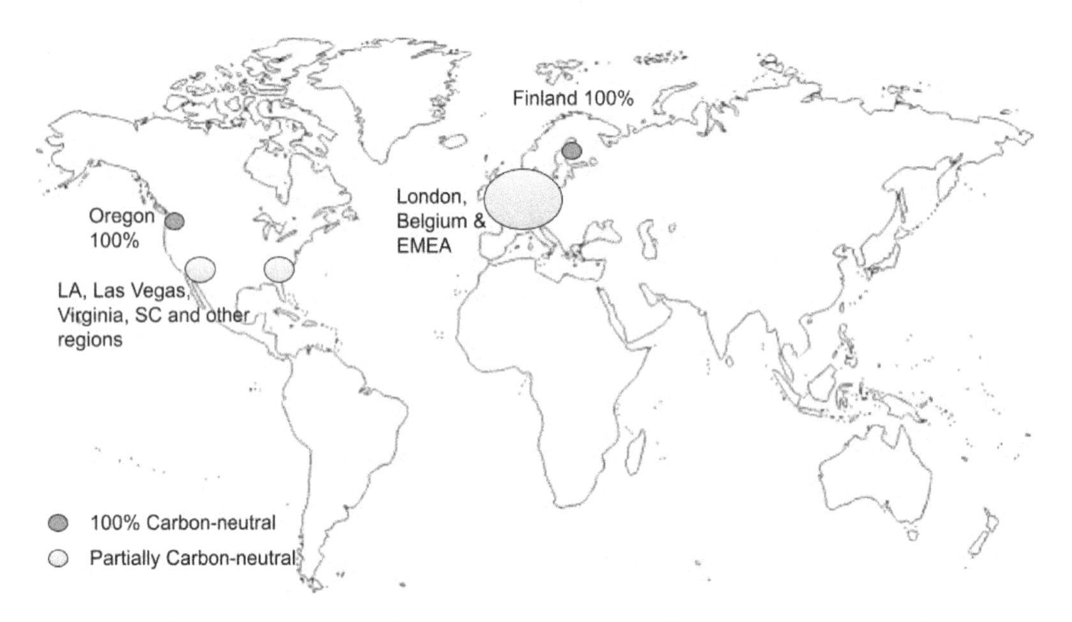


Figure 1.1 – The Google Workspace data centers, as of the second half of 2021, indicating the current progress toward carbon-neutral sustainability

As organizations look toward reducing their operating expenses and modernizing their legacy applications, the focus has turned to the energy used by servers for computational needs. Recent consumer surveys indicate that 79% of customers make purchasing decisions based on their perceptions of the environmental impact of a product (`https://www.globenewswire.com/news-release/2020/07/08/2059043/0/en/Capgemini-Press-Release-79-of-consumers-are-changing-their-purchase-preferences-based-on-social-responsibility-inclusiveness-or-environmental-impact.html`). The decision regarding selecting a sustainable infrastructure matters a lot these days, and by adopting and blending Google's sustainability commitment into an organization's operational model, enterprises can consequently attract more customers with carbon-free assurance.

With large data centers that are well connected through one of the world's largest networks, Google Workspace comes with the assurance of 99.99% availability for its users. The Google Workspace security whitepaper explains this in greater detail. That is, it explains how any data you create in Google Workspace – be it a small document, a drafted email, or even a checklist on **Google Keep** – is fully encrypted when it is stored and when in transit between an end user's computer and a data center. This prevents hacking and keeps your data safe and secure. We will look at this in more detail in the *Data security* section.

Now that we've discussed the evolution of Google Workspace, it's time to look at what is included in its portfolio.

# Google Workspace – what's included?

Google Workspace is a bundle of services that help users stay productive by completing tasks in an efficient way while staying connected with their co-workers. These services also allow users to access information from any device, at any time, and from anywhere. The core services in Google Workspace include the following:

- **Gmail**: This is an email service that allows an organization to deploy its communication emails using Google's servers. Google's advanced phishing and malware protection executes a predelivery scan that filters spam and viruses. Administrators have the functionality to create compliance rules based on content within email messages. Gmail boasts close to 4 billion users worldwide. It has native applications for **iOS** and **Android**.
- **Google Currents**: This gives users the capability to set up social collaboration among users in a domain. Communities within Google Currents can be used for posting discussions and topics. Users can follow topics, communities, or other users to keep up with all of the content being shared. Administrators can restrict interaction within the domain or allow users to interact with external communities as well. Currents was formerly known as **Google+**, the social networking platform from Google.
- **Google Calendar**: This is used for tracking personal goals, reminders, events, and tasks. It can be used for both personal work hours and corporate/organizational team calendars. It allows end users to view other calendars of peers, set up team calendars to be used by multiple users, use conference rooms, and attach meeting notes for each event.

- **Google Cloud Search**: This extends Google's search functionality for searching your organization's data. It can be used for searching Google Workspace data and third-party data sources as well. The search results will adhere to the security model of the organization - only users with the right access will be able to see and modify content.
- **Google Contacts**: This allows users to store the contact information of users they frequently work with. This information can be synchronized from the web with mobile devices as well. There are options to categorize the contact information based on business operations. Beyond name, email, and phone numbers, users can also store other custom information.
- **Google Docs Editors**: Google Docs, **Google Sheets**, **Google Slides**, and **Google Forms** are various services that help with creating different types of content, whether it is documents, large spreadsheets, or slides for meeting presentations. Each of these editors allows collaboration through sharing, and they include formatting options that aid with creating visually appealing content.
- **Google Drive**: This is the file storage and synchronization service. It not only allows users to work with Google Docs, Sheets, or Slides, but it also provides options for uploading files of non-Google formats such as **PDF**, **Microsoft Word**, and more. Certain editions of Google Workspace allow users to have unlimited storage, greater collaboration tools, fine-grained access, audit reporting, and advanced administration controls.
- **Google Groups for Business**: This allows users and administrators to create and manage groups for messaging multiple recipients at the same time. Beyond email messages, users can use Google Groups for Business for sharing calendars and content in Google Drive with the members of a group. This improves work efficiency by collaborating with multiple users at the same time without having to individually share with each user.
- **Google Chat**: Google Chat provides a quick way to communicate with recipients. Users can individually message each other or can set up a Google Chat room for messaging multiple users at the same time. It provides an enhanced thread-based conversation view that helps users stay focused on each topic of discussion. Chat allows integration with other third-party services using AI-powered **Chatbot** solutions.
- **Google Meet**: This provides an enterprise-grade, professional video-based communication tool for end users. It allows users to have breakout rooms, Q&A, and record meetings, which automatically gets saved into users' Google Drive accounts. Google Workspace administrators can choose which functionality to enable for the entire domain or for selected users.

- **Google Jamboard**: This is a smart display that is a digital interactive whiteboard. It allows collaboration by allowing multiple users to brainstorm ideas to action. These Jamboard files are automatically stored in Google Drive for future reference. Users can use web browsers or a mobile app to draw and create content. The Jamboard app for iOS and Android makes it easy for students and teachers to come together using the device of their choice.
- **Google Keep**: This allows users to create quick notes, share those notes with other users, and pin them for immediate retrieval. Google Keep can be used for preparing lists and drawings.
- **Google Sites**: This allows organizations to create multiple pages to host a Google Site. There are no limits on the number of pages that can be created for these sites. Content posted on sites can be restricted to internal viewing within the organization, or it can be published externally for other users to view. Google Sites can be used for embedding content from Google Drive, HTML, and custom scripts.
- **Google Tasks**: This is a productivity service that allows users to manage their activities with a due date. Tasks can also be created from within a Google Chat room, allowing members within the collaboration space to take ownership of the task.
- **Google Vault**: This helps the organization stay compliant with their legal requirements by allowing automated data retention from Gmail, Google Drive, Google Groups, Google Meet recordings, and Google Chat conversations. Administrators can delegate Google Vault administrator permissions to other power users that further enables them to search content from Vault for any e-discovery requests. Content in Vault can be retained for an unlimited period of time or for a specific period of time using retention policies. Retention policies are applied to content via labels.
- **Google Voice**: This allows organizations to replace their desk phones with an IP-based telephony service. Administrators can assign specific phone numbers for use based on the end user's country. This is an add-on service, and it supports SMS and voicemail for these users. Ring groups allow multiple users to set up a shift-based calling service.
- **Google Workspace Assured Controls**: This is an add-on service that allows organizations to stay compliant with defined legal standards. Organizations can work with Google support engineers located in the US region.
- **Google Workspace add-ons**: Taken together, these are Google Voice and Google Workspace Assured Controls.

## Additional Google services in Google Workspace

Other Google services, such as **YouTube**, **Google Classroom**, **DoubleClick**, **Google Scholar**, and **Google News**, are also available. Administrators can pick and choose which services are relevant for their organization, enabling them for a specific subset of users.

With this impressive product and set of features, Google Workspace already has a very strong presence in the market. To cater to different market segments, Google Workspace offers several licensing models that bundle different products and services. Let's take a look at that next.

# Google Workspace licensing models

Google Workspace is offered in three license tiers: *Education*, *Business*, and *Enterprise*.

Each of these tiers has further editions of licenses that best serve different types of customers. We will talk about each of these tiers in detail in the following subsections.

## Google Workspace Education editions

Google Workspace has been an integral part of educational institutions. More than 170 million users within educational domains are currently relying on Google Workspace tools and services. By introducing Google Workspace for schools and universities, Google has answered the diverse needs of K-12 institutions. Teachers and students were able to quickly adopt G Suite, and now Google Workspace. These students are evolving into the new workforce, already stepping into their careers with knowledge of Google Workspace, and this alleviates the need for extra training during new hire onboarding.

The Education tier has four license editions:

- **Google Workspace for Education Fundamentals**: This is the upgraded name for **G Suite for Education**. This edition has historically been offered for free and will continue to be free. Only schools and universities that qualify for a **.edu** domain are eligible for this license edition.
- **Google Workspace for Education Standard**: This was recently introduced, building upon the Fundamentals edition with enhanced security.
- **Google Workspace for Education Teaching and Learning Upgrade**: This provides additional video communication capabilities and an enhanced classroom feature that can be provisioned to the domain with the Fundamentals or Standard licenses.

- **Google Workspace for Education Plus**: This is the rebranded edition of **G Suite Enterprise for Education**. This secure edition is comparable to **Google Workspace Enterprise Plus**, including Security Center, Admin Logs in **BigQuery**, and so on.

There are some common features between the four Education license editions:

- Gmail
- Google Calendar
- Google Docs, Sheet, Slides, and Forms
- Google Classroom
- **Google Assignments**
- Google Tasks
- Google Meet (limits on the number of participants differ for each edition):
    - Features such as call-in for audio, moderator controls, hand-raising, and digital whiteboarding are available for all license editions.
- Google Sites
- Google Groups
- Security:
    - **Data loss prevention** (DLP)
    - Secure **Lightweight Directory Access Protocol** (LDAP)
    - Password monitoring
    - Alert center
- Google Vault

> **Pooled Storage**
>
> Google Drive storage differs for each edition, depending on whether it is pooled or individually assigned for each user.
>
> For example, if you have 10 users in Google Workspace Business Plus, this gives the entire domain a total of 50 TB storage (because 10 x 5 TB = 50 TB). However, this does not limit a user to 5 TB, and it allows you to have shared Google Drive files that are available to your group of users collaborating on a common task or project.

There are some differences between the four Education license editions, which are shown in the following table:

| Google Product | Feature | Education Fundamentals | Education Standard | Teaching and Learning Upgrade | Education Plus |
|---|---|---|---|---|---|
| Meet | Participants | 100 | 100 | 250 | 250 |
| | Polling and Q&A | X | X | ✓ | ✓ |
| | Breakout rooms | X | X | ✓ | ✓ |
| | Attendance tracking | X | X | ✓ | ✓ |
| | Noise cancellation | X | X | ✓ | ✓ |
| Drive | Storage | 100 TB pooled cloud storage | 100 TB pooled cloud storage | User 100 GB + 100 TB pooled cloud storage | 100 TB shared + 20 GB per user |
| Security | Dashboard, Investigation tool and Security Health | X | ✓ | X | ✓ |

## Google Chromebooks

**Google Chromebooks** are a new breed of laptops that have come into existence thanks to the power of Google Workspace. Chromebooks are powered by **Chrome OS**, which is a platform built around Google's cloud applications. Chromebooks have done extraordinarily well in the education sector due to their competitive pricing and the simplicity of the machines. Chromebooks require very little training, and their cost is small compared to other laptops.

Chromebooks work well with Google Classroom, which serve as a hub for classroom activities, including classroom discussions, attendance, and communication between parents and teachers.

Along with Google Workspace, Chromebooks have made modern operating systems accessible and easily provisioned for users. Teachers and educational systems are constantly looking for new ways to creatively engage students. With the move away from classic textbook based learning, several digital programs are being introduced globally for learning – schools are increasingly using Chromebooks as part of their teaching and learning programs. Chromebooks have rich feature sets and are affordable and secure with the **Chrome Enterprise Management** license.

Chromebooks also enable teachers and students to create new apps for immersive learning. Seeing the impressive adoption of Chromebooks in education, businesses have also gained confidence in issuing Chromebooks for their employees. Instead of spending $2,000 or more for each employee for devices, it has been economical to issue $500 worth of Chromebooks, which comes with great management capabilities for both users and administrators.

## Google Workspace Business editions

The following list shows the available Google Workspace Business editions:

- **Business Starter**: This is the first tier of the professional productivity suite of licenses, which allows users to have 30 GB of storage.
- **Business Standard**: This is the enhanced productivity suite of licenses, which allows users to have 2 TB of storage pooled for the domain.
- **Business Plus**: This is the advanced productivity suite of licenses. It has the most valuable set of features within this tier and allows users to have 5 TB of storage pooled for the domain.

Besides storage, each of these license editions comes with specific features and limitations. Companies can assess their needs and usage before selecting their ideal license edition.

The Business Standard and Business Plus licenses give you the option of having pooled storage across this domain.

There are some common features between the three Business license editions:

- Gmail
- Google Calendar
- Google Drive
- Google Chat and Chat rooms
- Google Meet
- Google Groups for businesses
- Google Tasks
- Google Sites
- Directory management/shared contacts
- Two-step verification for user identities

- IMAP/POP3 compatibility mode
- Offline access for Gmail and Google Drive
- Reports and audit logs

There are some differences between the three Business license editions, which are shown in the following table:

| Google Product | Feature | Business Starter | Business Standard | Business Plus |
|---|---|---|---|---|
| Drive | Storage | 30 GB | 2 TB | 5 TB |
| | Shared drive | X | ✓ | ✓ |
| | Visitor sharing (pin code sharing for non-Google users) | X | ✓ | ✓ |
| | Target audiences | X | ✓ | ✓ |
| | Advanced Google Drive audit reports | X | ✓ | ✓ |
| Meet | Meet participants | 100 | 150 | 250 |
| | Record your meetings in Google Drive | X | ✓ | ✓ |
| | Breakout rooms, hand-raising | X | ✓ | ✓ |
| | Tracking participant attendance | X | X | ✓ |
| Security | Google Vault for data retention | X | X | ✓ |
| | Advanced endpoint management | X | X | ✓ |
| | Fundamental data regions | X | ✓ | ✓ |

## Google Workspace Enterprise editions

This tier is offered for larger organizations with more than 300 users. It includes enterprise-grade features with additional security and compliance features to manage the users:

- **Enterprise Essentials**: This gives you the flexibility to use the full collaboration apps in Google Workspace while still retaining the existing mail infrastructure. Users can use Google Drive for content management and Google Meet for their communications. Users are allocated 1 TB of storage space.

- **Frontline**: This license extends collaboration tools for frontline workers who require productivity apps – it has a limit of 2 GB storage per user.
- **Enterprise Standard**: This offers solutions for large organizations with flexible storage and advanced video conferencing features.
- **Enterprise Plus**: This is the most valuable productivity and collaboration suite, with enterprise-grade functionality and security features to stay compliant with your organization's legal standards.

Organizations that are on a path to larger growth can investigate upgrading to the Google Workspace Enterprise editions.

Google gives you the flexibility of having multiple license editions from the Enterprise tier within the same domain, thereby allowing administrators to provide the relevant licenses for each subset of user groups.

Enterprise tier licenses also give you the flexibility to have the storage space needed for your domain. Users receive a scalable, reliable platform to have a large amount of content, which is required for a truly collaborative work environment.

There are some common features between the four Enterprise license editions:

- Google Drive:
  - Offline access using **Google Drive File Stream**
  - Visitor sharing (pin code sharing for non-Google users)
  - Interoperability with Microsoft format files, such as Word and Excel
  - Grammar and spelling suggestions
  - Version history
- Google Sites:
  - Unlimited web pages that can be published for domain users or externally for the public
- Google Meet:
  - Video conferencing
  - Recording meetings and saving to Google Drive
  - Enterprise features such as low-light mode, phone dial-in, real-time captions, background blur, and digital whiteboarding

- Security:
  - The Google Meet quality tool in the Admin console for troubleshooting

There are some differences between the four Enterprise license editions, which are shown in the following table:

| Google Product | Feature | Frontline | Enterprise Essentials | Enterprise Standard | Enterprise Plus |
|---|---|---|---|---|---|
| Gmail/ Calendar | Gmail and Calendar App | ✓ | X | ✓ | ✓ |
| Chat | Chat rooms with guest access | X | X | ✓ | ✓ |
| AppSheet | AppSheet for low-code app development | X | X | X | ✓ |
| Drive | Storage | 2 GB | 1 TB | As you need | As you need |
| | Shared drive | X | ✓ | ✓ | ✓ |
| | Document approvals | X | ✓ | ✓ | ✓ |
| | Connected sheets | X | ✓ | ✓ | ✓ |
| | Target audiences | X | ✓ | ✓ | ✓ |
| | Advanced Google Drive audit reports | X | ✓ | ✓ | ✓ |
| Meet | Meet participants | 100 | 150 | 250 | 250 |
| | Live stream | X | X | ✓<br>10 K viewers | ✓<br>100 K viewers |
| | Hand-raising | X | ✓ | ✓ | ✓ |
| | Tracking participant attendance | X | ✓ | ✓ | ✓ |
| | Audit logs in BigQuery | X | X | ✓ | ✓ |

| Google Product | Feature | Frontline | Enterprise Essentials | Enterprise Standard | Enterprise Plus |
|---|---|---|---|---|---|
| Security | Security center for Google Docs | X | X | X | ✓ |
| | Security sandbox | X | X | X | ✓ |
| | Access transparency report | X | X | X | ✓ |
| | Work insights reports | X | X | X | ✓ |
| | Google Vault for data retention | X | X | ✓ | ✓ |
| | Advanced endpoint management | X | X | ✓ | ✓ |
| | Data regions | X | X | X | ✓ |
| Support | Enhanced support | X | ✓ | ✓ | ✓ |

Now that we've reviewed the various features within each tier and each edition of the Google Workspace licenses, let's discuss how to decide on the best edition for your organization.

# Choosing the right edition

As a business owner, start by reviewing the differences of the editions in the previous section and categorizing your employees based on their types and the services they may consume. This will help in mapping the right type of users with the respective **stock keeping units** (**SKU**) license. For example, if there are temporary employees or interns who might not require all of the features of Google Workspace Business Plus, you can plan to have multiple license SKUs provisioned in your domain.

Let's review some sample user groups we generally see across various organizations:

- Certain user groups may serve as content creators, whereas others could be consumers of data.
- Field workers who are not consistently working from the same location may require additional security guardrails to ensure there is no accidental leakage of confidential information.
- Executive users who not only travel frequently but also have interactions with external users. These types of users require enterprise-grade video conferencing, the ability to chat with users who are external to the domain, access through mobile devices, and a highly secure, encrypted framework.
- Interns/temporary workers who do not create valuable content that requires data retention. These users would require active communication tools, mobile device management, and additional data loss prevention rules.

Beyond functional requirements, users can also be categorized based on geographical locations. This helps in deciding the data regions.

Once you have identified the license edition that would be best suited for your organization, it's time to decide the domain URL you would like to use to sign up for Google Workspace.

# Domain host versus Google Workspace

Now that you have decided and purchased your Google Workspace licenses, you will need a domain host with servers to house your content.

## What is a domain?

To set up a Google Workspace account, you need to own a **domain name** that represents your organization on the internet. In simplest terms, a domain name is the address for your organization on the World Wide Web.

This domain will appear in your email address after the @ symbol, for example, `user@company.org` or `employee@organization.com`, where `company.org` and `organization.com` are the Google Workspace primary domains.

Domains, once claimed, cannot be duplicated, which also means that if you have enrolled for a trial version of Google Workspace for a duration of 14 days, your domain verification will still be valid when converting to a full Google Workspace license.

## What is the DNS?

The **Domain Name System** (**DNS**) acts like the phonebook of the internet. It helps translate human-readable domain names such as `google.com` into the corresponding IP address so that browsers can route and load the correct resources.

DNS lookups involve multiple steps, outlined as follows:

1. A user types `google.com` into a web browser; a DNS resolver receives this query.
2. The DNS resolver then looks this up in a DNS root nameserver. As the name indicates, the DNS resolver's primary responsibility is to respond to the client with the IP address.
3. The root nameserver's primary purpose is to determine the address of a **top-level domain** (**TLD**) nameserver, which has the required information for its domains. Some of the popular TLDs include `.com`, `.net`, and `.info`.
4. In the preceding example, the DNS resolver then sends the query to the `.com` TLD.
5. The TLD server responds with the IP address of the domain's nameserver: `google.com`.
6. The DNS resolver then sends a query to the domain's nameserver.
7. The nameserver then returns the IP address of `google.com`, if found.
8. On a successful lookup, the DNS resolver responds to the web browser with the IP address of `google.com`.

It should be noted that configuring a DNS server on a device is an important decision. However, in most cases, the **Dynamic Host Configuration Protocol** (**DHCP**) configures the system to use the IP addresses of the ISP's domain nameservers. Due to this, a lot of users do not come across setting up DNS servers manually.

With the proliferation of web applications, DNS failure messages are seen by almost everybody. There are several reasons why a DNS lookup failure would occur.

The most common reasons for DNS failures are as follows:

- Users mistyping URLs
- DNS servers timing out
- Expired DNS caches on the devices

## Domain verification

Before configuring Google Workspace, users must verify the ownership of the domain so that no one else can claim ownership of it. This also ensures Google has permission to email as your domain [user@company.com] and no one else can email using your [`company.com`] email domain.

When you purchase Google Workspace, you will receive a verification ID, and this will need to be added to your domain host's DNS settings.

## How to verify a domain

There are a few things needed to verify a domain in Google Workspace:

- First, you will need to have the credentials to sign in to your domain host's control panel. If you do not have these handy, you may use the password reset feature on your domain host's control panel to reset the password.

> **Troubleshooting Tip**
>
> If you are not sure where you bought your domain, you can identify your domain host using **ICANN Lookup** (`https://lookup.icann.org/`).
>
> The **Internet Corporation for Assigned Names and Numbers (ICANN)** is a non-profit organization that collects domain information.

- Second, you will need to have a verification record or file from Google. The type of verification will be presented to you when you sign up for Google Workspace. The illustration in *Figure 1.2* shows the format of a verification record.
- Finally, you need to be able to edit and add records to your domain's DNS settings. If you do not have access to edit DNS records, you could alternatively add a meta tag or an HTML file that is reachable on the internet.

> **Troubleshooting Tip**
>
> If you are having trouble verifying your domain, this knowledge base article from Google on how to verify domains for several hosts will be very helpful: `https://support.google.com/a/topic/1409901`.

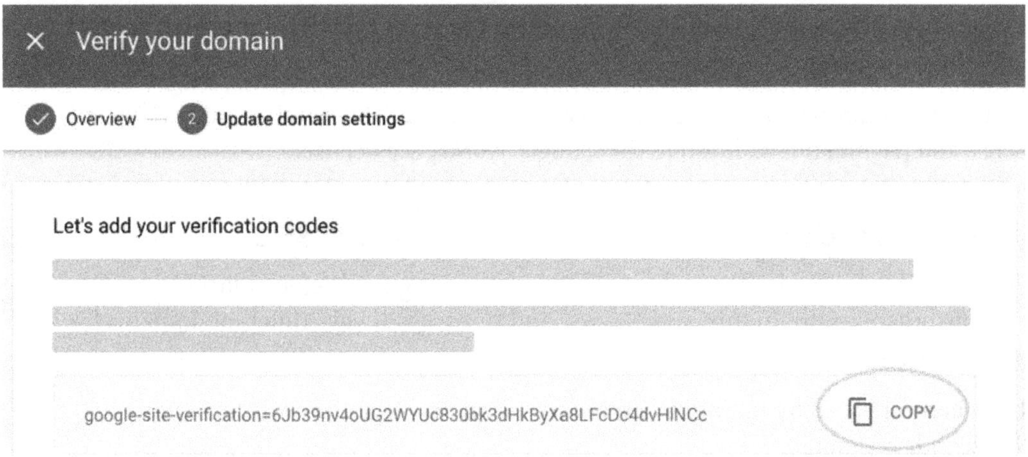

Figure 1.2 – Where to copy the verification code from the Admin console

The verification process usually takes 10 minutes, and once verified, the domain will show up as verified in the Admin console.

If your organization has additional sub-organizations that have a different name or prefer to use a different email address, you will have to repeat this domain verification process for each sub-domain that you add.

For example, consider the following:

The `company.com` domain name will be your primary domain.

The `abc.company.com` will be a sub-domain that allows users to have email addresses such as the following:

`user@abc.company.com`

Here are the steps to add a sub-domain:

1. Log in to your Google **Admin** console (`https://admin.google.com`).
2. Click on **Account** | **Domains**.
3. Click **Continue** to verify your domain with a TXT record.
4. In a different browser or tab, log in to your domain host account and follow the instructions for your DNS provider to add this copied TXT record within the DNS settings.
5. Now, log in again to your Google Workspace Admin console.
6. Click on **Verify** to verify your domain

This completes the verification process.

Google Support articles have host-specific instructions for each DNS provider, such as **GoDaddy** and **Enom**.

Organizations can also use Google's own domain service. This would require a separate license and payment in addition to the Google Workspace license.

## Secondary domains versus domain aliases

Imagine that the users named `User1` and `User2` belong to different subsidiaries within the same organization. In this case, `User1` and `User2` will have different domains for their email addresses.

This is accomplished by setting up a *secondary domain*. Organizations can add up to 599 secondary domains.

The following diagrams illustrate the differences between user email addresses when they choose between using a secondary domain or a domain alias:

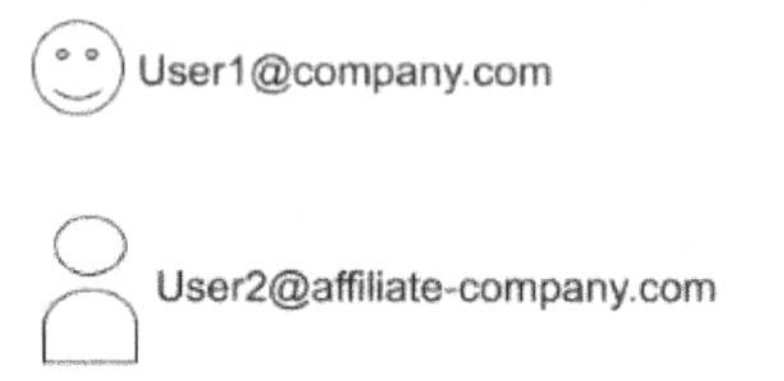


Figure 1.3 – Secondary domain email addresses

In the preceding setup with secondary domain, `User1` will have a different domain, while `User2` will have a different domain – however, they both will fall under the same organization:

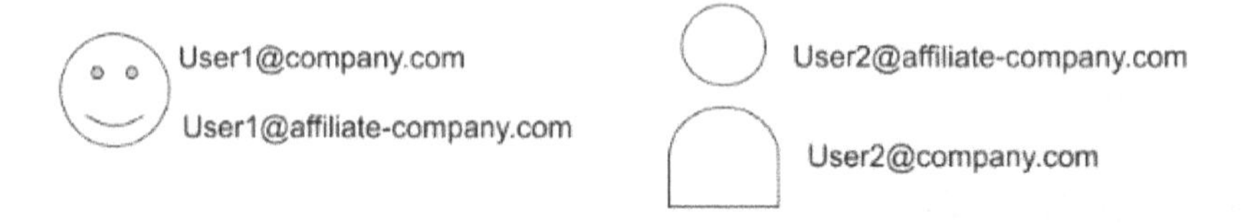


Figure 1.4 – Domain alias email addresses

If `User1` and `User2` would like to have two email addresses pointing to the same inbox, then this is accomplished by using a domain alias or a sub-domain.

Users created under a specific sub-domain automatically inherit the email alias of the primary domain name.

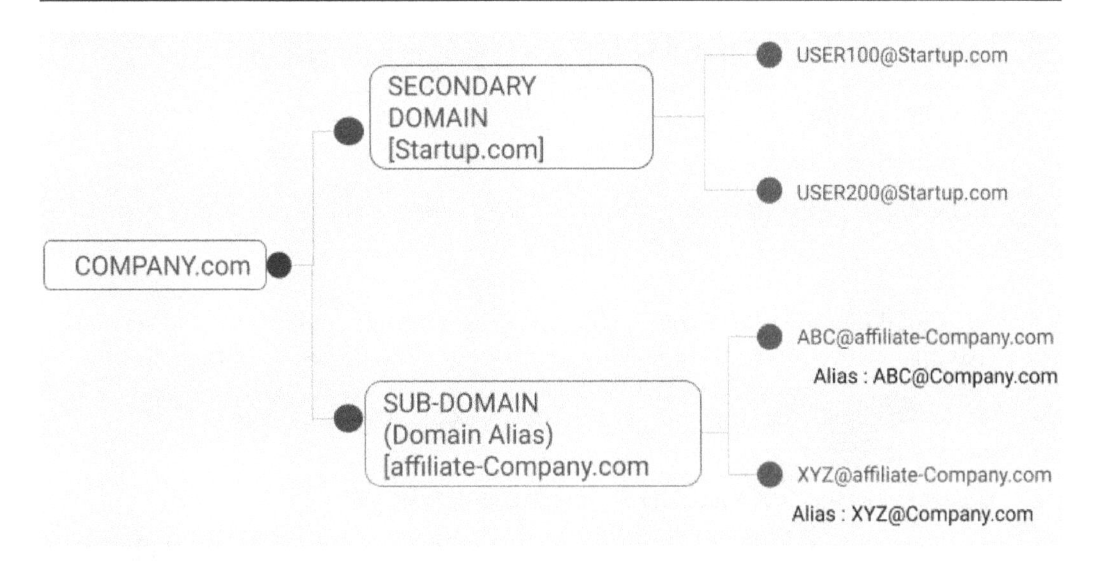


Figure 1.5 – Hierarchical domains with multiple affiliates

> **A Note for Power Users**
>
> Now that domain ownership has been claimed, administrators can grant login access to users.

As a Google Workspace user, you now have a **Google Cloud Identity** user account. We will get to know more about Cloud Identity in the next chapter.

To keep your account secure, Google provides you with a security management page that helps you manage the following:

- Passwords
- Recovery account:
    - If you lose your password and would like to recover the account, you can connect your Google Workspace account with another email to serve as your backup recovery.
- Privacy suggestions:
    - Google has a privacy checkup tool that can assist you in running a checklist of privacy settings against your account.

- Control which data about your activity gets stored, for example:
    - Searches you do
    - Websites you visit
    - Videos you watch
    - Places you go

Using your Cloud Identity user account, you can access multiple applications and services without having to enter multiple credentials. These services could be any of the following:

- Additional Google services such as YouTube, **Google Analytics**, and Google Classroom
- Data stored in BigQuery hosted on Google Cloud Platform
- Custom **Google App Engine** applications that are hosted on Google Cloud Platform

# Summary

In this chapter, we looked at the evolution of Google Workspace and its different editions. This chapter also laid the foundations for the core services and the different licensing models that are available. We also gave a brief introduction on how to get your domain for your company up and running quickly. This has set the stage for you to add users and configure apps within the domain in order to take full advantage of the Google Workspace offerings. We will learn more about configuring users and apps in the next chapter.

# 2
# Configuring Users and Apps

As applications move to the cloud, it becomes apparent that certain traditional security paradigms should be reimagined and must be built from scratch to provide cloud-native features. Every organization should be aware of the security threats they are facing and should be prepared to realize and mitigate them. When people hear of a cybersecurity threat, they immediately think of common attack vectors emanating from hostile nations, hacker groups, corporate spies, and so on. However, your organization's data could be under threat from someone as simple as a disgruntled employee or someone who recently got fired. It becomes very important to have appropriate entitlements across your user base and auditability and observability features to detect quickly when things go wrong. This security perimeter starts with **Cloud Identity**, where we manage the relationships between users and their cloud resources. Google Cloud Identity is an identity, device, and access management platform that helps maximize user and **information technology** (**IT**) efficiency. This is termed **Identity as a Service** (**IDaaS**).

This chapter will introduce you to Cloud Identity and admin roles; this is foundational to an understanding of the relationship between users and their roles with applications. As an administrator, this understanding is critical for defining **access control policies** (**ACPs**) for users and troubleshooting if problems arise in the future. We will also peek into **Google Cloud Directory Sync** (**GCDS**), a provisioning tool that will be effective in synchronizing the existing user base.

In this chapter, we will learn about the following topics:

- Google Cloud Identity and admin roles
- Configuring **organizational units** (**OUs**) in Cloud Identity
- Configuring users in Cloud Identity
- Configuring users in Google's Admin console and using Google Cloud Directory Sync
- Configuring applications in Workspace
- Sharing resources via Calendar

# Google Cloud Identity and admin roles

The traditional way of managing access for users who are confined to just the office premises has disappeared. People are now increasingly becoming digital nomads and are working from anywhere. The definition of *users* used to be employees; however, that has now expanded to customers, vendors, partners, and so on. And since the office perimeter has expanded, along with different types of devices, the need for a powerful **identity management system** (**IMS**) is more important than ever. Legacy **virtual private network** (**VPN**) solutions used to access information on a corporate network may work well on a laptop; however, the experience can get clumsy on a mobile device.

Organizations today are under increased pressure to undergo digital transformation since the way we work has transformed. Added to this, there is an increased threat in the form of new cyberattacks, as well as a need to keep company data secure across a plethora of devices and to extend the security policies to **Bring Your Own Device** (**BYOD**) as well.

Google Cloud Identity is built to solve several of these problems. Let's now turn our focus to some of the key features that Cloud Identity offers.

## Cloud Identity features

In this section, we will cover important features of Cloud Identity, such as Single Sign-On, multi-factor authentication, groups, and device management. Let's get started.

### Single sign-on

**Single sign-on** (**SSO**) provides seamless access to thousands of pre-integrated apps, both in the cloud and on-premises, which enables users to work from any place and any device.

### Multi-factor authentication

**Multi-factor authentication** (**MFA**) is used to ensure that users are who they say they are, with at least two pieces of evidence. You may have already seen this in action when you try to log in to a bank account, for example. If MFA is enabled on the account, you will need to enter your username and password, followed by a **one-time passcode** (**OTP**) that the bank authentication application sends you. You will gain access only if both the factors (password and OTP) are correct.

The need for MFA is more important than ever, as the traditional way of authenticating using only passwords could be easily compromised. Interestingly, it's the users themselves who make it easier for hackers by choosing words that are far too common, using the same passwords across multiple applications, not changing passwords for a long period of time, and sharing them in an insecure way.

Cloud Identity supports the following MFA verification methods:

- Push notifications
- Google Authenticator
- Titan Security Keys
- Using Android/iOS devices as a security key

### Device management

Cloud Identity offers a robust device management feature set that allows organizations and users to work with different types of devices seamlessly. Device Management offers capabilities such as the following:

- **Passcode enforcement**: The ability to enforce a screen lock or password on managed devices.
- **Remote sign-out**: If a device is stolen or an unrecognized device exists in the **Admin** console, you have the ability to sign out from the device remotely.

- **Remote account wipe**: If a managed device goes missing, users can choose to wipe work or school data from the device.
- **Device approval/blocking**: Provides capabilities to administrators to review user-owned devices that request access to network and data.
- **Context-aware access**: Context-aware access gives the ability to create access policies based on location, **Internet Protocol** (**IP**) address, device security status, and user identity.

Device management offers several other capabilities as well, and we will learn more about configuring devices and using the device management **application programming interface** (**API**) in the next chapter.

## Groups and dynamic groups

Cloud Identity also supports groups, whereby users who should have similar functional responsibilities will be grouped together under a name. The entitlements will be applied to a group, rather than an individual user.

There are different types of groups supported by Cloud Identity, the most prominent ones being Google Groups, dynamic groups, and security groups. A detailed description of different types of groups and their characteristics can be found at `https://cloud.google.com/identity/docs/groups`.

> **Cloud Identity versus Identity and Access Management**
>
> You may come across these two different terminologies as you work with Google Cloud. In short, Cloud Identity defines who users are, while **identity and access management** (**IAM**) defines what those users can do within **Google Cloud Platform** (**GCP**).
>
> Cloud Identity offers centralized user administration—a mechanism to add/suspend/delete users, set up MFA, or create/edit groups in Workspace.
>
> IAM provides policies, roles, and permissions that can be applied to users or groups at different levels that define the scope of access across GCP.

With the core feature set of Cloud Identity well defined, let's turn our attention to how these features are bundled across different segments.

## Cloud Identity editions

Google offers two editions of Cloud Identity: **Premium edition** and **Free edition**. Understandably, the Premium edition has more features than the Free edition. The following table showcases the feature set supported across the two editions:

| **Features** | **Premium edition** | **Free edition** |
|---|---|---|
| Fundamental endpoint management | Full support | Full support |
| Advanced endpoint management | Full support | Full support |
| Enterprise endpoint management | Full support | Does not support |
| Directory | Full support | Partial support |
| Advanced security features | Full support | Partial support |
| SSO and automated provisioning | Full support | Partial support |
| Reporting | Full support | Partial support |
| Billing and support | Full support | Partial support |

For more granular details on features that are supported across these two editions of Cloud Identity, please refer to `https://cloud.google.com/identity/docs/editions`.

Now that Cloud Identity has been conceptualized, it becomes apparent that this is where Google Workspace OUs and users are housed and their access and entitlements are managed.

# Configuring OUs in Cloud Identity

Before setting up users, OUs must be configured in Cloud Identity. These help in categorizing users and enabling respective apps for each OU. Apps such as Gmail, Drive, Meet, and Chat can be selectively enabled for the OU, and further security settings within each of these apps can be applied to sub-OUs.

In the previous chapter, we went into detail about subdomains versus secondary domains. Users across multiple domains or subdomains can be set up under any OU.

Root-level or top-level OUs take over the primary domain name. All child OUs will automatically inherit settings defined for the root OU, but these can be changed by overriding the settings.

For example, if the root OU is `Company.com`, administrators can configure sub-OUs with various names such as *IT Staff*, *Executives*, and *Field Workers*. Within these sub-OUs, there can be nested OUs as well. Users are created as leaf nodes in this hierarchical setup. Those users can belong to either the sub-domain or the primary/secondary domain. Irrespective of which domain the user is set up with, all security settings and app configurations are inherited based on the OUs the user belongs to.

The following screenshot shows a representation of an OU:

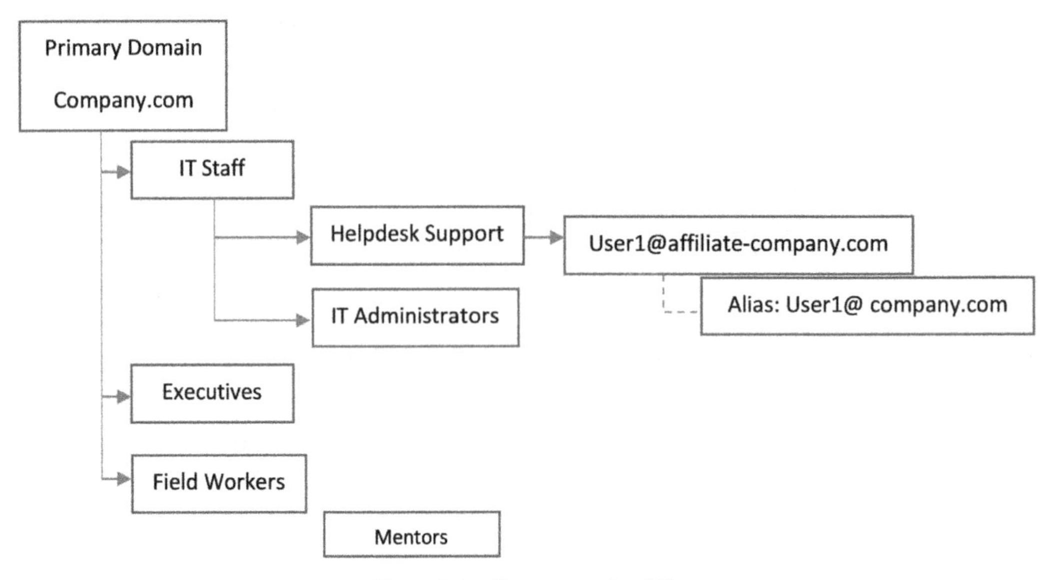


Figure 2.1 – Representative OU

Administrators can move users from one OU to another OU. If users are moved from one OU to another OU, the respective security settings defined for each OU will be applied to the users within the destination OU.

If your organization uses GCDS, OUs can be synchronized from **Active Directory** (**AD**) to the Google Admin directory. This is installed locally on a server that authorizes both source and destination.

OUs can be created in a bulk manner using the Admin directory API. Administrators have the option of changing the name of OUs or rearranging the hierarchy of the OU structure, as illustrated in the following screenshot:

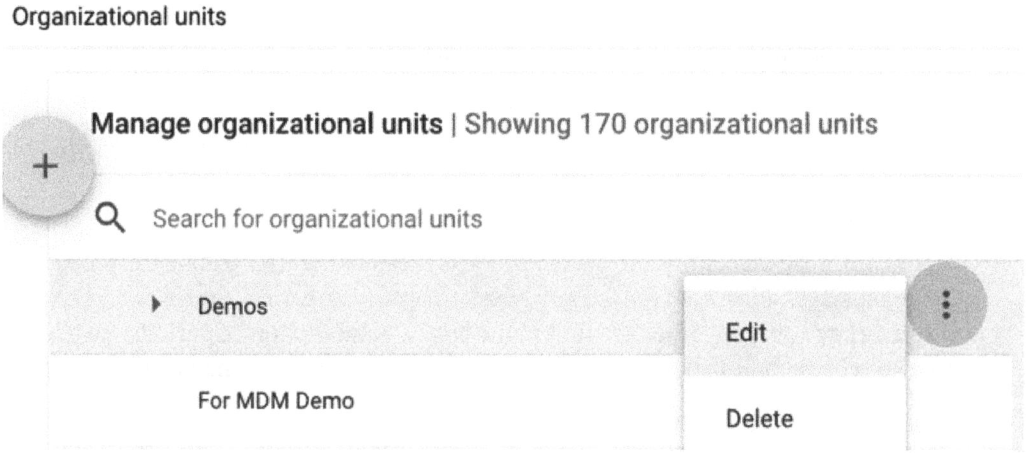

Organizational units

Manage organizational units | Showing 170 organizational units

Search for organizational units

Demos

Edit

For MDM Demo

Delete

Figure 2.2 – Renaming an OU in the Admin interface

The preceding screenshot shows that you must click the kebab (three dots) icon to pull up the interface to rename an OU.

# Configuring users in Cloud Identity

Cloud Identity has a few options available to add users, as follows:

- If there are few users to add, then the Google **Admin** console could be used to add users individually.
- If you are adding several users at once, a **comma-separated values** (**CSV**) file could be used to upload and create users in the system.
- If you are a large organization, GCDS could be useful for keeping users in sync with your existing **Lightweight Directory Access Protocol** (**LDAP**) directory.

It is important to come up with a naming convention for users that potentially results in username conflict resolution, prior to getting users uploaded to Cloud Identity. An organization-level standard will help users get standardized email addresses that are easy to remember. Administrators also have the option to review and edit user-defined usernames/email addresses.

Google Cloud Identity has certain rules when it comes to assigning usernames, as outlined here:

- Usernames can contain letters (`a-z`), numbers (`0-9`), dashes (`-`), underscores (`_`), apostrophes (`'`), and periods (`.`).

- Letters in usernames must be lowercase. All uppercase letters that are entered when creating a username are converted to lowercase letters.
- Usernames can't contain more than a single period (`.`) in a row, accents, accented letters, ampersands (&), equals signs (=), brackets (< , >), plus signs (+), or commas (`,`).
- Periods (`.`) are not ignored in usernames in the way they are ignored in Gmail accounts. If a user account called `username` is created, the user will be unable to receive messages addressed to `user.name@company.com`, or `us.er.na.me@company.com`, or any other account name with a combination of periods. To allow a user to receive mail with these variations, we should create an email alias for them.
- Usernames can begin or end with non-alphanumeric characters, but not with periods (`.`); usernames can have a maximum of 64 characters.

# Adding users to Cloud Identity

As we saw earlier, Cloud Identity offers several ways to add users within your domain. You could do this one by one, do it in bulk, or do this through user federation.

The next steps explain how to add users with these options.

## Manually creating users

The following steps show how to provision a user in Cloud Identity manually:

1. Log in to the Google **Admin** console.
2. From the home page, click on **Users**.
3. Click on **Invite new user/Add new user**.
4. Fill out the form to invite the user. This will add the user to the domain and send login credentials to the user to their off-domain email address—typically their personal email.
5. Administrators also have the option of autogenerating a password or setting a specific password for these users.

## Adding users in bulk

The following steps show how to provision users in bulk in Cloud Identity:

1. Log in to the **Admin** console.
2. From the home page, click on **Users**.

3. Click on **Bulk Update Users**. This option allows you to download a template.
4. Using this template, fill in and format user details in appropriate columns.
5. Save this in CSV format.
6. Now, open the page in *Step 2*, and upload the CSV file.

> **Note**
> Administrators will have to go through the same process if they would like to update any user information in the domain.

## Syncing users' data with your LDAP server

For large corporations, users and groups from LDAP servers such as Microsoft AD can be synchronized to Google using GCDS. We will learn more about this feature in the next section.

## Merging users who already have an unmanaged Google Account

There may be scenarios where users sign up to have a Google Account with their work domain as an email address. These user accounts are unmanaged accounts and administrators will have to use a special workflow to convert these accounts as managed accounts to preserve their data. A typical workflow for merging users with unmanaged Google Account is illustrated in the following bullet points:

- Google gives you the option of registering for a Google Cloud Identity account for your work email. Even if the organization does not use Google Workspace for their business, users can still sign up for a Google Account.
- Later, when the same organization decides to purchase Google Workspace, these users who previously have a Google Cloud Identity account end up having **conflicting accounts**.
- Administrators have the option of searching for such existing conflicting accounts and being sent an invite that merges the account into a managed Workspace account with the user's consent.

Why is this workflow necessary? For the following reasons:

- If the same user email is created in a Google Workspace domain, the conflicting user's data created within the conflicting account will be lost.
- By receiving consent from the user, we are converting the user account into a managed user within the Workspace domain.

Here are the steps for this workflow:

1. Log in to the **Admin** console.
2. From the home page, click on **Users**.
3. Click on **More** | **Transfer tool for unmanaged users**.
4. This unmanaged user page lists all such existing user accounts.
5. Select the users you'd like to request consent from and click **Invite**.

   Users who receive this invitation to merge the account can choose to click **Accept** or **Decline**. This results in the following:

   - If users click **Accept**, the unmanaged user account will be converted into a Workspace user account.
   - If users click **Decline**, administrators can proceed with creating this same user as a "new user" in the Workspace domain. The conflicting account will receive a prompt to rename the account to avoid further conflict.

# Deleting users

Administrators can delete or suspend users. Let's look at a practical use case. If an employee is going on temporary leave for reasons such as short-term disability, maternity, or paternity, with the intention of staying dormant for a short term, but eventually will be active after a certain period, then this user will need to be in a *Suspended* state.

If an employee is being terminated or leaving your organization, you would want to delete the user, freeing up the license for reassignment. While this is required, collaborators would also want to retain access to the data. Besides data retention through Vault for legal reasons, Google provides you with an option to transfer the ownership of the content from the ex-employee to another user.

Mistakes may happen, and employees may bounce back and rejoin your organization. Users who are deleted can be restored within 20 days.

> **User Deletion Deletes Content**
>
> If a user account is indeed going to be deleted, you should know that data such as Gmail, Drive, and Sites created by this user will also be deleted by default unless it is explicitly transferred. Groups that the user was part of, however, will not be deleted.

The following steps indicate how a user will need to be deleted from the **Admin** console:

1. Log in to the Google **Admin** console.
2. Search for the user or click on **Directory | User**. Then, select the user.
3. Click on **Delete User** from the left-side panel.

As part of the user deletion workflow, administrators are provided with an option to transfer data from the to-be-deleted user to another user. Administrators are presented with options such as this:

**Transfer user's data**

**Data in Gmail**

1. Migrate the user's existing email
2. If you want to keep receiving future emails sent to this address, here are your options
   - Reuse this users email address **(Recommended)**
     You can make this user's current email address an alternate email (email alias) for another user 24 hours after this user is deleted. Learn more
   - Set up email forwarding for incoming messages

**Data in other apps**

Transfer Don't transfer data

Select the user you want to transfer **Jane CloudIdentity's** data to (for example, a manager)

Search for a user

Select data to transfer :

Drive And Docs

Include files that are not shared with anyone.

Calendar

Also release all calendar resources booked in events organised by the user
Only future non-private events with at least one guest/resource shall be transferred. Learn more

Brand Accounts
Brand Accounts and their data will be transferred to a new owner.

Data Studio

Include assets that are not shared with anyone.

All data not transferred will be deleted, including YouTube and Vault data. Learn more

Once you delete this user their license will be removed.

CANCEL DELETE USER

Figure 2.3 – Transferring content to others on user deletion

If a user is leaving the organization or is being deleted, you can transfer the ownership of content to the user's peer or manager. This helps retain Drive content and any weekly/daily team calls scheduled by the user. Others can still have access to it.

As already mentioned, if this user is deleted by mistake or if the user chooses to get rehired, you can recover the deleted user. Here are the steps to do so:

1. Click on the **Admin** console | **Directory** | **Users.**
2. Select **Filter** to pick the **Recently deleted** option.
3. This shows all the recently deleted users and you can recover from there. You can see the **Recently deleted** filter in the following screenshot:

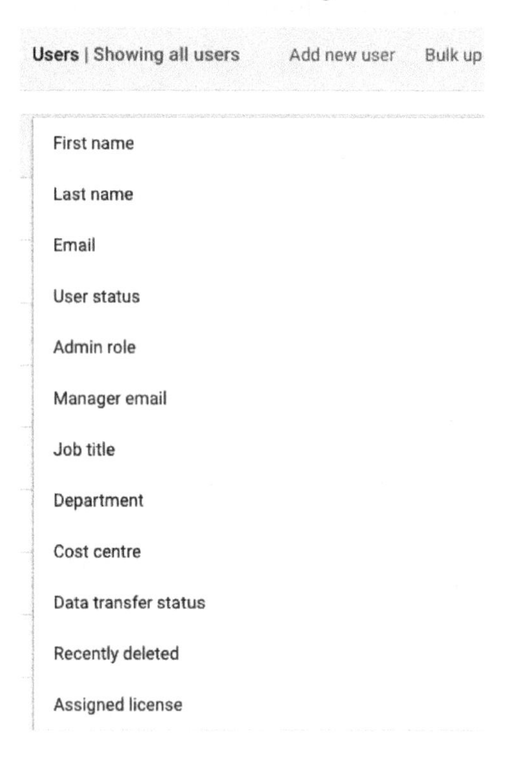


Figure 2.4 – Recently deleted filter on the Admin console

Administrators will be presented with a screen like this one as part of the **Recover user** workflow:

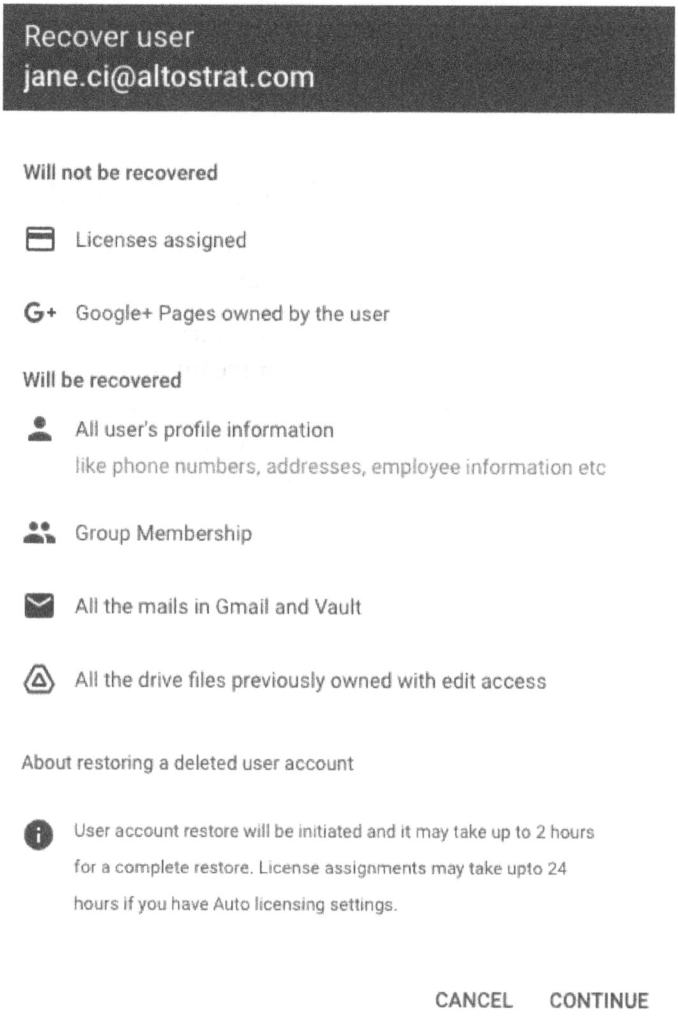

Recover user
jane.ci@altostrat.com

Will not be recovered

Licenses assigned

Google+ Pages owned by the user

Will be recovered

All user's profile information
like phone numbers, addresses, employee information etc

Group Membership

All the mails in Gmail and Vault

All the drive files previously owned with edit access

About restoring a deleted user account

User account restore will be initiated and it may take up to 2 hours for a complete restore. License assignments may take upto 24 hours if you have Auto licensing settings.

CANCEL CONTINUE

Figure 2.5 – Recovering a deleted user

Recovering a user is not simple, and Cloud Identity has some restrictions on when a deleted user can be recovered. Firstly, the user should not have been deleted over 20 days ago; secondly, there should be enough licenses to cover when the recovered user is restored; and finally, the username or email alias should not have been reallocated to someone else.

With user configurations well established, it's time to move on to look at how users can start working with Google Workspace applications.

With the ability to configure users squared away, let's turn our focus to the GCDS service, a useful service that helps you import users, groups, and a few other entities from your existing LDAP directory service to Google Workspace.

## Using Google Cloud Directory Sync (GCDS)

Organizations typically have all their users in an AD that refers to a list of users stored as a directory of information. AD organizes the users in an OU.

User identities can be directly created in Google's Cloud Identity or they can be integrated from various sources, such as **human resource information systems** (**HRIS**) (**Workday**, **Systems, Applications, and Products in Data Processing** (**SAP**), and so on), or other **identity providers** (**IdPs**), such as Okta, Ping Identity, ForgeRock, and Azure AD using federation. We will dive into federation techniques in the next section when we talk about SSO.

These identity systems serve as the *source of truth* for user identities and integrate with all applications that require user-login authentication. Google Cloud integrates with all these sources of identities seamlessly using GCDS and makes your move to Google Workspace easy, as illustrated in the following diagram:

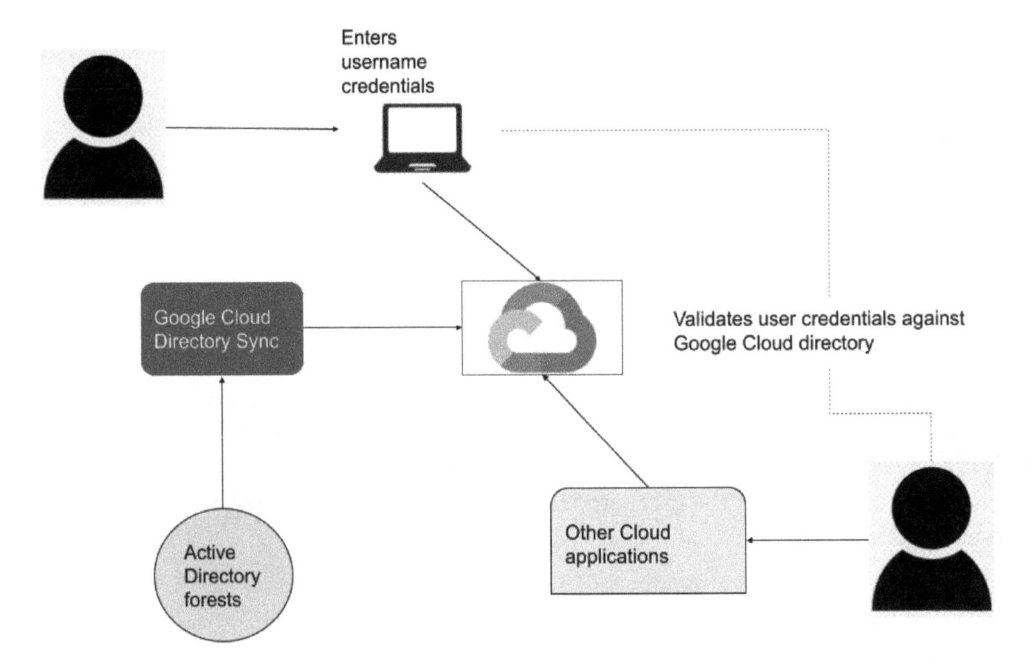


Figure 2.6 – Overview of GCDS

From a user's point of view, they do not have to remember multiple passwords or credentials across each app they use. Users who enter their password for logging in to their respective computers are validated against the AD, and their passwords are synced from AD to their respective email inboxes. This ensures that users enter their credentials only once when logging in to their computer, and that's it. They can open a browser and access all Workspace data from each app.

Administrators wish to retain AD LDAP information and continue authorizing users to their Workspace accounts using AD authentication. When GCDS syncs LDAP information from AD, these users get a Cloud Identity account created in a Google Domain and further can be configured to have a Workspace license applied as well. Administrators can download GCDS from this link: `https://tools.google.com/dlpage/dirsync`.

You can see an overview of GCDS here:

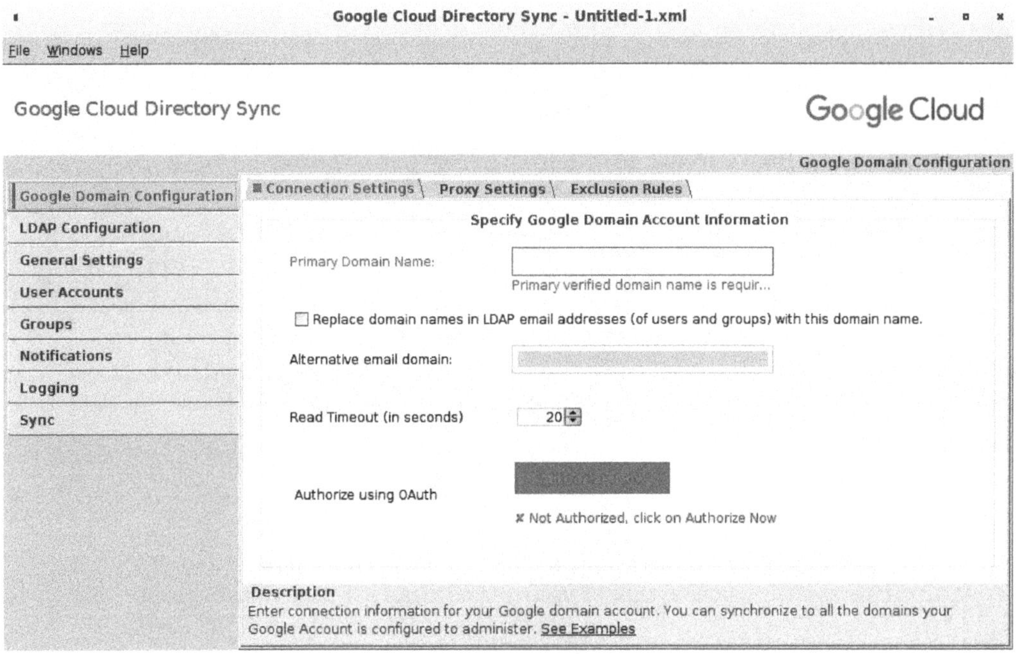

Figure 2.7 – GCDS of users

GCDS is a client-installed application that may run in a standalone server and is authorized to connect both the AD and the destination Google Workspace domain.

GCDS can perform one-way sync on the following:

- OUs
- Users:
    - User aliases
    - Extended user profile information such as address, phone number, employee **identifier** (**ID**), or any other LDAP-based custom information that is unique to an organization
- Groups:
    - Groups of users that can be used for granting access to Drive content or Sites
- Contacts:
    - This can be employee contact information or other commonly used contact information such as shared contacts
- Passwords
- Calendar rooms

GCDS automatically populates several default settings based on source AD/LDAP versions, which makes it easier to configure. It also provides an ability to perform custom mapping, which can come in handy when—say—user profiles have a slightly different name across these two systems; for instance, custom mapping could be as simple as username naming conventions or `EmployeeID` from `AD` to the `EID` field in the user profile. These mapping rules can also be used if specific users and groups need to be excluded from the migration.

**GCDS Is Safe**

It is important to call out that GCDS does not migrate any content such as email messages, calendar events, or user-created files. GCDS executes one-way sync between your AD/LDAP source to Google Workspace and does not alter any data in your current LDAP configuration.

# GCDS configurations

GCDS has options for custom rules that help administrators select which users need to be synced to the Google Workspace domain. Similarly, if you end up creating users directly in Google Domain, GCDS might delete them because those users do not exist in the source AD. You can create an exclusion rule for that OU within the Google domain. That will ensure GCDS does not compare those users against your AD.

The following screenshot shows the GCDS configuration screen:

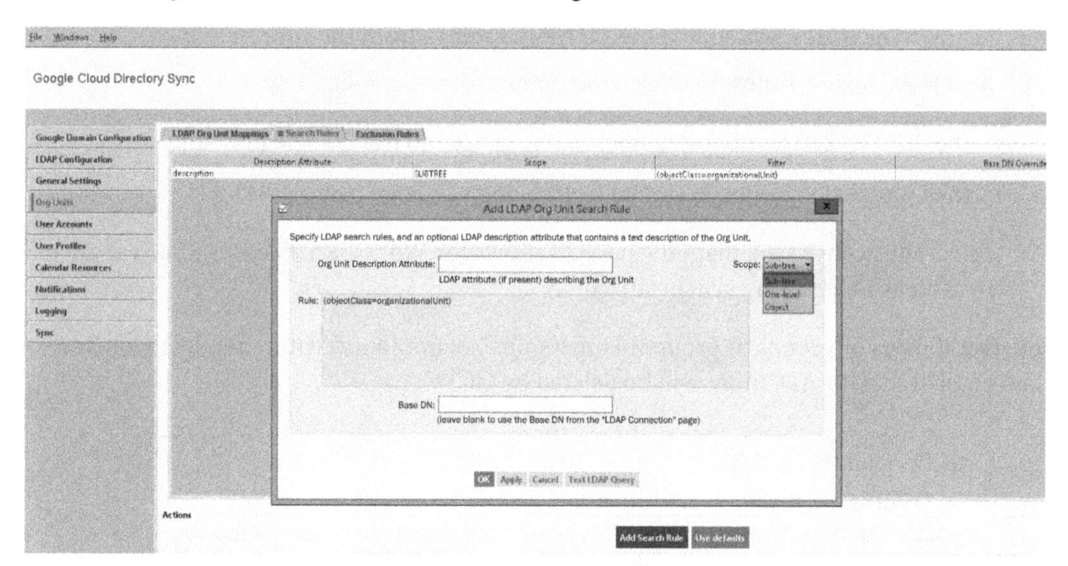


Figure 2.8 – GCDS configuration screen

Here is a quick step-by-step checklist for GCDS:

1. Install GCDS on a server. Both Windows and Linux servers are supported.
2. GCDS uses **Open Authorization** (**OAuth**) for authentication, and the refresh token is typically stored as a configuration file in the **Extensible Markup Language** (**XML**) format.

   On the server where GCDS is locally installed, it requires access to write into one folder at the minimum to keep its configuration XML file updated with the latest OAuth refresh token.

3. Enter your Google domain user credentials. This is the user authorization used for executing GCDS.

   A best practice is to create a user account called `GCDS Admin` and use that to authorize this GCDS execution. This helps in auditing any user/group updates in Google Domain. Ensure this user account has a comfortable session expiration duration or does not require a password change until the sync finishes running.

4. Set up **General Settings** by selecting what would you like to sync.
5. Set up **Sync Rules**, which include LDAP mappings from the source.
6. Set up **Exclusion Rules**. You have the option to do the following:

   - The AD OU can be excluded from being synced to the Google domain.
   - The Google OU can be excluded from being validated against AD.

7. Select the license sync mapping. GCDS allows for Workspace licenses to be assigned to users who are being synchronized.

Note that if users or groups or group memberships are not found within Google Domain when compared with AD, those will be deleted by GCDS.

> **GCDS Simulation Mode**
>
> GCDS offers a simulation mode that shows administrators the result of a sync, without performing a sync. This helps administrators to understand what the outcome will be and whether they would like to go ahead with the synchronization. Administrators are encouraged to take advantage of this feature and tweak configuration settings so that they feel comfortable before performing the actual synchronization.

> **GCDS Scheduled Sync**
>
> The GCDS tool can be scheduled to run at regular frequencies to keep the `User` directory up to date with the latest profile and directory information. It is important to note that any changes that are performed at Google Workspace for these users will need to be reflected in the source AD/LDAP systems, otherwise the subsequent GCDS run can wipe out the changes that were performed on the Google Workspace OUs.

Now that users have been created and synced with Google Workspace, let's move on to license management—an important area that dwells on how users are assigned licenses so that they can start consuming Google Workspace services.

# Managing licenses

A user needs a license to use Google Workspace services.

When users are created, they automatically acquire a Cloud Identity-Free license and then become eligible to be assigned a Google Workspace license. If organizations prefer not to have all users in Google Workspace and would like to have only a few of them assigned Cloud Identity accounts, then that is possible as well.

For example, this situation may be applicable for short-term employees who are the recipients of Google Drive content, interns who read data but do not create content of their own, or for other employees who require access to applications that are hosted on GCP. Anyone who does not require Gmail access or authorization to create content can use Cloud Identity.

Google has clearly laid out the requirements for how users will be mapped to a service, as outlined here:

- If an organization has more than one Google Workspace subscription or a mix of Cloud Identity and Cloud Identity Premium subscriptions, then administrators can only enable automatic licensing for one of those subscribed products' **stock-keeping units** (**SKUs**). Only one service will be eligible for automatic licensing.
- Once automatic licensing has been turned on for all users, the ability to remove an individual user's license will be lost. If an individual user license needs to be removed, then administrators will have to turn off automatic licensing and then remove the license for the user.
- Automatic licensing can be set up for specific OUs when you have multiple OUs.

Also, note that once automatic licensing has been turned on, it may take up to a day to take effect.

We discussed previously how users can be federated using GCDS. If your organization is using GCDS, you must choose one of the following ways to automatically assign licenses:

- Using the option in the Google **Admin** console described in the *Configuring users in Cloud Identity* section
- While configuring GCDS

The following screenshot shows **Auto-licensing** being enabled on an OU:

Auto-licensing: OFF for everyone ? Override for specific organizations

| Overriding Organizations | Auto-licensing | Remove All |
| --- | --- | --- |
| MTV > **Zoom Marketing** | ON (Google Apps Vault) | × |
| ... > Zoom Marketing > **Marketing Vendor Team** | OFF | × |

Figure 2.9 – Auto-licensing is enabled on an OU level

## How to enable automatic license assignment?

The following steps will walk you through on how to enable automatic license assignments:

1. Log in to your Google **Admin** console.
2. Click on **Billing | License settings**.
3. Click on the service you want to assign licenses for.
4. Click the section option to be **On**.
5. If you have multiple subscriptions of the same service, choose which subscription to use for automatic license assignment.
6. Click **Save**.

The following screenshot shows what administrators will see when automatic licensing has been turned on:

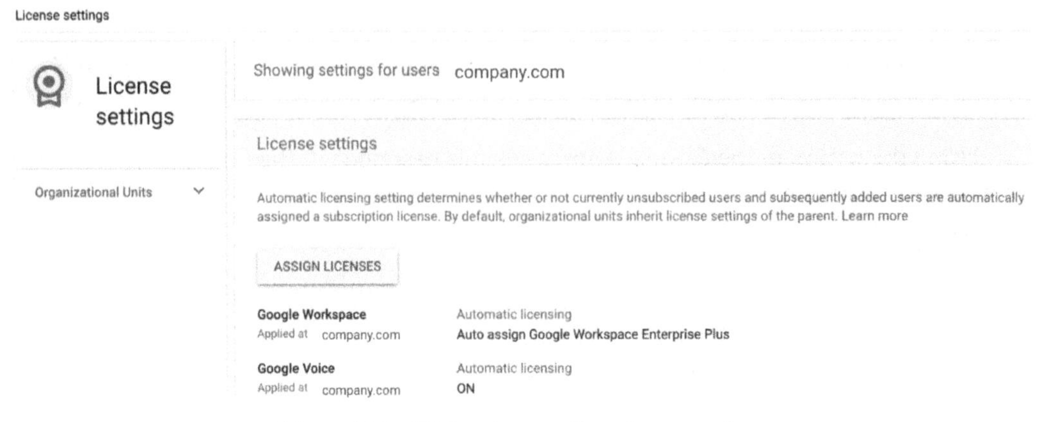


Figure 2.10 – With automatic licensing turned on

## How to manually assign licenses to users?

The following steps narrate how to manually assign licenses to users:

1. Log in to your Google **Admin** console.
2. Navigate to **Users**.
3. Next to each user's name where you want to assign or remove a license, check the box.
4. At the top, click on **More** and select **Assign Licenses** or **Remove Licenses**.
5. Navigate to **Subscription** and then select **Assign** or **Remove**.

This will automatically take effect by granting or revoking these users' access to Workspace services. However, it is to be noted that unassigned licenses might take up to 24 hours to be available for reassignment to a different user.

If the Workspace license is removed for a user, the user will default to being a Cloud Identity user while still retaining access to additional Google services such as YouTube and Google News. Similarly, if organizations use other third-party cloud apps such as Salesforce, DocuSign, and Workday, those are pre-integrated within Google Cloud Identity. They do not require a Workspace license.

Practically speaking, users can log in to their computer using their credentials and open the browser to access Gmail, Drive, and so on from Workspace, and further can also access other integrated apps without having to log in again.

# Configuring applications in Workspace

As we know already, Google Workspace is a collection of productivity and collaboration apps that enable you to run your teams efficiently. The Google Workspace application suite can be broadly classified into the following three segments:

- Core applications developed by Google
- Additional Google services that fall outside of the core applications
- Marketplace or third-party applications

The following table shows the different categories of applications and some popular applications in each category:

| Core services | Additional Google services | Popular marketplace applications |
|---|---|---|
| Gmail | AppSheet | Timer for Google Forms |
| Meet | Blogger | Kami |
| Chat | Brand Accounts | Pear Deck |
| Calendar | Classroom | LucidChart |
| Drive | FeedBurner | Zoom |
| Docs | Google Ads | EasyBib |
| Sheets | Google Books | Form Mule |
| Slides | GCP | Slides Translator |
| Forms | Google Data Studio | Copy Down |
| Sites | Google Domains | Presence for Meet |
| Currents | Google Trips | Fluency Tutor |
| Keep | Individual Storage | Classroom Share |
| Apps Script | Material Gallery | Stava Rex |
| Cloud Search | Socratic | CLOZEit |
| Jamboard | YouTube | PlagiarismCheck.org |

Google Workspace allows you to enable various apps included within the Workspace suite of services and provides integrations to extend its capabilities to other third-party apps. This list is ever-growing. There are hundreds of Marketplace applications.

**Marketplace Apps**

Marketplace apps are applications developed by aspiring developers or product owners trying to integrate their product with Google Workspace and help extend its functionality beyond Google Cloud.

For example, if a legal team uses an e-signature service such as DocuSign frequently, administrators can install the eSignature add-on from Marketplace. This will allow users to use the add-on within the Gmail or Drive **user interface** (**UI**).

Another example would be a sales team using marketing apps such as Salesforce frequently; installing add-ons can allow users to add/fetch relevant information from third-party applications quickly.

The following screenshot shows the different app categories available on the Admin console:

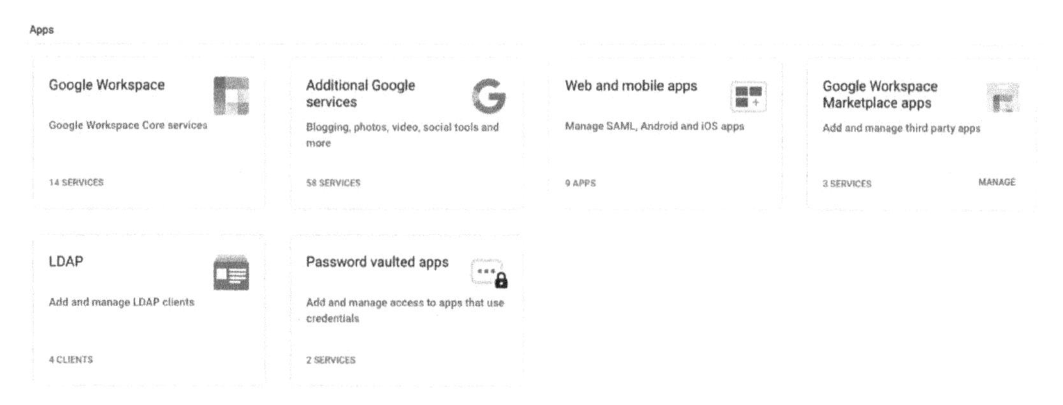


Figure 2.11 – App categories in the Admin console

We will review Marketplace apps, managed LDAP clients, and password vaulted apps in our next chapter. Let's focus on Google Workspace apps and additional Google services in the next section.

# Google Workspace core services

The Google **Admin** console provides a nifty way to turn any of the Google Workspace core services on or off. Let's look at the setup process to configure Google Workspace core services, as follows:

1. Log in to the Google **Admin** console.
2. Click on **Apps**.
3. Click on **Overview**.
4. Now, click on **Google Workspace** to see a full list of OUs in the left panel and a list of Google apps on the right side.

   By now, you will have a list of users and the required services that need to be enabled for each user. To make this convenient and efficient, you are recommended to have a user categorized already into OUs.
5. Select an OU, and then select the app that you would like to enable or disable.

6. Click on the kebab icon (3 dots) to enable or disable the service, as illustrated in the following screenshot. These changes can take up to 24 hours to propagate to all users:

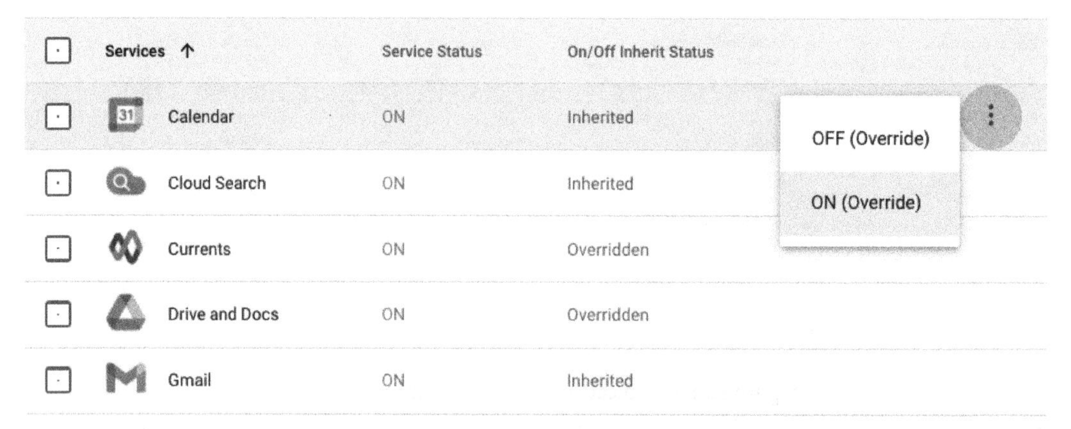


Figure 2.12 – Using the kebab icon to enable/disable service

Once you have completed enabling or disabling the service for each OU, it determines whether the sub-OUs are inheriting the permission of the root OU or whether it is being overridden.

# Google additional services

Similarly, organization owners can also enable additional Google services so that their users can benefit from the Google product portfolio and the cloud services it has to offer.

Administrators have the option of enabling or disabling certain apps for respective OUs or Google access groups.

During Google Workspace deployment planning, it is a best practice to segregate your users into functional groups and then make a checklist of which apps are required for each of those clusters of users. This makes the configurations easier to implement, and any OU-specific exceptions can be handled via groups.

OUs can be set up to have restricted access, and security groups can be further used to allow exceptional access for even more granularity.

Here is how to enable additional Google services:

1. Log in to the Google **Admin** console.
2. Click on **Apps**.
3. Click on **Overview**.
4. Now, click on **Additional Google Services** to see a full list of OUs in the left panel and a list of additional Google apps on the right side.

Turning the services on/off is rather a relatively simple exercise. However, configuring apps is not so straightforward. There are several app-specific entries you may need to keep handy for easier setup.

In the next section, you will learn about how to configure a popular core service—Gmail.

## Enabling Gmail

Configuring Gmail in your domain involves setting up and configuring routes via **mail exchanger** (**MX**) records. MX records are responsible for receiving emails for this domain. Until MX records are defined, emails sent to these users will not reach the user's inboxes. While the **Domain Name System** (**DNS**) helps reach the content for this domain's website, MX records serve as the address for the mailbox.

When configuring MX records, we would define several MX records, typically pointing to an array of mail servers for load balancing and redundancy.

MX records are typically defined within the domain host provider settings. Note that this is the same DNS host provider from *Chapter 1*, *Introducing Google Workspace*, where we have entered the **TXT** record.

The following steps will help navigate and set up MX records with your domain host:

1. Log in to the domain host provider control panel.
2. Within the control panel of the domain host provider, open the settings to configure the domain's MX records:

    I. Remember to delete any existing MX records before you configure your domain's MX records.

    II. If you can't delete existing MX records, change their priority number to a higher value—typically over `20`. The priority that you set when you add an MX record specifies the sequence in which an email server receives emails. The lower the number, the higher the priority.

3. Add new MX records for the Google mail servers.

   If your domain host places a limit on the number of MX records, then only add the first two records shown in the following table of Google Workspace MX records:

| Name/Host/Alias | Time to Live (TTL*) | Record type | Priority | Value/Answer/Destination |
|---|---|---|---|---|
| @ or leave blank | 3600 | MX | 1 | ASPMX.L.GOOGLE.COM |
| @ or leave blank | 3600 | MX | 5 | ALT1.ASPMX.L.GOOGLE.COM |
| @ or leave blank | 3600 | MX | 5 | ALT2.ASPMX.L.GOOGLE.COM |
| @ or leave blank | 3600 | MX | 10 | ALT3.ASPMX.L.GOOGLE.COM |
| @ or leave blank | 3600 | MX | 10 | ALT4.ASPMX.L.GOOGLE.COM |

4. Save your changes.

   Skip the following step if you already verified your domain by another method (such as a TXT or **Canonical Name (CNAME)** record).

5. If you need to verify your domain, in the **Admin** console, scroll to the **Get your verification code** section and click the **COPY** button, as illustrated in the following screenshot:

| MX SERVER ADDRESS | PRIORITY |
|---|---|
| ALT1.ASPMX.L.GOOGLE.COM | 5 |
| ALT2.ASPMX.L.GOOGLE.COM | 5 |
| ALT3.ASPMX.L.GOOGLE.COM | 10 |
| ALT4.ASPMX.L.GOOGLE.COM | 10 |

**Note**: Each address is for a Google mail server. We provide several servers in case one becomes unavailable.

**5. Get your verification code**

Figure 2.13 – Verification code in the Admin console

6. Paste the value into the **Value/Answer/Destination/Target** column.
7. Ensure the record's priority is set to **Low** or to `15` or greater.

8. Open the Google **Admin** console.
9. Within the **Setup** tool under **Manage Domains**, a red circle highlights the **Activate** option in the Gmail section.
10. In the Gmail section, click **Activate**.
11. Verify that you've created all user email addresses for Gmail. Click **Continue**.
12. On the next page, click **Activate Gmail to complete the configuration**.

Once this is completed, you can send and receive messages at your new Google Workspace email address in less than 6 hours (at the latest by 48-72 hours).

To avoid spam and make sure your emails do not get spoofed, best practices for email authentication suggest that you set up the **Sender Policy Framework** (**SPF**), **DomainKeys Identified Mail** (**DKIM**) for digital signatures, and **Domain-based Message Authentication, Reporting, and Conformance** (**DMARC**).

We will review these settings in the next chapter.

## Sharing resources via Calendar

Google Workspace allows any shared resources in an organization to be effectively suggested and shared among users. These resources could be anything—conference rooms, company cars, bicycles, game rooms, and so on. Calendar provides a nifty way to let administrators add these resources under different categories and allow them to be surfaced via the Calendar interface.

Administrators typically start by adding a building first, then adding more resources such as rooms and **audiovisual** (**AV**) systems inside those buildings. Once complete, for instance, users would be able to reserve a room with Jamboard that is in Building 2, conference room 3.

Google Calendar's **artificial intelligence/machine learning** (**AI/ML**) feature works with shared resources that fall under the category of **Meeting Space** to automate room booking suggestions based on user preferences. The AI/ML feature looks at various heuristics, such as total participants in a meeting and the proximity to buildings, and suggests meeting rooms accordingly. This can be very helpful as users don't have to keep hunting across several rooms that match their criteria.

Google Calendar configuration options and sharing settings will be discussed extensively in the next chapter.

# Summary

This chapter laid a great foundation of Google Cloud Identity and how it integrates with Google Workspace. We also saw a step-by-step overview of creating or migrating users into Workspace and how to assign licenses to them. We dwelled upon GCDS in detail to understand how it helps migrate users and other entities from existing identity systems over to Workspace. Once users are in place, we looked at how to assign licenses to them so that they start consuming Workplace services. This chapter concluded by looking at different types of services that are made available and how to activate them for users or groups. Now, it's time to peek under the hood at how user data is managed by Workspace and which security options are available across services in the next chapter.

# Part 2: Data Security

In this part, you will learn how Workspace keeps your data secure. As bad actors evolve their techniques over time, Workspace has also evolved to keep up with the different attack vectors that target your data. We will talk about security configurations that are available in different layers of Workspace. The part will also talk about how Workspace satisfies some enterprise compliance needs.

This part comprises the following chapters:


- *Chapter 3, Application Security*
- *Chapter 4, Automated Security Auditing*

# 3
# Application Security

Google Workspace has evolved over the years, introducing an increasing number of security features that are necessary for customers of all sizes, from small-to-medium businesses to large enterprises. Google has a security-first culture when it comes to building applications. To achieve defense-in-depth, security features should be in place at every level of the application. Security should never be an afterthought, especially for SaaS products; these products are accessible by almost everyone across the globe. The applications and their infrastructure must undergo continuous improvement, and any new vulnerabilities that are identified must be patched.

In Google Workspace, data protection is incorporated within every layer of the technology stack, beginning at the very bottom of the stack, where infrastructure is purpose-built and every server is embedded with a Titan chip. These chips have proven extremely difficult to be hacked, providing a secure operational model with additional physical protection for data centers and encryption across the network path. Furthermore, data stored in Google Workspace can be kept secure by configuring advanced malware and spam protection, content compliance rules, secure sharing settings, and automated alerts powered by AI/ML systems. We will take an extensive look at the security configurations that are available for different core services and applications in this chapter.

In this chapter, we will cover the following topics:

- Context-Aware Access
- Google end-user security
- Single sign-on
- Google security settings for integrated Marketplace apps

# Context-Aware Access using Cloud Identity

As Google was growing globally, there was a need to redesign the security models and access policies that would allow employees from various geographies and devices to access their data securely. The intent was to implement a zero-trust security process, enabling users to work from anywhere without the need for a traditional VPN.

This model is called **BeyondCorp**.

With the design of such secure system, security and pragmatism should go together; otherwise, security could deter users from using the product. Employees are your assets, and these security options should allow employees to work from anywhere; they should not be a hindrance. The solution should provide excellent auditability and traceability when things go wrong. With a diverse workforce including field workers, parents, part-time workers, and traveling executives, the BeyondCorp model needed to be flexible and cater to different user needs. Google opened up this BeyondCorp model for its Workspace users under the brand name **Context-Aware Access**. Context-Aware Access is bundled with Cloud Identity's Premium license:

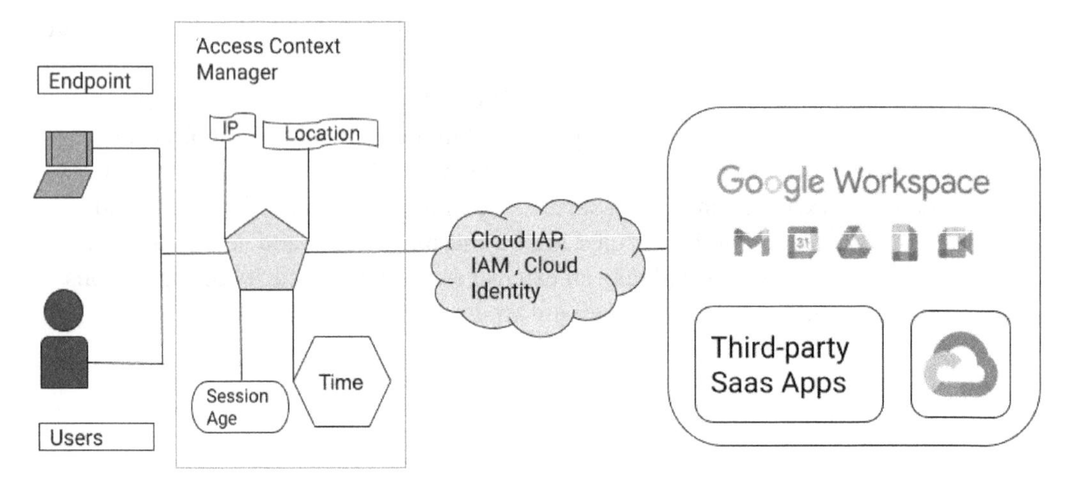


Figure 3.1 – Context-Aware Access conceptual model

Context-Aware Access kicks into action the moment a Workspace user connects to their work data from any device. Context-Aware Access provides true zero-trust functionality, it determines the apps that user can access based on their device and security policies. Users could be logging in from various services such as `gmail.com` or `drive.google.com` or through **single sign-on** (**SSO**) using third-party SaaS applications. Regardless of the service users choose to log in from, Context-Aware Access executes its core zero-trust tenet. It accomplishes this by factoring in multiple constraints, such as the user's device type, IP address, and service type to evaluate this authentication.

Context-Aware Access also uses access policies defined by the administrator, which are then assigned to users in OUs as access levels. These access policies are evaluated by the rules engine every time the user logs in. There is no implicit assumption that allows the user to log in. This ensures that employees truly get the agile experience of using any device, anywhere, to be able to access their work data.

> No Need for VPNs
>
> Typically, enterprises use **virtual private networks** (**VPNs**) to allow secure work access. Using Context-Aware Access alleviates the need for VPNs.
>
> Access policies can be used to restrict access to Workspace apps in the corporate network. Access policies can also be applied to integrated apps to exclude a subset of users within the corporate network.

Next, let's take a look at how to configure Context-Aware Access.

# Configuring Context-Aware Access

Context-Aware Access can be configured using the Workspace **Admin** console using the following levers:

- **Access Policy**: Access Policy is based on a combination of the following:
  - Geolocation
  - IP address
  - Mobile device policy such as OS version, OS type, and so on
- **Access Levels**: The defined access policy can be assigned to Workspace services and for specific OUs as well.

- **Error Message**: Here, you can configure the error message that users will see when their access to a service is denied. We do not want the user to feel clueless when they get an authentication error:

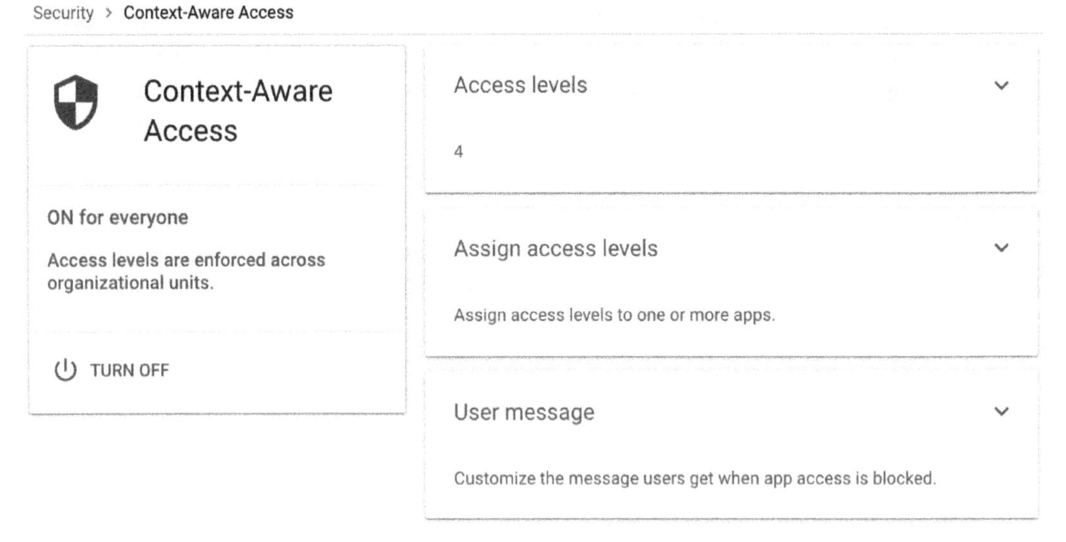


Figure 3.2 – Configuring Context-Aware Access

While Context-Aware Access is intelligent enough to understand the dynamics of where the user is accessing data from and what they are accessing, it is a shared responsibility between the user and Google Workspace to keep accounts secure. Google Workspace provides several options to protect user accounts from unauthorized access. We'll review them in the next section.

# End-user security

Google Cloud Identity users have the option to self-serve their account security settings on the Workspace **Admin** console. All users should be able to set up **2-step verification (2SV)**, view their login history, look at their registered devices, and look at their active sessions.

Besides these end-user settings, administrators can also mandate certain security settings for users or manage sessions, cookies, and password settings. Administrators have the power to do the following:

- Reset a user's password.
- Reset a user's session/cookies, forcing the user to log in again.

- Check on the user's 2SV enrollment.
- Revoke access to any third-party applications. Irrepsective of whether access is granted directly with the user's Cloud Identity or through an application-specific password, both can be managed by the Administrator.

Next, let's look at how Google strives to keep users secure via password monitoring.

## Password monitoring

One of the challenges with username/password combinations is that users are the weakest link. Google's products may be secure and have the best-in-class security, but if users decide to use the same password across multiple websites and if one of the websites gets compromised, Google's products will be compromised as well.

There are a couple of ways to overcome this challenge:

- Administrators can enforce certain policies to ensure users have a strong password that has a minimal probability of being hacked.
- Google Chrome also has a password monitoring extension called *Google Password Manager*. This extension restricts users from reusing the same password they are currently using for their organization's Google Workspace account across any other personal websites, such as banking and retail.

Here are some recommendations for password monitoring:

- **Enforce strong passwords**: From the **Admin** console, administrators can enable the enforcement of strong passwords for user passwords. Google uses a password strength-rating algorithm to confirm a strong password. Strong passwords have better password strength – strong passwords are effective against guessing or brute-force attacks by bad actors. Google's algorithm eliminates commonly used phrases or easy passwords such as `myPassword` or `Password123`, and it also checks for randomness in the alphanumeric password characters to gauge the password's strength.
- **Enforce password length**: Administrators can enforce passwords to be between 8 and 100 characters long.
- **Password expiration**: This is set to ensure the current password expires after a certain period of time, prompting users to redefine a new password. This expiration happens at regular frequencies and can be configured to allow/prevent users from reusing their old passwords.

## 2-step verification

With threats and security vulnerabilities across the internet growing, protecting Google accounts with a username/password combination is just not enough. As we noted earlier in the *Password monitoring* section, users can reuse passwords and are prone to several hacking attempts, such as **rainbow table** attacks.

Google allows users to have an additional layer of security with an authentication key, besides a password. This is called 2SV, which is also called *multi-factor authentication* or *2-factor authentication.*

When an Administrator enforces 2SV, users are given a period to enroll and configure their choice of 2SV. Once 2SV has been configured, all future logins from this user require the additional second key to be used during every login.

When selecting the key for 2SV, the following options are available:

- **SMS**: Users receive a code on their mobile phone via a text message. Carrier charges may apply for receiving text messages.
- **Phone call**: Users receive a phone call from an automated system that spells out the 2SV code.
- **Backup codes**: After setting up 2SV, users can generate backup codes to be used for authentication when they lose their device.
- **Google prompt**: Push notifications are sent to users of Android or iOS mobile devices. This is a much safer option as this requires both the Google account credentials and access to the mobile device that's connected to this account.
- **Google Authenticator app**: A mobile app by Google that helps users configure and generate a one-time password as the 2-factor key. This app can be configured to serve as 2SV for more than one Google account.
- **Security key**: This is the most secure option for 2SV. This is a physical security key that is inserted into your computer to authorize access to your Google accounts. These devices are direct defenses against credential phishing.

> **Credential Phishing**
>
> Credential phishing occurs when hackers trick users into sharing their username/password combination. Depending on the type of key (a Titan Security Key or a generic hardware security key), it can be connected using USB, Bluetooth, or **near-field communication** (**NFC**) to pass the second factor of authentication.

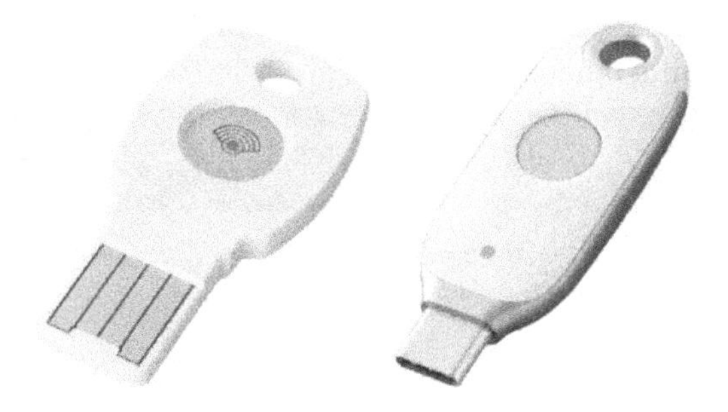

Figure 3.3 – Titan Security Keys

So far, we have looked at the capabilities of Context-Aware Access and how it enables administrators to provision and secure users with Google Workspace. In the next section, we will deep dive into how Google handles SSO through industry-standard protocols.

# Single sign-on

SSO is an authentication process that allows users to log into multiple applications or systems using a single set of credentials. SSO works on a trust-based model that's established between the system that has user credentials, called the **Identity Provider (IdP)**, and the service/application that the user wants to access, called the **Service Provider (SP)**. Typically, the SSO mechanism is implemented using the **Security Assertion Markup Language (SAML)** protocol.

Google Workspace supports SSO via the SAML protocol. This typically means that you will have to log in just once to be able to access all the supported applications.

As we noted in the previous chapter, **Google Cloud Directory Sync (GCDS)** can be used to sync user details and credentials from AD into Google Cloud Identity. Besides AD, other IdPs such as Ping Identity and Okta can be configured as the user directory and sync identities to Google Cloud.

Administrators can remove dependencies on other IdPs and choose to use Google Cloud Identity as its IdP. To extend this functionality beyond the core services offered in Google Workspace, there are 300+ pre-integrated apps included in Google Cloud's integration portfolio that support SSO using SAML.

To enable pre-integrated apps in your domain, follow these steps:

1. Go to the Google **Admin** console.
2. Click on **Apps** from the left-hand side panel and select **Web and Mobile Apps**.

3. Click on **Add App** to see the available options. An Android or iOS app or custom SAML app can be added here:

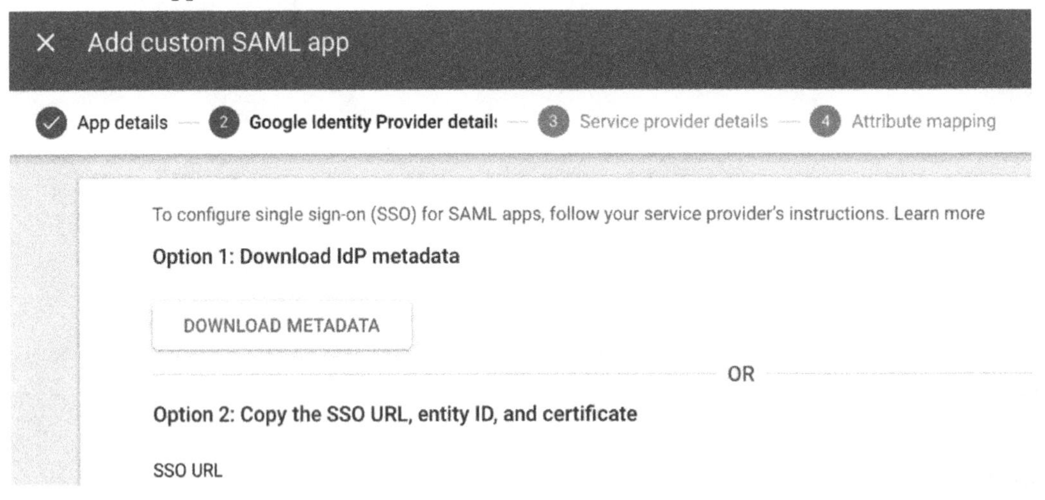


Figure 3.4 – Adding a custom SAML app

By adding these apps, domain administrators can let users directly access these apps without having to log in to each app individually.

The following link provides the full up-to-date list of all the pre-integrated apps:

`https://support.google.com/a/table/9217027?hl=en&ref_topic=7556794`

In this section, we learned how to integrate with other apps beyond Google Workspace using SAML-based authentication. However, some organizations have legacy applications that are built in-house that require credentials and do not support SAML-based authentication. Let's dive into how Google Workspace handles them.

# Password vaulted apps

In the previous two sections, we covered how Google Workspace support SSO IdP and password vaulted apps. However, some organizations have legacy applications that are built in-house that require credentials and do not support SAML-based authentication.

Google Workspace extends the SSO functionality through its **password vaulted apps** capability. This service saves login credentials for applications and assigns those credentials to users through group association. Users will need to be part of a group to be able to log into the app via the Google user console. Groups provide an elegant way to segregate users and control access.

A typical workflow for using password vaulted apps is highlighted here.

The first step in setting up password vaulted apps is group creation. Users can be added or removed as needed from these groups:

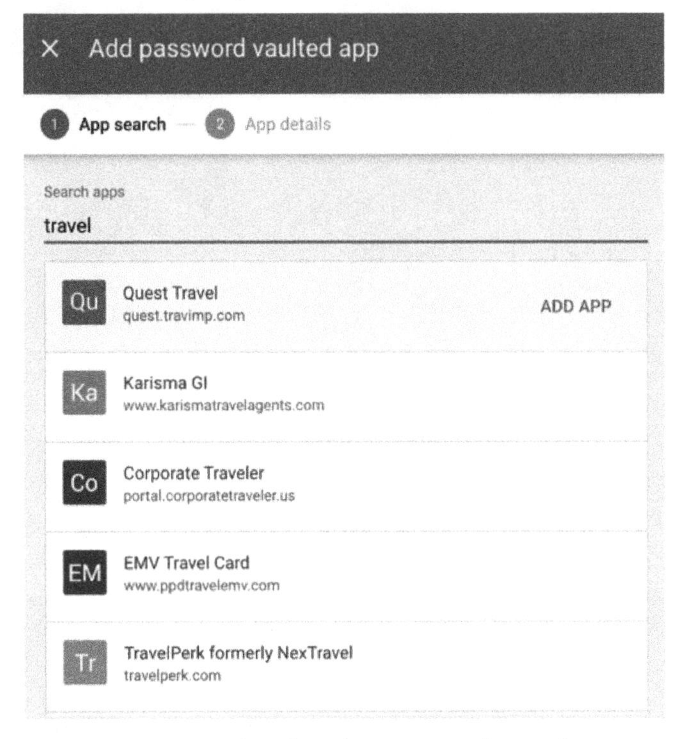


Figure 3.5 – Searching for apps using keywords

Once a group has been created and an app has been selected, administrators can assign the app to groups and add credentials for tying up all three factors of this functionality:

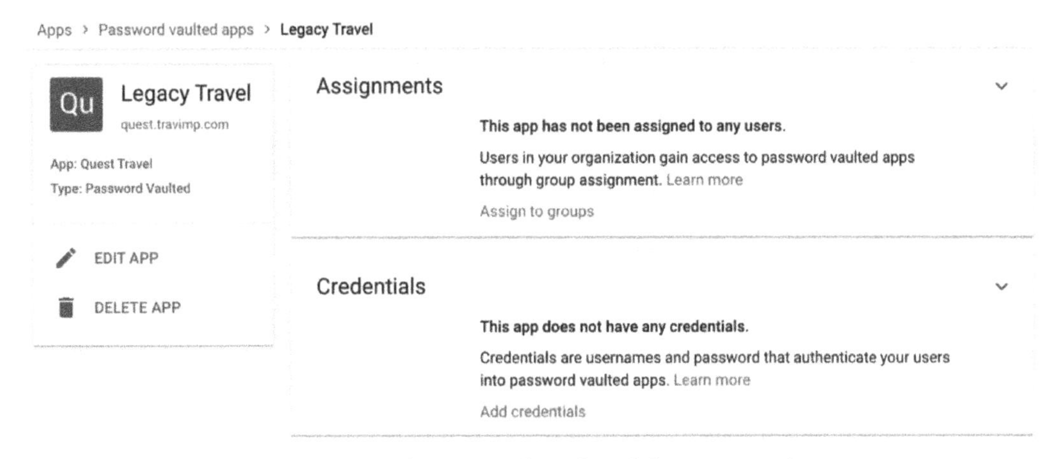


Figure 3.6 – An app showing credentials and their associated groups

In this example, an existing app was added from the app library using the search functionality. Administrators can also add custom apps:

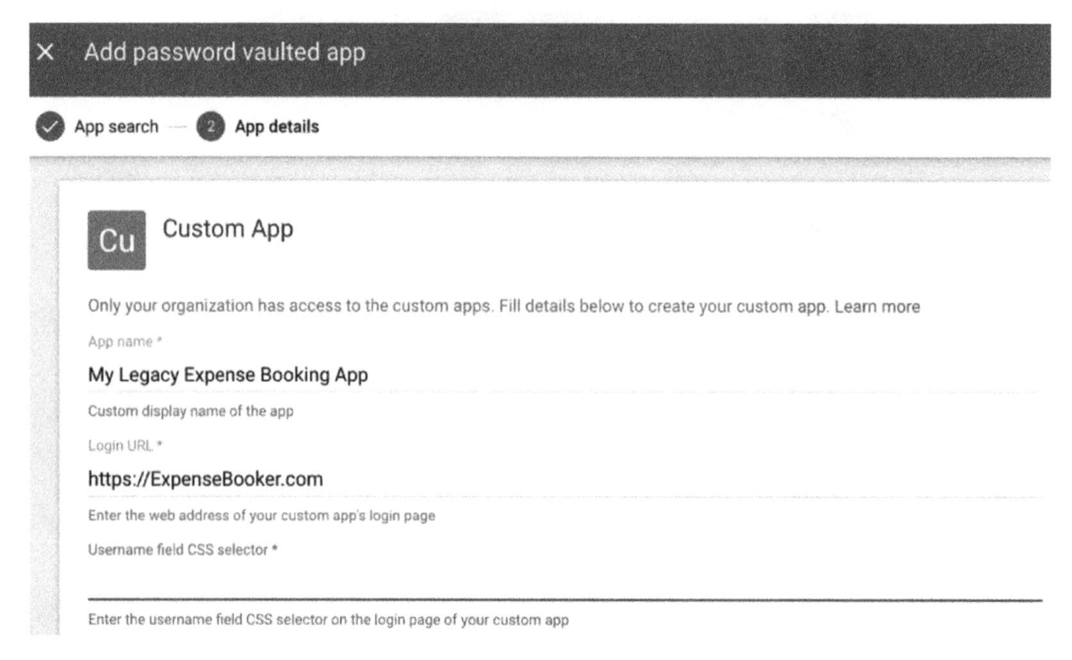


Figure 3.7 – Adding a custom app with a URL

Finally, for users to be able to sign in using the Google user console to these apps, a Chrome extension is required. Users will have to install the *Cloud Identity Account Manager* browser extension for Chrome. This extension can be downloaded from the following link:

`https://chrome.google.com/webstore/detail/cloud-identity-account-ma/bepedphhpelcmjancenhicofcbepgmpk`

## Secure LDAP

In the previous two sections, we covered Google Workspace as an SSO IdP and password vaulted app. Now, let's review integrations for LDAP-based authenticated apps.

Users' Cloud Identity accounts can be used as cloud-based LDAP servers for authenticating with applications. IT teams have traditionally used on-premises LDAP servers that manage user directories.

Allowing the use of LDAP enables organizations to use apps that are hosted on any cloud environment, such as GCP, AWS, or Azure.

By using secure LDAP, Google Cloud exposes directory objects to LDAP clients for the authentication of users. To enable secure LDAP, follow these steps:

1. Go to the Google **Admin** console.
2. Click on **Apps** from the left-hand side panel and select **LDAP**.
3. On this page, click **ADD CLIENT**.
4. Specify a name in the LDAP client name field, for example, `Expense Tool`.
5. Optionally, type in a description for the LDAP client, for example, `Expense entry app for sales department employees`.
6. Click **CONTINUE**.

Once the app has been added, various access configurations are defined. Once complete, a secure LDAP digital certificate is generated, which serves as the authentication for the LDAP client. This certificate should be downloaded and uploaded into the LDAP client that is being integrated with Google Workspace.

Not every LDAP client might support an LDAP digital certificate for authentication – if a client does not support certificates, a third-party proxy such as a *stunnel TLS proxy* can be used.

Once all the secure LDAP configurations have been set up, as a final step, enable the app by setting its service status to **ON** in the console.

Once it has been enabled, administrators can do a connectivity test using LDAP tools such as **ldapsearch**.

As we have seen, with Context-Aware Access and end-user security, Google Workspace has taken great care to permeate security into its product at almost all levels. This paves way for a robust security infrastructure that can be leveraged by all the applications that are built on this platform. Now, let's move on and look at security configurations that are available for admins and users for some of the core Google Workspace services.

# Google apps security

In this section, we will learn about the security settings that are available across all the applications in Google Workplace. This section will cover the application and security settings for Gmail, Drive, Calendar, Google Chat, Google Meet, Sites, Vault, Jamboard, and Marketplace applications.

# Gmail

The previous chapter walked through how to set up **mail exchange** (**MX**) records and enable them. This confirms that incoming and outgoing emails will flow through without interruptions for the domain.

As a next step, administrators will have to decide which group of users will need to have the Gmail service enabled. Once enabled, these users will have their own Gmail inboxes.

Here's how you enable Gmail for users:

1. Log in to the Google **Admin** console.
2. Click on **Apps | Google Workspace | Gmail**.
3. Click on **Service Status** and select the top-level OU you'd like to enable.
    - All the sub-OUs will automatically inherit the same enabled status.
    - If there are exceptions where a sub-OU is required to have this service disabled, then select the specific OU from the left-hand side panel and then change the service status. This will override the parent-OU setting.
4. Click **Save**.

This will enable Gmail for all the users in the OU. Administrators can then apply fine-grained access controls across the user base:

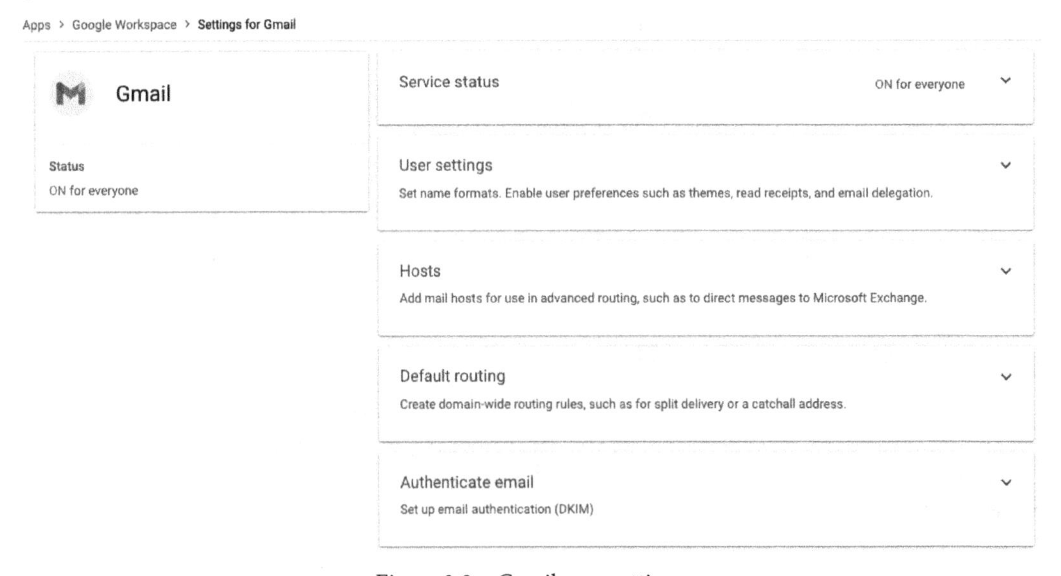


Figure 3.8 – Gmail core settings

Within Gmail, administrators can configure special rules for handling various types of incoming and outgoing emails:

- **User Settings**:

  There are a bunch of configuration options available to choose from that can be applied to each OU or a group of users. This includes settings such as the following:

  - **Mail delegation**: Allows users to grant access to other users to access their mailbox. For example, managers can delegate mail access to their executive assistants. Another example would be elementary school students delegating mail access to their class teachers.
  - **Offline mode**: Allows users to access Gmail in areas without internet connectivity.
  - **Themes for the UI**: Helps users visually customize their views of the inbox.
  - **Confidential mode**: Allows users to send emails with content expiration and SMS passcodes.
  - **Smart Compose**: When users type a few words in the Gmail compose window, Google's artificial intelligence and machine learning technology will auto-complete these sentences.

- **Hosts**:

  Generally, within Workspace, all emails are configured to be delivered to the respective user's mailbox. However, in some situations, where the domain is in the middle of deploying Google Workspace, some users will remain in their old mail servers while a subset of users may have been deployed in Google Workspace. In these situations, setting up hosts can direct emails to another server.

  Hosts are configured as the recipient IP addresses of the on-premises mail server.

  This configuration also allows emails to be routed to the MX server or requires that emails be transmitted through a TLS connection.

- **Default routing**:

  This allows admins to set up a domain-wide routing policy that is applicable for all incoming emails. Administrators can alter the incoming email by prepending a custom subject or changing the route for specific emails or routing spam, among other things.

  There can be multiple routing rules, and these should be ordered based on their priority. If there are conflicting rules, the rules that are configured as higher priority will take precedence.

- **Quarantines**:

  When administrators define compliance policies to prevent data exfiltration, email messages can be stored in a quarantine location for additional review before being delivered to the recipient. Multiple quarantines can be set up for various types of policies. Administrators shouldn't be overwhelmed by having to do this additional review. This can be delegated to other **power users** who have elevated privileges as *Quarantine Reviewers*. This privilege is available within **Admin Roles**. Create a custom admin role, add this privilege, and assign it to users who choose to be a Quarantined Reviewer.

  Messages in quarantine will be automatically deleted once the retention period expires if no action is taken on these messages. The typical retention period is 30 days.

- **Safety**:

  Advanced spam and phishing protection can be enabled for selected users within a domain through the **Safety** setting.

  There are additional controls to prevent spam filtering for specific senders or recipients. For example, if organizations have an internal mass email application, then you can set that sender address to bypass spam filtering since mass emails typically would be classified as spam.

- **End-user access**:

  Configurations are available to allow users to use third-party mail clients to access emails using POP3 and IMAP.

  If users are accustomed to using MS Outlook, they can continue using this to access their Gmail inbox.

  Administrators can also enable a setting to implicitly warn users when they receive emails from external users. This will train the users to be more cautious in opening those emails or attachments.

- **Compliance**:

  Administrators can define rules to handle email messages that contain specific keywords, sensitive information, **personally identifiable information** (**PII**), or national identification numbers.

  These content compliance rules can either reject the emails from being delivered to recipients or store the emails in quarantine for additional review.

Now that we've covered some of the basic Gmail settings, let's turn our attention to advanced email authentication methods, including **Sender Policy Framework** (**SPF**), **Domain-based Message Authentication, Reporting, and Conformance** (**DMARC**), and **DomainKeys Identified Mail** (**DKIM**).

## Sender Policy Framework

SPF is a configuration of IP addresses that are allowed to send emails on behalf of the domain. Setting this up prevents someone from spoofing or impersonating a user from that domain. Harmful content that can easily trick a recipient can be avoided using SPF. This is configured within the Domain Host in the Google **Admin** console.

To understand the need for SPF, let's look at a real-life example:

When a user scans a paper using an internet-connected scanning device, the device emails the scanned file to the user's inbox. How is the scanning device emailing the file? It is obvious that the scanning device is connected to the internet and that by adding the scanning device's IP address to SPF, emails from this device are trusted and forwarded to the user's inbox.

SPF is a great technique for adding authentication to your emails. The mail receiver will use the *envelope from* address of the email to confirm that the sending IP address was allowed to do so.

These days, email authentication techniques have evolved and have led to features such as DKIM and DMARC. We will talk about these in the subsequent sections.

## DMARC

Administrators can request DMARC reports from the email server to learn about authentication issues or to figure out a list of malicious content that is being sent to the domain. This helps in identifying the repeat offenders, fixing the mail configuration, and preventing spam on the domain.

DMARC can be defined with steps on how to react if such malicious emails are received.

The following is an example of a DMARC policy record. The `v` and `p` tags must be listed first; the other tags can be in any order:

```
v=DMARC1; p=reject; rua=mailto:adminReview@myCompany.com,
mailto:dmarc_review@myCompany.com; pct=100; adkim=s; aspf=s
```

### DKIM

DKIM is an email standard that ensures emails are not being intercepted or altered and checks whether emails originate from the source user.

By setting up DKIM for the domain, outgoing emails can have a secret digital signature that prevents emails from being spoofed.

> **Spoofing**
>
> Spoofing an email means impersonating another user by presenting that name on the message header in combination with an incorrect email address.

Besides DKIM, it is a best practice to set up SPF to prevent spoofing and DMARC to specify policies to track suspicious messages. All these settings work together to secure your inboxes.

Gmail is an important core service and must be configured properly if you wish to have an optimized experience across the user base in your organization. With that taken care of, let's look at Google Drive.

## Google Drive

Google Drive is a core Google Workspace service that is used for storing and synchronizing content across multiple devices. We'll take a look at the two types of drive spaces within Google Drive: **My Drive** and **Shared Drive**.

### My Drive

Files and content that's created or uploaded by users appear under **My Drive**. Even if the content is created by another user and shared, it will still appear under the **My Drive** or **Shared with me** label. Users can create folders within **My Drive** to collaborate with other users. The content that's created by users and that is stored within **My Drive** consumes storage that's been allocated for the user.

You can determine what a user can do to a file or folder by designating the user any one of the following roles:

- **Viewer**: Users with this role can only view the content.
- **Commenter**: Users with this role can view and highlight a line to post a comment. They can also respond to other comments.
- **Editor**: Users with this role can view, comment, and edit the content. This role also allows users to share the document with other users, as well as make a copy of the document.

The following are some additional controls:

- **Expiring Access**: This setting allows content owners to share the content with *Viewers* and *Commenters* with an expiration date. After this expires, the collaborators will lose access to this content automatically.
- **Information Resource Management (IRM)**: IRM controls prevent *Commentators* and *Viewers* of a file from making a copy and downloading the file. It also restricts the file from being shared with other users.

Owners can transfer ownership of their content to other users. We will review the **Security Investigation Tool** in the upcoming sections, where we will learn about how Administrators can audit the access permissions of a file.

## Shared Drive

Shared Drive, on the other hand, is a different way of organizing content. All collaborators who have access to Shared Drive will be able to contribute to the Shared Drive folders:

> **Note**
>
> Data such as files, Google Docs, Sheets, Slides, and more that are created within Shared Drive count toward the overall domain's storage capacity. They do not count toward the user's storage consumption.

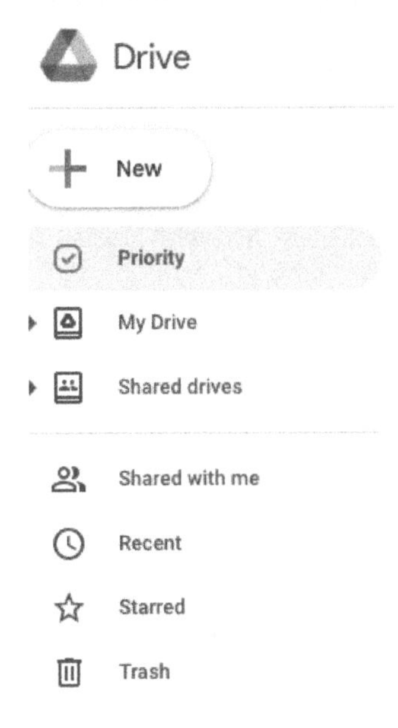


Figure 3.9 – Drive, Shared drives, and various labels

Shared Drive provides the following access roles for users:

- **Manager**:
    - Full access to add or remove files or folders
    - Full access to add or remove collaborators
- **Content manager**:
    - This is the default role for new members who gain access to Shared Drive.
    - Full access to add or remove files.
    - Limited access for adding collaborators to this Shared Drive.
- **Contributor**:
    - Full access for content creation
    - Restricted access for deleting content or adding people to folders
- **Commenter**:
    - Can view all files and comment on those files
- **Viewer**:
    - Can only view the files within Shared Drive:

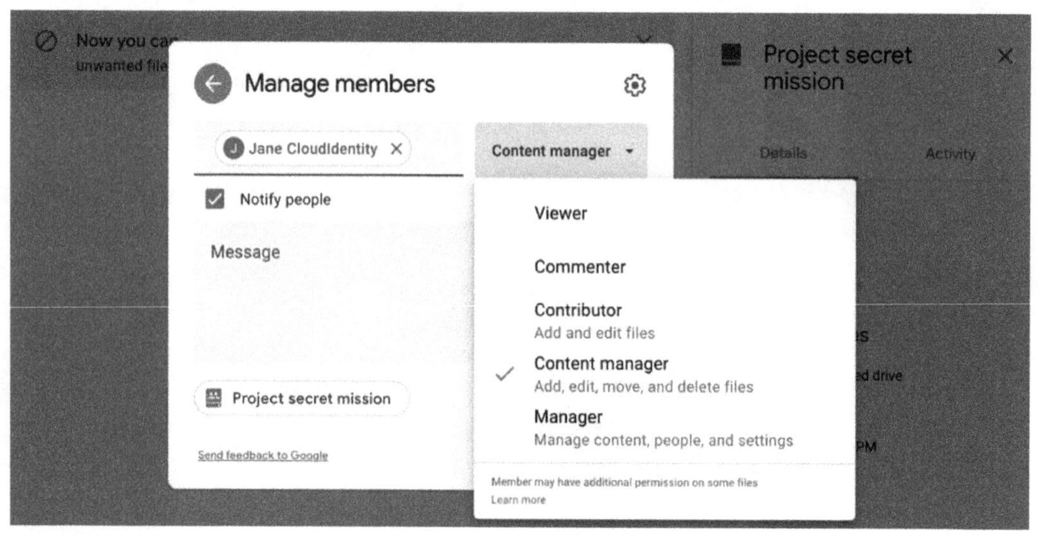


Figure 3.10 – Roles in Shared Drive

To manage the main Google Drive settings, log into Google Drive, click the **Settings** icon at the top right, and choose **Settings**. The following settings typically show up for Administrators:

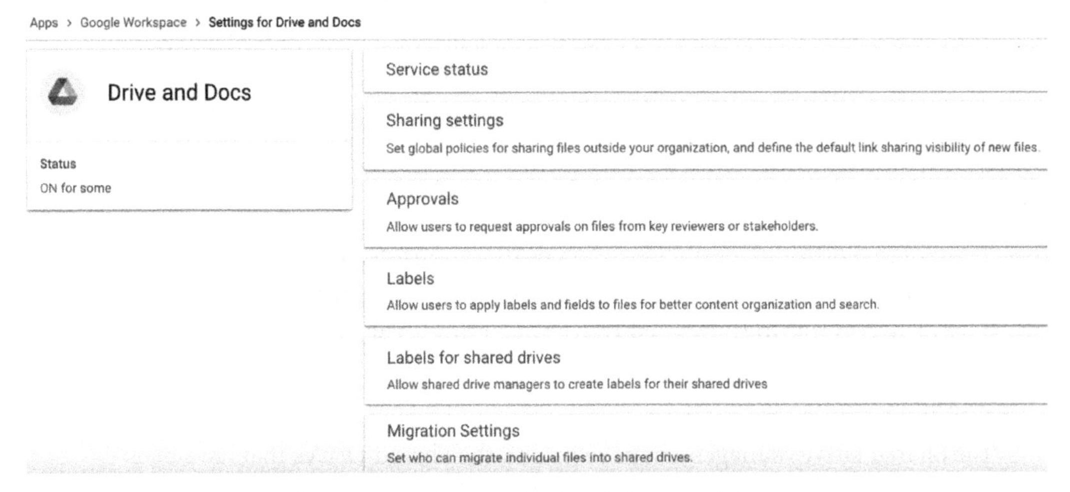
Apps > Google Workspace > Settings for Drive and Docs
Drive and Docs
Status
ON for some
Service status
Sharing settings
Set global policies for sharing files outside your organization, and define the default link sharing visibility of new files.
Approvals
Allow users to request approvals on files from key reviewers or stakeholders.
Labels
Allow users to apply labels and fields to files for better content organization and search.
Labels for shared drives
Allow shared drive managers to create labels for their shared drives
Migration Settings
Set who can migrate individual files into shared drives.

Figure 3.11 – Settings for Google Drive and Docs

Let's expand on some of the important settings for Google Drive and Docs:

- **Sharing settings**:
  - **External sharing settings**: This allows users to share their content that's stored in **My Drive** folders with external recipients.
  - **Target audiences**: This is a feature that helps set up a virtual guardrail that enables users to share content with a specific audience. For example, let's consider a scenario where a company has interns and they are paired up with mentors. Here, you can set up audiences as *Mentors* and allow *Interns* OU users to only share Drive content with *Mentors*. In doing so, the drive content will not be visible to others.
- **Shared Drive settings**:
  - **Creation**: Administrators can prevent users from creating a Shared Drive on their own. Instead, users will have to request administrators to create Shared Drives on their behalf.
  - **Sharing externally**: Prevents users external to this domain from accessing Shared Drives within this domain.
  - Apply IRM controls for files within Shared Drive.

- **Labels**:

  Labels are used for organizing and classifying your data in Drive. It is important to note that all content can be labeled, regardless of its format or its source of origin. This setting allows administrators to enable or disable labels for users.

  Administrators can also use the **Manage Labels** link to create new labels, disable labels, or delete labels. Labels that are created from this page are visible to users and can be used by users to organize their data.

- **Shared Drive Management**:

  Shared Drives that are created by users or the administrator are centrally owned by the domain and not owned by any specific user. Users who are managers or have an access role to the Shared Drive can perform various content management activities. However, the Shared Drive will not contribute toward the user's storage consumption.

  The Shared Drive Management page lists all the Shared Drives that have been created within this domain and allows administrators to audit users' access and roles.

- **Offline Access**:

  This setting allows administrators to grant offline capabilities to users.

- **Drive for Desktop**:

  A synchronization application that is used for uploading local files stored on a device into Google Drive. Administrators can choose to enable or disable the use of **Drive for Desktop**.

  **Drive for Desktop** is installed locally on the user's computer and authorized to its respective Google Workspace account. It pulls files stored locally from the computer and uploads them to Google Drive and vice versa.

- **Smart Compose within Documents**:

  Google Docs has the embedded capability of predicting words as they are typed. This is powered by ML and AI to help users finish their sentences without having to type long sentences, thereby finishing mundane documentation tasks quicker than usual. This setting can be enabled or disabled for users.

- **Add-ons**:

  Google Drive has a few formatting menus on the top of the page. One of the menu options is called **Add-ons**. Add-ons help users extend their Docs or Sheets functionality with additional features. These add-ons are created by developers and published in add-on stores such as Google Marketplace.

- **Drive SDK API**:

  Google Drive has an extensive API available for developing applications or automating tasks programmatically. By enabling this setting, administrators can allow users to use Drive API to develop customized applications.

- **Transferring ownership**:

  Using this feature, administrators can transfer files that are owned by one user to another user. The previous owner will still retain **Edit** access to those files.

  This is useful for situations such as when a user is going on extended leave or is transferring to a different team.

- **Templates**

  When users are creating content, they don't have to start from scratch. Administrators can set up templates for various business purposes.

  This setting allows users to create a document and submit this as a template for future recurring use. Submitted templates will be shared with other users.

Google Drive offers robust settings that can help any organization create and share content securely and effectively.

Now, it's time to look at the settings for another important Workspace service: Calendar.

## Calendar

Calendar management covers three types of calendars:

- The user's primary calendar
- Secondary calendars that have been created for group usage
- Calendar resources for video conference rooms

Administrators can restrict how much calendar information is shared by a user external to their organization. They can also allow users to share calendars externally but not to specific domains, for example.

Secondary calendars show up on the user's calendar but are different from the primary calendar. These come in handy when there is a need for the separation of events across the primary calendar and other shared calendars.

For example, if a user is working with a team and would like to create a calendar to track team members' vacation days, the user can create a secondary calendar. This can then be shared with all group members so that they can create events in this secondary calendar.

Calendars themselves have a user setting page that allows you to tweak the time zone, 3-day or work-week view, working hours, and more. These settings can be applied by users to their primary or secondary calendars:

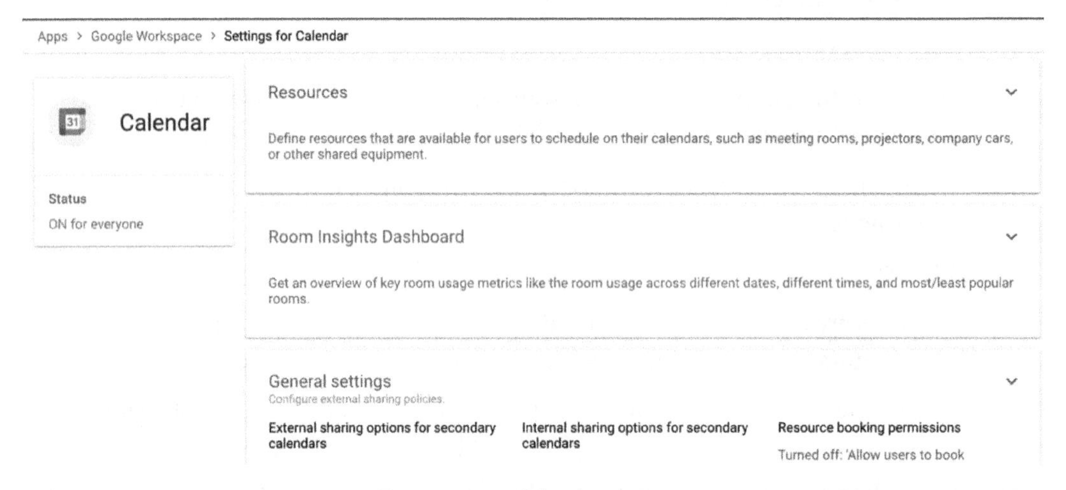


Figure 3.12 – Calendar settings

The Google Workspace **Admin** console has several settings for calendar management that combine both users' calendars and conference rooms set up as calendar resources. It's time to deep dive into these:

- **General Settings**:
  - While we cover sharing primary calendars under the **Sharing** settings, this setting covers secondary calendar sharing to external users.
  - Calendar room booking can be restricted for users. If there are special rooms allocated for executive use, those calendar resources can be allowed or restricted for the relevant users to use.

- **Sharing Settings**:
  - The work location for users: Users can set up the locations where they are working from, setting the time zone for the calendar.
  - Sharing calendars with external users.
  - Control sharing primary calendars with internal users.
  - Users can choose to be warned/prompted when event invitations are sent to external guests.
  - Allow users to set their working hours. For instance, employees can set up part-time working hours, or field workers can exclude their travel time from working hours.
- **Advanced Settings**:
  - **Transfer Events**:
    - Using this feature, administrators can transfer events that have been organized by one user to another user.
    - You can release any conference rooms that have been booked for those events.
    - Administrators can also cancel events that have been organized by a **deleted user**. This is especially useful when an employee is going on extended leave, transferring to a different team, or for terminated employees who no longer work for the organization.
  - **Resources**:

    Conference rooms in an organization are treated as **Calendar Resources** in Google Workspace Calendar. These resources can be added with *Building* information and *Features* for the conference resource, such as the following:

    - The capacity of the resource
    - Floor – total number of floors and floor numbers
    - Types of resources – meeting space, projector, vehicle, and so on
    - Video conferencing capabilities

- **Room Insights Dashboard**:

  Room Insights Dashboard provides insightful information about conference room usage for meetings in this domain. The metrics include items such as booking rate, hours booked, booking distribution, most used rooms, and least used rooms:

  - Administrators or office planners can review which rooms are least used and derive information as to why that might be the case.
  - Rooms that are booked for meetings but never get used or are hard to find in the office building can be revived:

Figure 3.13 – Room usage metrics

- **Interoperability**:

  This setting comes in handy when organizations have some employees in Google Workspace, while the remaining users use Microsoft Exchange, and there is a need for sharing calendar availability information. This helps facilitate meetings across both sets of participants.

  By establishing a trusted connection between the Exchange Server and Google Workspace, users can check availability information across both environments.

  This interoperability is not just limited to users but can be extended to booking conference rooms on the Exchange Server.

  More than one trusted Exchange connection can be configured with Google Workspace.

With the Calendar settings squared away, let's move on to the next service – Google Chat.

## Google Chat

Google Chat is currently going through a transition from the classic Google Hangouts to the new Google Chat, which provides more features and improved collaboration. It also features a new user interface that is designed to increase user adoption.

Unlike the classic Hangouts, Google Chat gives users the flexibility to set up a chat space with multiple members for threaded conversations. For example, if four users are chatting about a topic, the fifth user can start a new thread on a separate topic without interrupting any ongoing conversation.

Chat can be used within the Gmail view's side panel, by using a separate browser tab and navigating to `chat.google.com` or by using the desktop client's **Progressive Web App** (**PWA**).

> Progressive Web Apps
>
> PWAs are web applications that have capabilities like a native platform app and can also be installed on a device. Once installed, these PWA apps can be launched from a user's home screen or dock. PWAs can handle different file types and can also be programmed to interact with other applications.

The individual choice of where to use Chat is left to the user's discretion. These settings cannot be enforced by administrators.

Administrators, however, have the following settings to play with to customize what users can do and see:

- **Smart Features**:
  - Here, you can enable or disable personalization features such as **Smart Compose**, which predicts chat replies based on ML and AI, Summary Cards, and more.
  - **GIFs**: This setting controls whether users can add animated images to Chat or prevent them from doing so. These animated sequences of images are the vogue in user expression.
- **History for Chats**:

  1:1 conversation among peers is retained for the user's view. This is called **Chat History**. Users have the option of turning off Chat History and going off the record when chatting with others. This setting will enforce Chat History to be **ON** for all 1:1 conversations.

- **History for Chat Spaces**:

  Like 1:1 conversations, when a Chat Space with an unthreaded room is set up with multiple users, those conversation histories can also be retained. This setting allows administrators to enable or disable Chat History to enforce the capturing of conversations for future references. Chat Spaces with *threaded rooms* will have **Chat History** enabled by default. This cannot be turned off.

- **External Chat**:
  - **External Chat setting**: This setting allows or restricts users from chatting with external users who do not belong to this domain.
  - **External Rooms**: This setting allows or restricts users from joining Chat Spaces created by external domain users. One use case where this setting may come in handy would be when an organization works with vendors or partners frequently, so there may be a need to set up a Chat Space for users in both organizations to collaborate.
  - **User warning**: These warnings implicitly remind users when they are about to send a message to a recipient who is external to this domain.
  - **Status**: When users are busy, unavailable, or stepping away from their computer, they can use **Status** within Chat to reflect their current whereabouts. This setting controls the privacy of users and allows administrators to control whether the status message should be visible to external users or not.

- **Chatbots**:

  These are automated tools that simulate human conversations and execute tasks. They can be designed to follow Dialogflow commands. These chatbots can be programmed to do mundane tasks and fetch information from third-party integrated applications such as Salesforce and ServiceNow.

  This setting controls whether users are allowed to use chatbots or not.

## Google Meet

The recent pandemic has accelerated the need for video conferencing, allowing people to connect and conduct work without having to go to their workplaces.

Google Meet allows people to securely connect, collaborate, and connect from anywhere. People can safely join high-quality video meetings for groups of up to 250 people.

Depending on the Google Workspace edition, the number of participants that are allowed for Meet differs from 100 to 250. Users joining a Meet call can use either a web browser, a mobile device with iOS or Android, or dial in via telephone. Irrespective of which device a user is logging in from, the experience is consistent, high definition, and user-friendly.

Google Meet has the following configuration options:

- **Telephony**:

  This setting controls the addition of telephony dial-in on Meet events by default. Meet allows users to dial into the call using a passcode. These dial-in phone numbers have international numbers as well. Users from outside of the US can also dial into the meeting.

- **Recording**:

  Meetings can be recorded by meeting organizers. These recordings are saved in Google Drive automatically when the meeting ends. They are automatically shared with other participants of the meeting. This setting allows or restricts users from recording their meetings. Some organizations may have strict compliance regulations that prevent users from recording their meetings.

- **Live Stream**:

  When the organizers of a meeting want to host a large audience beyond 250 people, a live stream is launched. Depending on the Google Workspace edition, the number of viewers ranges from 10,000 to 100,000.

  Live stream viewers can view and hear the speakers through a high-quality video stream that is done in real time.

- **Virtual Backgrounds**:

  As users are connecting to Google Meet from various locations, there is a need for virtual backgrounds to achieve a professional non-intrusive experience.

  Users can use sample images provided by Google or use images of their own. For example, employees may want to use their organization's banner or logo as a background.

- **Interoperability**:

  Similar to the Calendar interoperability with Exchange, Google Meet gateways can be configured to use Pexip to extend the connectivity across other devices. Pexip is a piece of middleware that converts a Meet URL into a compatible link that can be used across devices from different vendors. For instance, organizations using Cisco or Polycom devices don't need to invest in other peripheral devices. Pexip, Cisco, and Polycom devices can be used to handle Google Meet calls.

- **Meeting safety**:

  - **Host Management**: Meeting organizers can restrict participants from unmuting, screen sharing, or posting a chat message during a meeting.
  - **Access to join meetings**: The organizers of a meeting can control who can join and participate in a meeting.

- **Meet Quality Tool**:

  This shows a detailed dashboard of all the meetings that are being hosted by a domain's users. The details include a list of all participants, their duration of presence, which device they logged in from, and detailed network information, such as packet loss, network congestion, delays, and jitter.

Google Meet is a real differentiator that makes Google Workspace popular. The adoption of Google Meet across international audiences is a true testament to its staying power in the market and helps in the adoption of other Workspace services.

# Sites

Google Sites allows teams to create high-quality websites quickly for projects or events. Sites offers an editor that lets users quickly create content using drag-and-drop features and allows them to interact with other collaborators in real time. Sites have sharing features that are very similar to Google Drive or Google Docs.

Sites has recently been upgraded from classic Sites to new Sites. These configurations help control Sites creation and sharing:

- **Sharing Settings**:

  This setting controls the sharing setting that determines the visibility of a Site page for external users. Site editors can display or hide user information about who updated the page last.

- **Templates**:

  Similar to Google Docs, Sites has the option of creating templates to use a formatted UI on the Site page. Users don't need to create content from scratch.

  Administrators can name template categories for organizing various templates.

- **Custom URL**:

  Site pages can be hosted on a custom URL that is easier to remember:

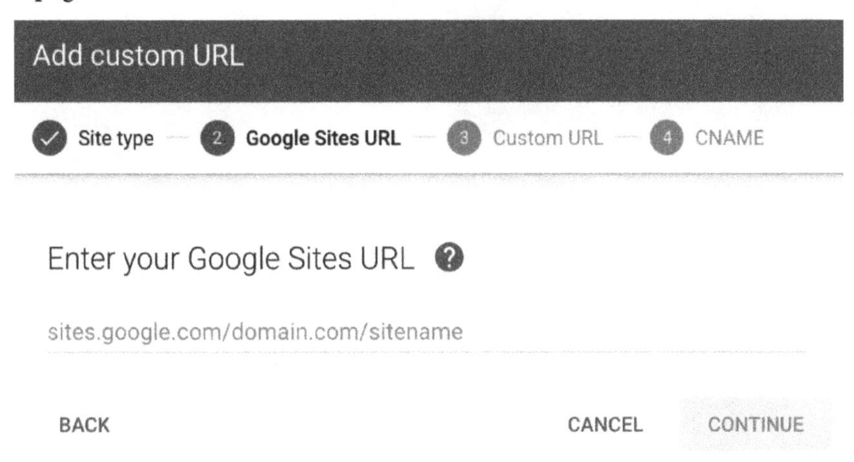


Figure 3.14 – Adding a custom URL in Sites

With its simple-to-use editor and real-time collaboration capabilities, Sites allows a web page to be put together really easily.

# Vault

Vault is one of the Google Workspace services that automatically retains data for eDiscovery purposes. As with all Google Workspace services, Vault also has built-in search capabilities that help with fuzzy searches and various other keyword operators to support the search. Auditors can use this to fetch the relevant content that is required for any litigation or auditing evidence.

Vault is configured using a **Default Retention** or **Custom Retention** policy. If there is a need for an audit, *Holds* are created against a user. A *Matter* is used for searching and exporting content.

**eDiscovery Lingo**

For the uninitiated, eDiscovery is a process by which electronic evidence in a legal case is preserved, collected, and reviewed, following the model recommended by the Electronic Discovery Reference Model. *Matters* serve as a container in a Vault to store files and display holds, searches, and exports. *Holds* are used to preserve Gmail messages indefinitely in Vault to meet legal obligations.

Please note that a misconfigured Vault retention policy can result in data being purged forever. This is irrevocable:

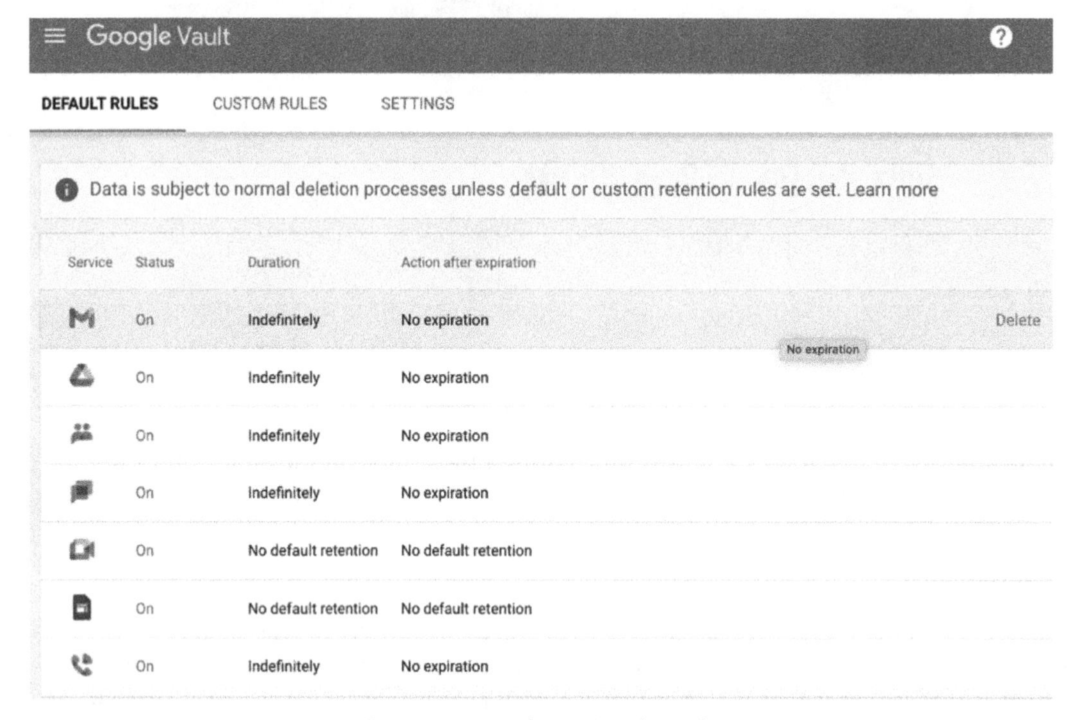


Figure 3.15 – Rules in Google Vault

Vault can be accessed via `vault.google.com`. It cannot be accessed from within the Google **Admin** console.

On this Vault configuration page, administrators can define a **Default Retention** policy. This blanket policy covers the following:

- Gmail messages
- Chat conversations
- Meet recordings
- Drive files
- Groups
- Voice SMS messages

Google does not restrict any duration for retention, which means administrators can set up an indefinite retention policy that never expires. You can only have one default retention policy.

If there are unique use cases to be covered, you can set up a custom retention policy.

There can be more than one custom retention policy that covers various OUs or specific users, among other things.

Holds are similar to custom retention rules; however, Holds will retain data indefinitely until the Hold itself is deleted. Holds are applied to users or OUs in response to a specific investigation.

Please note that the retention policy or Hold with the farthest expiration will take effect and have precedence over other custom retention rules. Data that is searched can be exported in MBOX or PST format.

## Other services

We reviewed all the core services that have multiple security settings that determine how data is stored and shared with other users. Some services such as Keep, Jamboard, and Groups have minimal configurations for service enablement and sharing data that's external to the domain. They do not offer granular security options due to the nature of the product.

Clicking on the **Settings** option will display the domain's OUs, allowing administrators to selectively enable this service for a specific OU. All nested sub-OUs will inherit their parent OU settings.

Administrators have the option of overriding the service enablement for nested sub-OUs if needed. For instance, consider a use case where there are multiple OUs with very few users within each OU requiring Jamboard services to be enabled. Administrators can then use Google Groups as security access groups to grant these users access to services or to override specific security settings.

It is also a best practice for administrators to begin organizing users functionally, which will eventually help in navigating these settings for each Google Workspace core service:

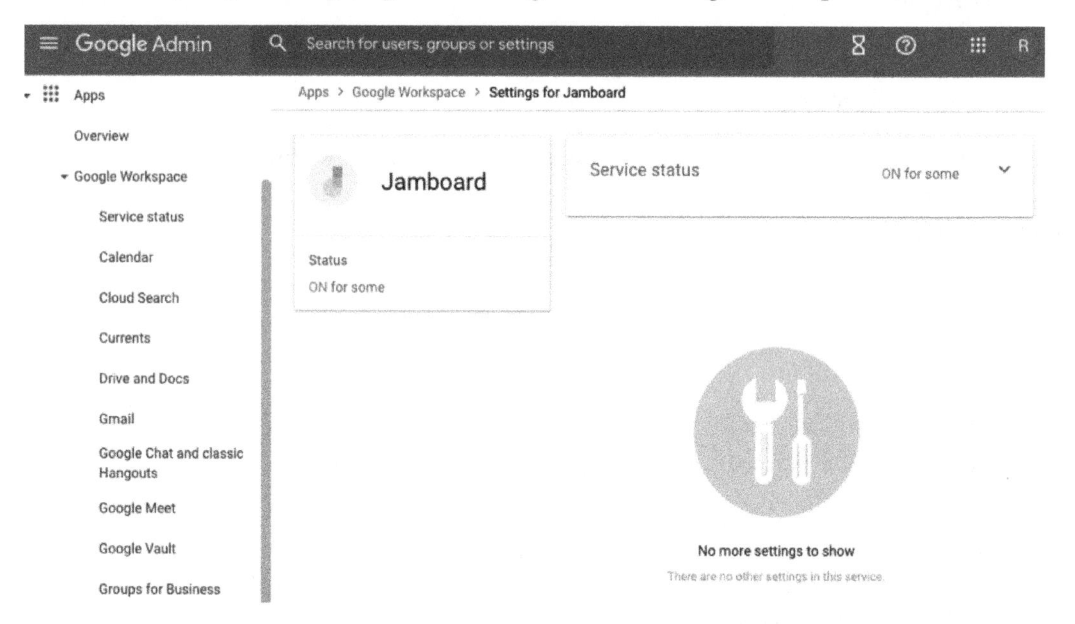


Figure 3.16 – Showing the Jamboard setting with status set to ON

As you may have realized, core services have a ton of functionalities and levers to make the experience optimal and secure for users. With core services dealt, let's motor on to Marketplace apps.

## Marketplace apps

In *Chapter 2, Configuring Users and Apps*, we learned about Google Workspace's core services, additional Google services, and Marketplace apps.

Administrators can either allow users in an organization to install any Marketplace app or just publish a selected list of apps that are allowed:

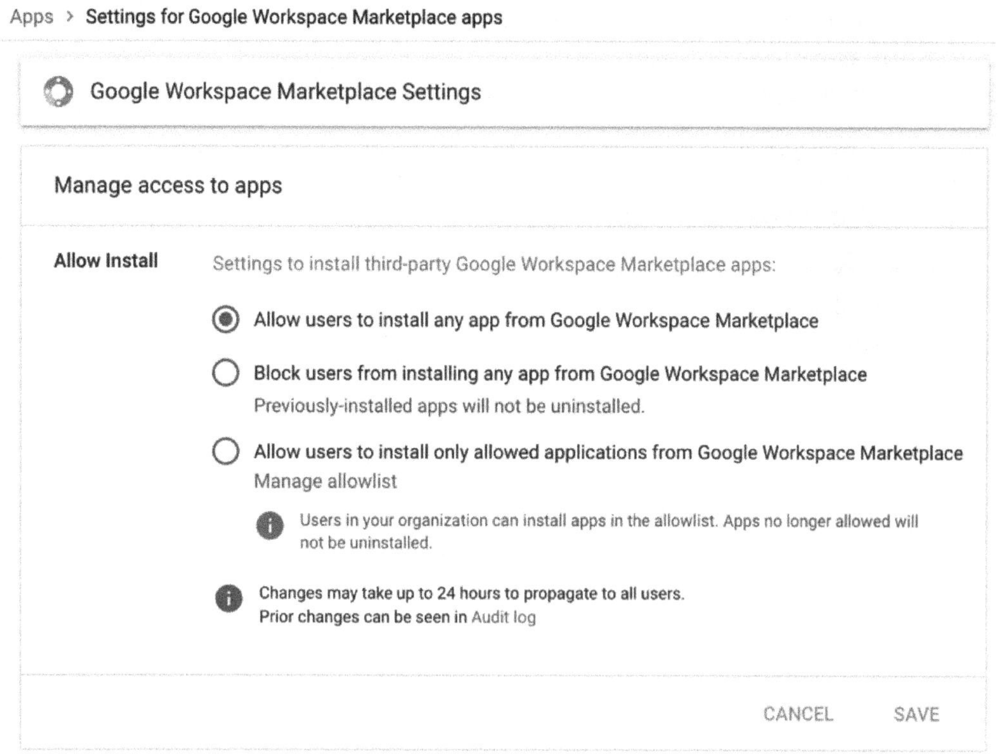

Apps > **Settings for Google Workspace Marketplace apps**

Google Workspace Marketplace Settings

Manage access to apps

**Allow Install** Settings to install third-party Google Workspace Marketplace apps:

(●) Allow users to install any app from Google Workspace Marketplace

( ) Block users from installing any app from Google Workspace Marketplace
Previously-installed apps will not be uninstalled.

( ) Allow users to install only allowed applications from Google Workspace Marketplace
Manage allowlist

Users in your organization can install apps in the allowlist. Apps no longer allowed will not be uninstalled.

Changes may take up to 24 hours to propagate to all users.
Prior changes can be seen in Audit log

CANCEL SAVE

Figure 3.17 – Marketplace settings

You can find these settings within the **Admin** console, under **Settings for Google Workspace Marketplace Apps**.

As a security measure, administrators can control which Marketplace apps can be installed, as well as access for users in the domain. For this, administrators have to select the third option from those shown in the preceding screenshot, and then prepare an **allowlist** for users to use:

1. Go to the Google **Admin** console and click on **Apps** from the left-hand side panel.
2. Click the **Google Workspace Marketplace apps** apps list.
3. Click **Google Workspace Marketplace allowlist.**
4. Click **Add app to allowlist.**
5. Search for the app. Once the app has been identified, click **Add to allowlist.**

Similarly, if an app is no longer allowed for users to use, then remove the app from the allowlist.

This further fulfills any compliance standards that are required for an organization by setting up virtual guardrails, which allow users to use other third-party apps. However, not just any random app can be used, as this may result in data leakage.

These apps are using OAuth2.0 authentication standards to connect to the user's account to fetch and update data. Administrators have additional controls that will ensure these apps have limited or extended access through Google's API.

For example, let's assume that a power user has created an app or an add-on that will convert all Gmail attachments into a Google Drive file. Administrators can restrict this app to access only to Drive and Gmail data through the API:

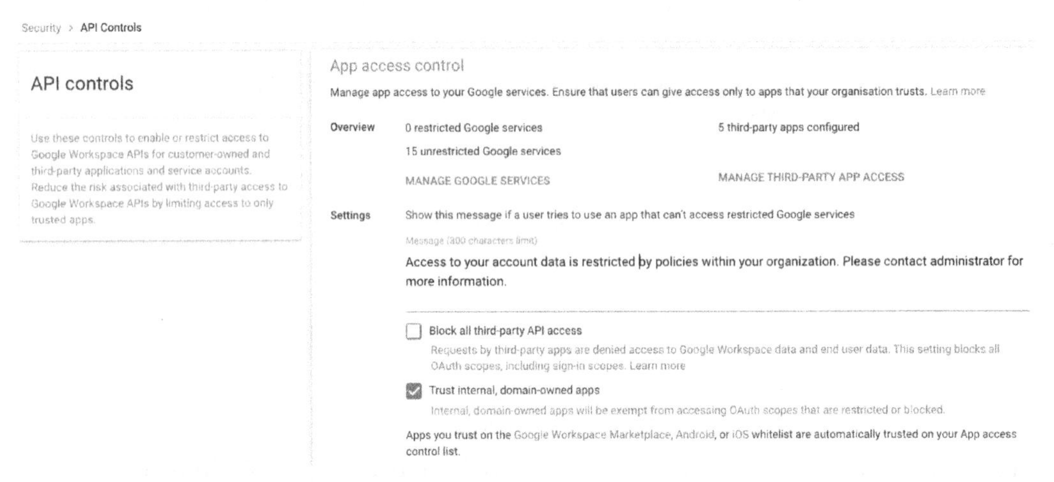


Figure 3.18 – API controls

By setting up these configurations for third-party apps, we are only allowing certain actions that the app intends to execute. Administrators can also add a detailed descriptive message that will be displayed for users.

As an administrator, it is good to keep a close check on what apps are installed or authorized by users. You can find this information by following these steps:

1. Go to the Google **Admin** console.
2. Click on **Security** from the left-hand side panel and select **API controls.**
3. Within the **App access control** section, select **MANAGE THIRD-PARTY APP ACCESS.**

   This displays details the apps that are being used by this domain's users. The details include **App name**, **Type**, **ID**, **Requested Services** (which are scopes that have been defined), and **Verified Status**.

Using this information, Administrators can determine whether it is a necessary app and whether users should continue using it.

A more detailed introduction to Marketplace apps, how to enable them, access rights, and security will be described in detail in *Chapter 5, Beyond Workspace*.

# Summary

In this chapter, we learned how to configure several core Workspace services. Configuring them the right way is critical not only for an optimal user experience but also for enhanced security. The security for users in a domain starts with proper configuration in the Cloud Identity system, and Context-Aware Access sets the stage for it perfectly. Single sign-on capabilities enable users to sign into multiple services with a single credential set, which aids in a simplified user experience. Password monitoring allows users to protect themselves from not reusing their passwords, thus improving the security posture for their domains.

Next, we talked about important Workspace services and the different options the administrators and users of these services have to make them their own. Gmail has in-depth security configurations that keep users' inboxes free of spam, spoofing, phishing, and other fraudulent attack vectors that users could easily fall prey to.

By integrating conference rooms into Calendars as resources and providing interoperability with MS Exchange resources, Google Workspace Calendars offers extended support when users have to book meetings for their teams. With Google Meet offering video conferencing capabilities and its seamless integration with Calendar, setting up a Calendar invite with Google Meet is a breeze.

We also looked at configuring Marketplace apps and other services such as Keep and Jamboard. At this point, you should understand that security is at the forefront of Google Workspace and that every service and every configuration option is designed to keep user data safe.

Now, it's time to take to move on and look at how to automatically audit the security capabilities that are available with Google Workspace.

# 4
# Automated Security Auditing

As enterprises move their resources and data to the cloud and consume cloud-native SaaS solutions such as Google Workspace, their auditing and compliance story needs to be rewritten. The auditing, monitoring, and observability of these applications and data are very important, and enterprises are expected to adhere to stricter compliance by governments and law enforcement.

Auditability gives us the chronological sequence of events that led to a change. This is typically achieved via an activity log that applications pump out with every event. The ability to stitch together these logs and gather insights is crucial for maintaining a good security posture. Several compliance standards such as SOC 2 heavily enforce auditability; this standard mandates that audit logs conform to integrity, confidentiality, and privacy requirements.

Monitoring typically tells us what is broken and why. Monitoring functions are important for analyzing long-term trends, capacity planning, understanding resource utilization, and, most importantly, reacting to system failures promptly. Observability complements monitoring and often helps you understand why a system is broken. Observability typically happens via logs, metrics, and traces.

In this chapter, we will learn about how Google Workspace enables enterprises and administrators to maintain a good compliance posture, gain insights into a system's state and failures, and how to act when things aren't right.

In this chapter, we will cover the following topics:

- Google Workspace security center
- Data loss prevention techniques
- Segregation of data by regions
- Endpoint and device management
- Various reports that provide business and security insights

Let's start with the security center.

# Google Workspace security center

The Google Workspace **security center** is a unified security dashboard that provides actionable security insights such as external file sharing, visibility into spam and malware threats, and metrics about security effectiveness in a single comprehensive interface. The security center also provides security health recommendations that, when acted upon, improve the security posture and keep users, systems, and data safe.

> **Important**
> The security center dashboard is only available with the Enterprise edition, Education Standard, and Plus licenses.

Administrators and operational teams receive thousands of alerts and emails every day. Many of them may not be actionable; however, it would be too risky to dismiss them as just noise. How can the signal versus noise ratio be improved so that only actionable alerts surface to the top? Could the monitoring system have the intelligence to apply correlation and understand the type of events and notify only those that need attention?

Meet the security center.

The security center has been thoughtfully designed with various components, each having a purpose. Administrators can set up alerts, review dashboards, validate the current security posture, investigate an incident, remediate the incident, and set up data loss prevention policies to guard the domain's content.

In the previous chapter, we learned how individual users can be configured with security policies and how sharing settings can be configured for individual apps in Google Workspace. In this chapter, we'll investigate how we can take advantage of the security center to modernize mundane auditing activities.

Google Workspace has multiple security services that are bundled within the security center:

- Security health
- Security dashboard
- Security investigation tool
- Data protection
- Security rules
- Alert center

It's time to look at each of these services in detail.

# Security Health

**Security Health** provides a full list of all the security settings across all Google Workspace services and all OUs. This is a single pane of glass view that shows OUs that may have a risky security configuration and are vulnerable.

The following screenshot shows the **Security Health** page and how it intuitively showcases settings across different OUs:

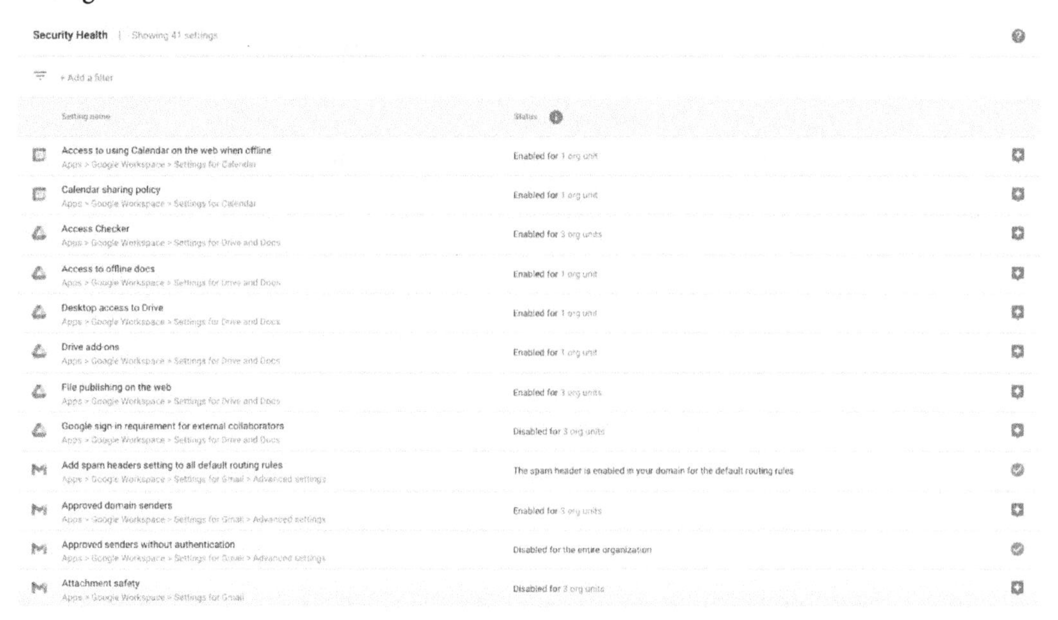


Figure 4.1 – The Security Health page showing various security settings

This page not only lists all the security settings, but also the values that have been defined for this Google Workspace domain. It shows a green checkmark to indicate the setting that's been defined is secure, as per Google's best practice recommendations.

The status column shows how many OUs have this setting enabled. When administrators are dealing with multiple OUs or working with a nested OU structure, it can be easy to forget which OU has a setting overridden or inherited from a parent OU. Having this information in a quick snapshot view can be useful to validate the intended setting versus the actual configuration.

**A Few Quirks**

Interestingly, the security health feature is available for the Enterprise edition, along with the Essentials and Cloud Identity Premium editions. While the Enterprise edition customers get to see all the security settings in the Security Health section, the Essentials and Cloud Identity Premium editions only list a subset of the security settings on this page. It should also be noted that any security setting changes within the Admin console might take 24 hours to be reflected on the Security Health page.

Let's review the different security settings that are displayed on the Security Health page across the core Google Workspace services:

| Core Service | Settings | Google Workspace Editions |
|---|---|---|
| Calendar | • Calendar sharing policy | Enterprise Plus, Education |
| | • Access to Calendar when offline | Enterprise Plus |
| Drive | • Drive sharing settings<br>• Warning for out-of-domain sharing<br>• Access Checker<br>• Drive add-ons<br>• Access to offline docs<br>• Desktop access to Drive<br>• File publishing on the web<br>• Google sign-in requirement for external collaborators | Enterprise Plus, Education |

| Core Service | Settings | Google Workspace Editions |
|---|---|---|
| Gmail | • Automatic email forwarding<br>• Comprehensive mail storage<br>• Bypassing spam filters for internal senders<br>• POP and IMAP access for users<br>• DKIM<br>• SPF record<br>• DMARC<br>• Approved senders without authentication<br>• Approved domain senders<br>• Email whitelist IPs<br>• Add the spam headers setting to all default routing rules<br>• MX record configuration<br>• MTA-STS configuration | Enterprise Plus, Education |
| | • Attachment safety<br>• Links and external images safety<br>• Spoofing and authentication safety | Enterprise Plus |
| Groups | • Groups creation and membership | Enterprise Plus, Education |
| Marketplace apps | • Google Workspace Marketplace applications usage | Enterprise Plus, Education |
| Device management | • Blocking of compromised mobile devices<br>• Mobile management<br>• Mobile password requirements<br>• Device encryption<br>• Mobile inactivity reports<br>• Auto account wipe<br>• Application verification<br>• Installation of mobile applications from unknown sources<br>• External media storage | Enterprise, Education, Cloud Identity Premium |

| Core Service | Settings | Google Workspace Editions |
|---|---|---|
| Security | • Two-step verification for users<br>• Two-step verification for admins<br>• Security key enforcement for admins | Enterprise, Education, Cloud Identity Premium |
| | • Security key enforcement for users | Enterprise Plus |
| Sites | • Sites sharing policy | Enterprise Plus, Education |

# Security dashboard

**The security dashboard** lets administrators view security reports in one place. It also allows users to slice and dice data across various products with customizable time ranges across all the domains. It allows administrators to analyze trends and capture any anomalies that reflect changes in user behavior. The dashboard also allows users to compare current and historical data:

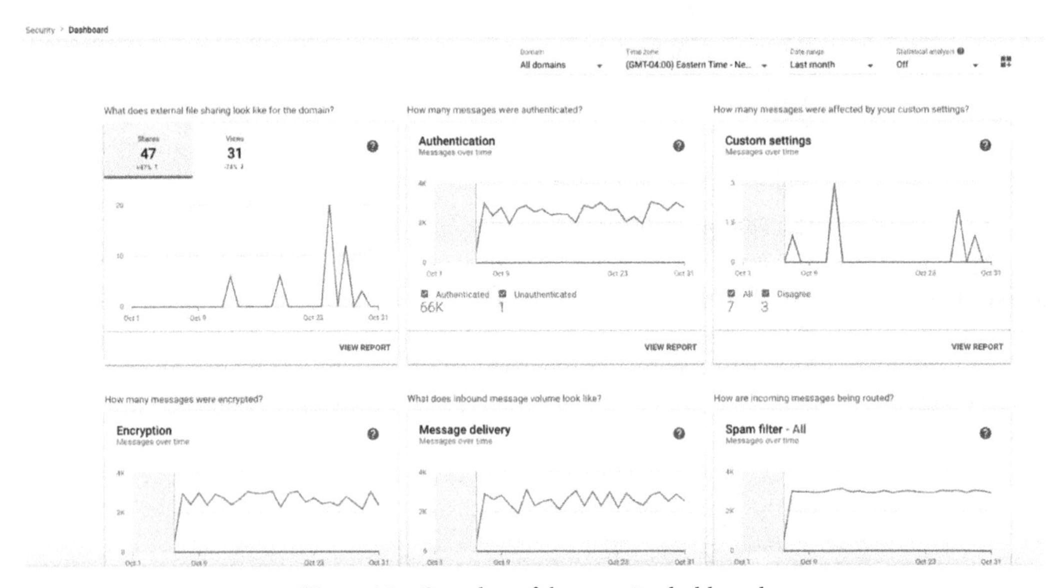


Figure 4.2 – Snapshot of the security dashboard

There are a few things to note as we navigate through the security dashboard:

- The availability of reports is based on the Google Workspace edition.
- The retention times of log data differ across reports. It varies from 30 days to 180 days.
- Usage data takes a while to propagate to the security dashboard for users to generate reports. It typically lasts between 1 to 4 hours.

The following table shows the list of reports that are available across Workspace editions:

| Google Workspace Edition | Report | Insights Gained |
|---|---|---|
| Enterprise Plus | File exposure | Report on the domain user's external file sharing |
| Enterprise Plus | Authentication | Report on messages that were authenticated |
| Enterprise Plus | Custom settings | Report on messages that were affected by the domain's custom settings |
| Enterprise Plus | Encryption | Report on encrypted messages |
| Enterprise Plus | Message delivery | Report on inbound message volume |
| Enterprise Plus | Spam filter – All | Report on incoming messages that are being routed |
| Enterprise Plus | Spam filter – Phishing | Report on potential phishing emails being routed |
| Enterprise Plus | Spam filter – Malware | Report on the volume of messages marked as malware |
| Enterprise Plus | User reports | Report on the number of users marking their emails |
| Enterprise Plus | Suspicious attachments | Report on the volume of messages containing suspicious attachments |
| Enterprise Plus | Spoofing | Report on messages showing evidence of potential spoofing |
| Enterprise Standard, Plus | DLP incidents | Report on the frequency of DLP rules violated concerning their severity |
| Enterprise Standard, Plus | Top policy incidents | Report on the top policies causing the highest number of incidents |
| Enterprise Standard, Plus, and Cloud Identity | Failed device password attempts | Report on the frequency of failed password attempts on devices |
| Enterprise Standard, Plus, and Cloud Identity | Compromised device events | Report on the number of detected compromised device events |
| Enterprise Standard, Plus, and Cloud Identity | Suspicious device activities | Report on detected suspicious device activities |
| Enterprise Standard, Plus, and Cloud Identity | OAuth scope grants by product (beta customers only) | Report on the number of OAuth scope grants |
| Enterprise Standard, Plus, and Cloud Identity | OAuth grant activity | Report on the number of apps with the highest change in OAuth grant activity |
| Enterprise Standard, Plus, and Cloud Identity | OAuth grants to new apps | Report on the number of OAuth tokens granted to new apps |

| Google Workspace Edition | Report | Insights Gained |
|---|---|---|
| Enterprise Standard, Plus, and Cloud Identity | OAuth grants to new apps | Report on the number of OAuth tokens granted to new apps |
| Enterprise Standard, Plus, and Cloud Identity | User login attempts | Report on the number of login challenge methods used in this domain |
| Enterprise Standard, Plus, and Cloud Identity | User login attempts | Report on the frequency of failed user login attempts |
| Enterprise Standard, Plus, and Cloud Identity | User login attempts | Report on the number of suspicious user login attempts |
| Cloud Identity | Chrome threat protection summary | Report on the number of Chrome threat activities |
| Cloud Identity | Chrome data protection summary | Report on the number of Chrome incidents for each data protection rule |
| Cloud Identity | Chrome high-risk users | Report on the number of Chrome users who have encountered the most threats |
| Cloud Identity | Chrome high-risk domains | Report on the number of domains that are the riskiest for Chrome users |

Finally, depending on the need, the security dashboard user interface allows users to customize reports. Let's take a look:

1. Click on the **Customize dashboard** button at the top-right corner of the **Security Dashboard** page.
2. From the panel on the right, add the required widgets by clicking and dragging them in.
3. The security dashboard can be rearranged by dragging the individual reports as well.

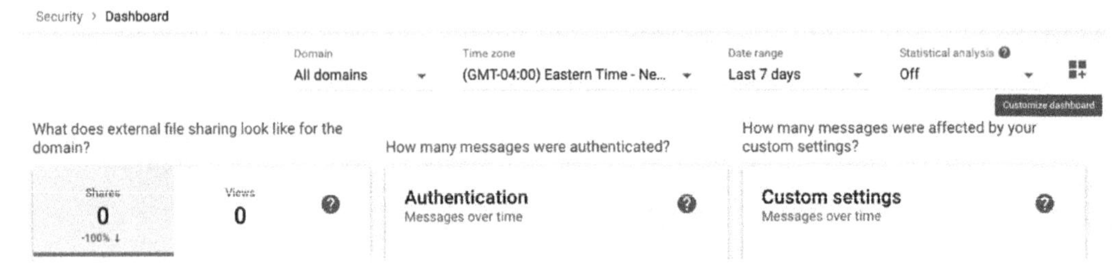


Figure 4.3 – Customizing the security dashboard

Now, let's move on and investigate the next item in our toolkit – the security investigation tool, which is an administrator's best companion in determining and remediating security incidents.

## Security investigation tool

The security investigation tool allows administrators to respond to security incidents effectively by allowing them to identify, triage, and remediate security issues in their domain.

This tool spans almost all core services, including Gmail, Drive, Devices, Calendar Log Events, and Context-Aware Access Logs. The tool allows administrators to select one of these data sources and run a search using conditional filters. The result set can be used to observe anomalies and direct administrators to deep dive into specific areas. This query and its results can be shared with other users as well.

The search functionality is very robust; it allows administrators to add nested queries to get multiple events from different services combined.

Here is a typical use case where the security investigation tool can come in handy:

1. A user has received a spoofed email and has promptly reported that to the administrator.
2. The administrator then can initiate an investigation using the security investigation tool to determine the sender of the phishing email.
3. The administrator can then choose to block the sender or remove the phishing email from the user's inbox, among other things.

4. Furthermore, administrators can perform a pivot on the results to search for users that may have received the same phishing email from the offender. Those emails could then be purged from all impacted user inboxes to prevent further damage.

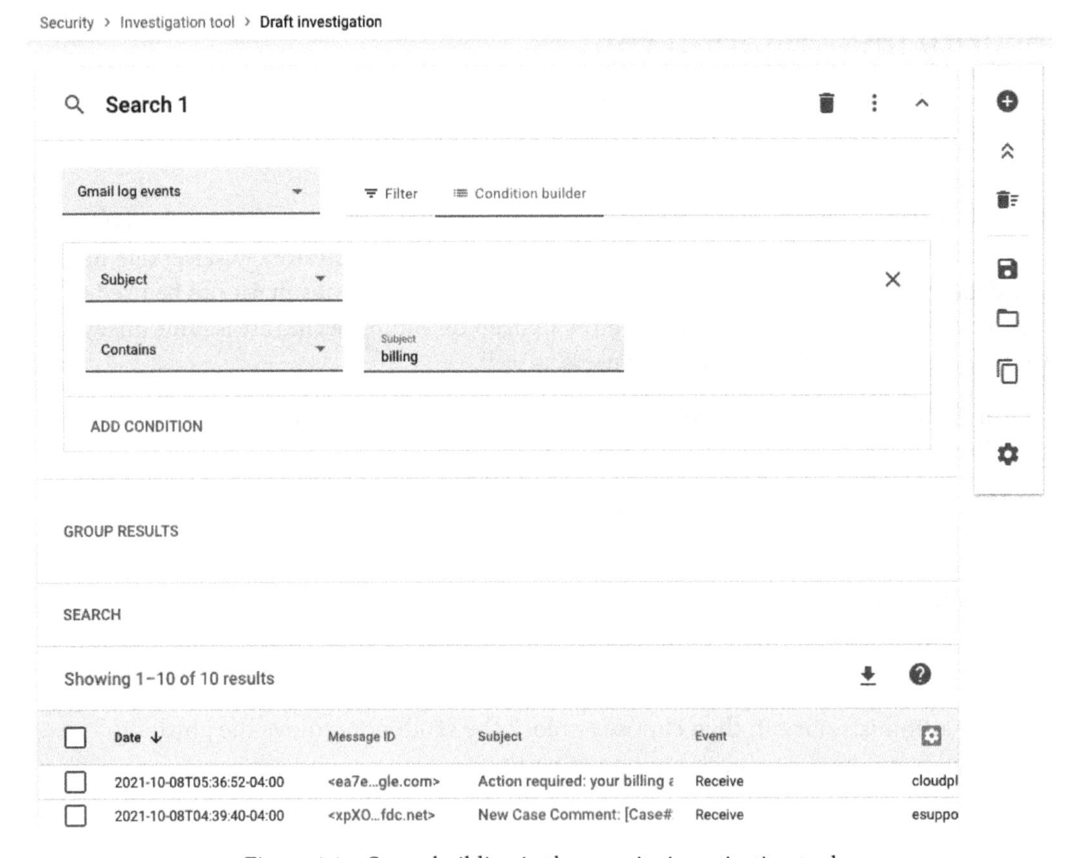


Figure 4.4 – Query building in the security investigation tool

Click on the kebab icon (3 dots) against each column, as shown in the following screenshot, to run a pivot search across other log events:

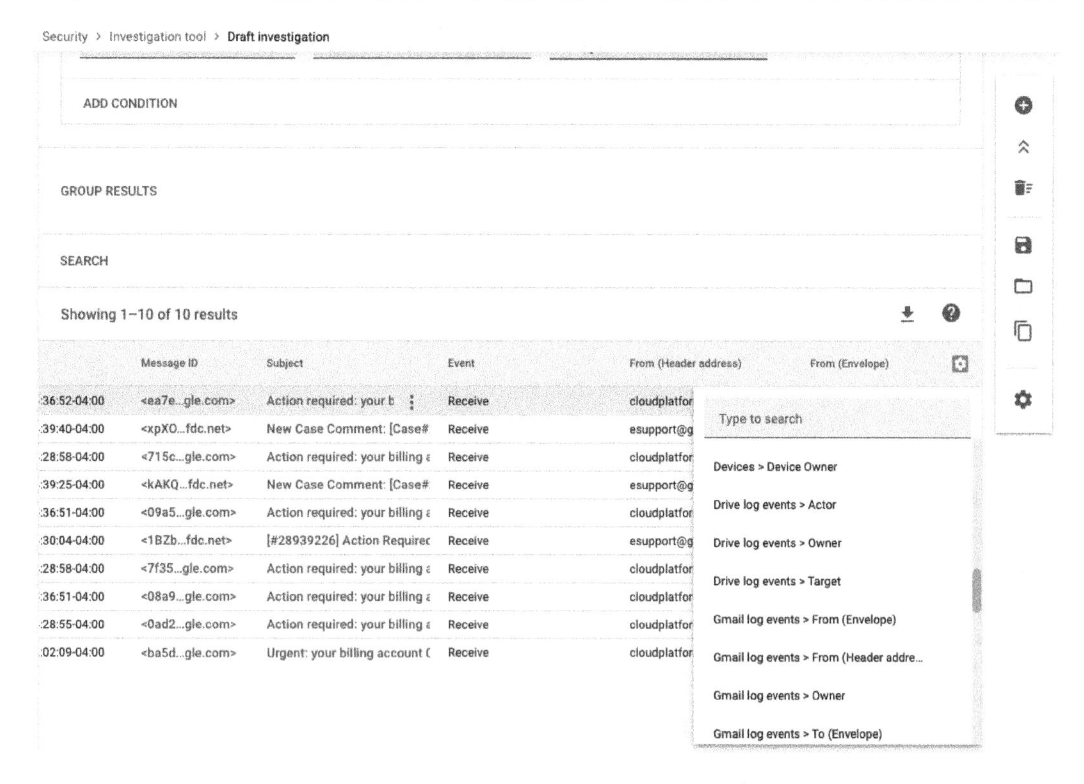


Figure 4.5 – Audit event type to search for in the security investigation tool

Administrators can get a wider picture of how many users were affected by this malicious email and send a targeted notification to these users.

The security investigation tool offers several options for administrators on how to remediate this incident. To limit the attack surface and damage within the tool, administrators can choose to do any of the following:

- Delete the offending message.
- Mark it as phishing.
- Select **Mark as spam** to move the email into the Spam folder within the user's mailbox.
- Restore the message.
- If the message was originally in the spam folder, selecting **Send to inbox** will move the message to the user's inbox.

- Move the message into quarantine for additional review using the **Send to quarantine** option.

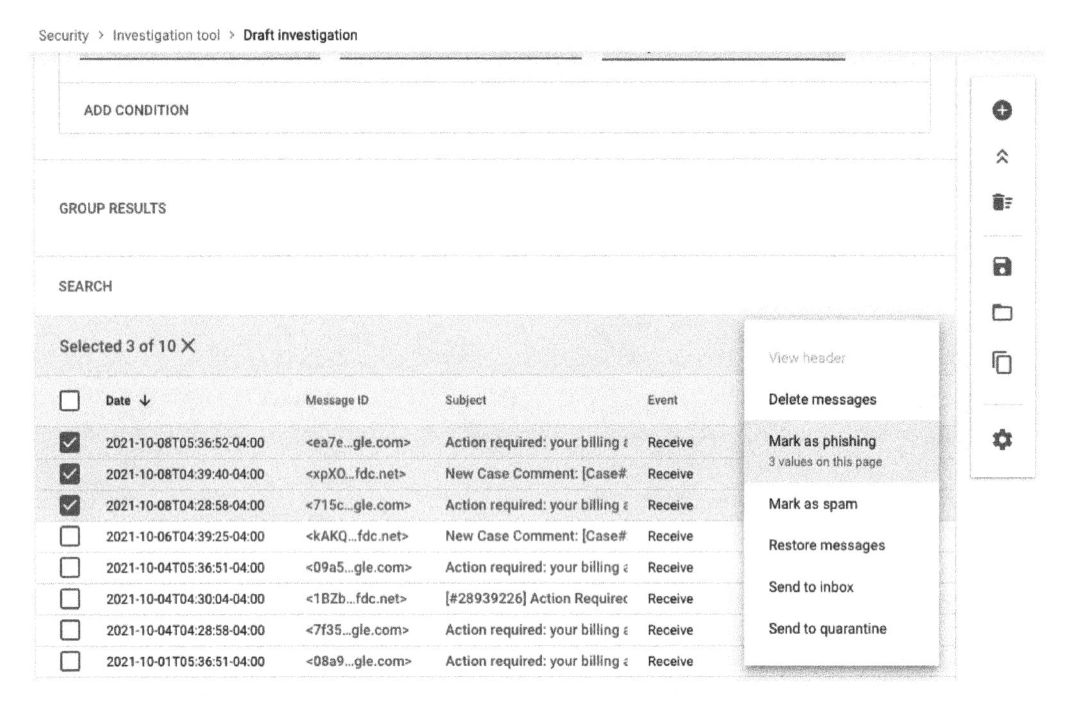


Figure 4.6 – The options that are available for remediation

To understand how the investigation tool can be helpful, let's look at another real-life scenario. Let's assume that a user owns several important documents in Google Drive. The user has recently left the company and the user has been marked as *suspended* in Google Workspace. Let's also factor in that the documents that are owned by the user are shared with collaborators.

A new employee in the same team wants access to the documents that are titled `Legal`. Since the owner is no longer active, none of the other collaborators who have *Viewer* or *Commenter* access can extend access to this new employee. The new employee now reaches out to the administrator to gain access.

The administrator can run a search on the Drive data source to locate the files that have been shared:

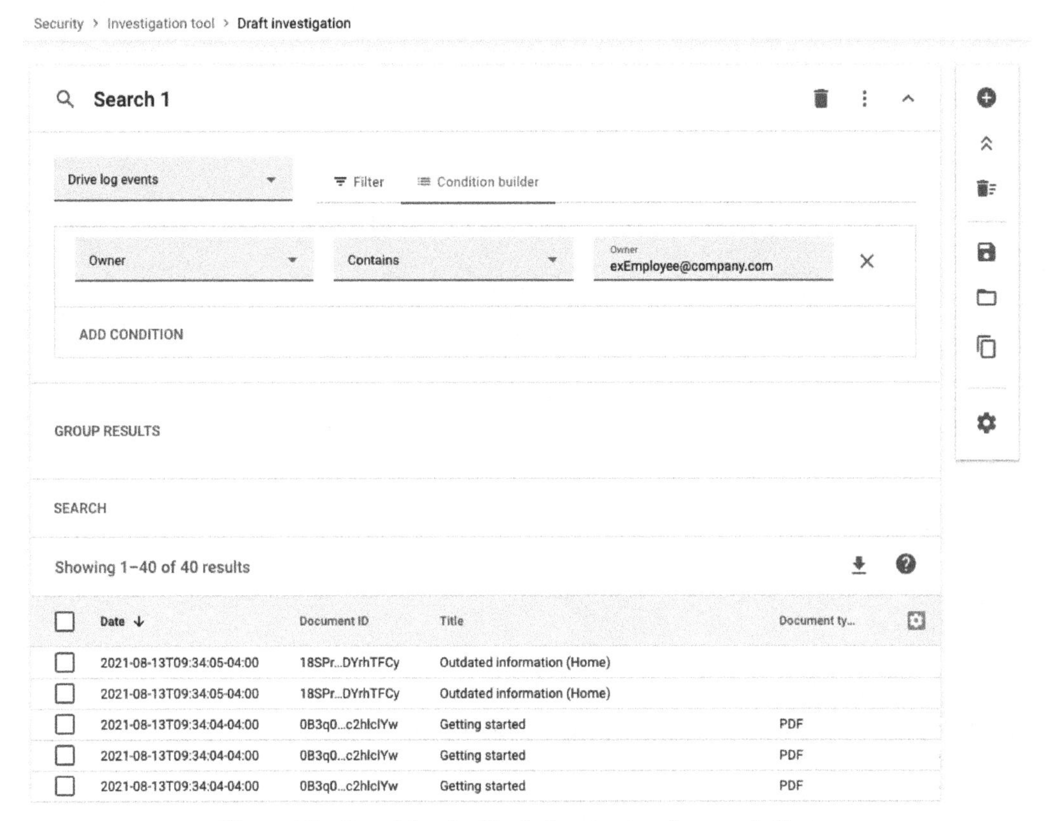


Figure 4.7 – Searching for files belonging to a "suspended" user

The administrator then applies additional filters to search for content titled `Legal`:

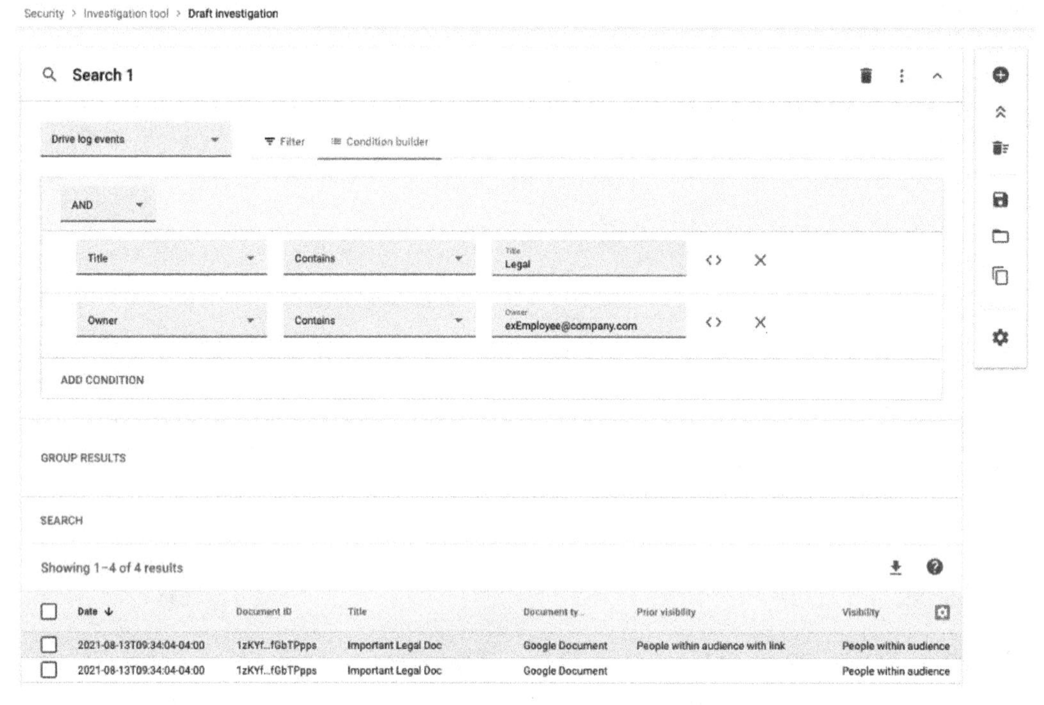


Figure 4.8 – Query build to search for content titled "Legal"

Once the files that are titled `Legal` show up in the search results, the administrator can then select these files to act on them. There are a few options at the administrator's disposal, as follows:

- **Add users**
- **Audit file permissions**
- **Change owner**
- **Disable download, print, copy**
- **Remove users**

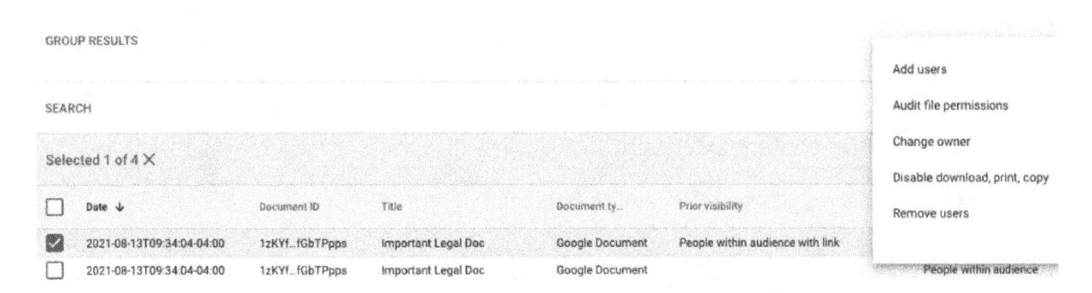


Figure 4.9 – Options available for an administrator to act on Drive file contents

In our use case, the administrator could then add the new employee as a collaborator to this document.

As we have elaborated, the security investigation tool is a powerful tool for an administrator to have in their toolkit, and it comes in handy in several common scenarios in an organization. With that, let's look at **data loss prevention** (**DLP**) software.

# Data loss prevention

DLP is a technique that Google has woven into its products to detect and alert users and administrators about sensitive data that needs to be safeguarded within the company and not shared externally. This is a critical feature that improves the security posture so that administrators and users can sleep peacefully at night.

There have been so many instances where employees accidentally lose data – for example, perhaps they share a file that contains social security numbers to people that should not be seeing them. Or it could be users that intentionally leak data, or hackers that could be looking for the weakest link and trying to steal data. In all these instances, it is imperative that data be handled and stored carefully at rest and when sharing it.

DLP helps companies prevent data loss. It allows administrators to define policies that can detect sensitive data. These policies could be based on any of the following:

- **Predefined detectors**: These can be national identification numbers or **personally identifiable information** (**PII**) such as mailing addresses or phone numbers.
- **Regular expressions**: Unique content such as employee numbers or special codes can be defined as regular expressions.
- **Word lists**: You can define a list of words that are confidential to the organization.

If there is Drive content that has any of these detectors, then the DLP rule will take effect and act based on the defined policy. The policy can be configured in such a way that users can be warned when sensitive content is shared externally. The users can also be restricted from sharing sensitive content externally.

Here are some scenarios where DLP can be helpful:

- Warn the user when a sheet with several addresses and phone numbers is being shared externally to the domain. Addresses are classified as PII.
- Restrict users when a document that contains confidential project information is being shared externally to the domain. This could be defined via a custom word list that's specific to the domain.
- Restrict users from sharing files that contain credit card information. DLP software is smart enough to detect credit numbers using the **Luhn algorithm**.

> **Luhn Algorithm**
> The Luhn algorithm is a checksum formula that's used to validate various commonly occurring numbers in business, such as credit cards, social security numbers, and IMEI numbers.

The following steps will show you how to create a detector using the DLP interface:

1. Log in to the Google **Admin** console.
2. Open **Security** from the left-hand side panel and click on **Data Protection**.
3. Click on **Manage Detectors**, then **Add a Detector**:

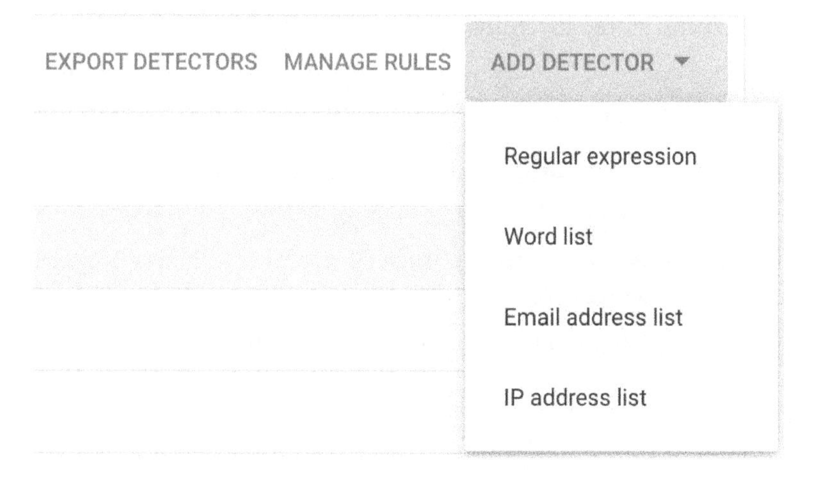


Figure 4.10 – Adding detectors in DLP

This setting gives you the option to add specific detectors that can be used across multiple rules:

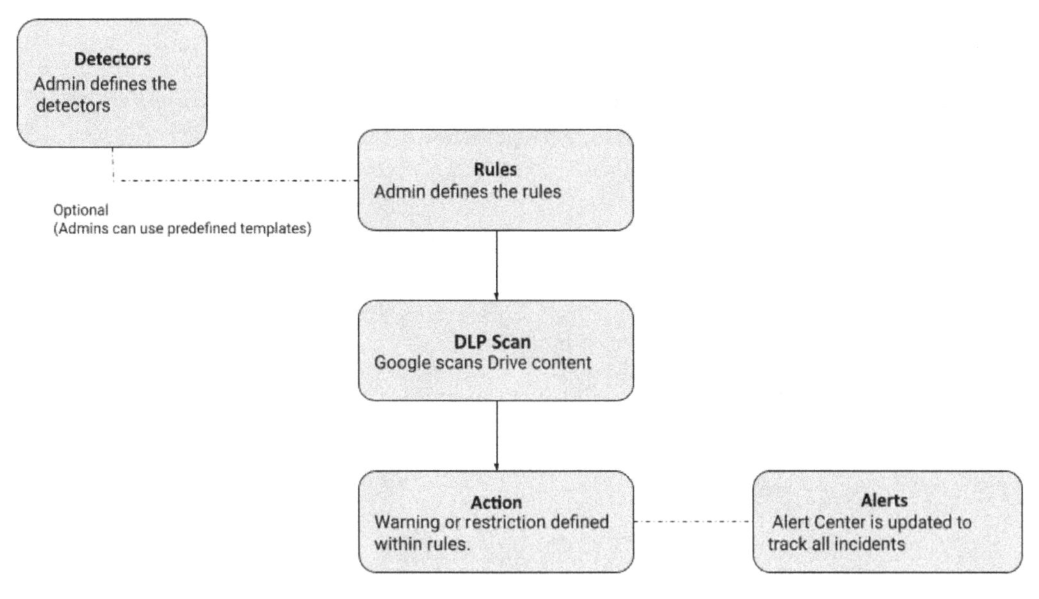


Figure 4.11 – Workflow of DLP

Once the detectors have been defined, rules can be configured and applied to targeted users within OUs or groups.

Rules are scalable and can scan non-Google format file types such as `.bmp`, `.eps`, `.fif`, `.gif`, `.img_for_ocr`, `.jpeg`, `.gzip`, `.rar`, `.tar`, and `.zip`. It is important to note that image and video file types are not scanned for DLP.

## Creating a rule from a template

Google Workspace makes this easier for administrators by providing templates of frequently used DLP rules. Admins don't need to start from scratch and can use a template to quickly configure detectors and actions:

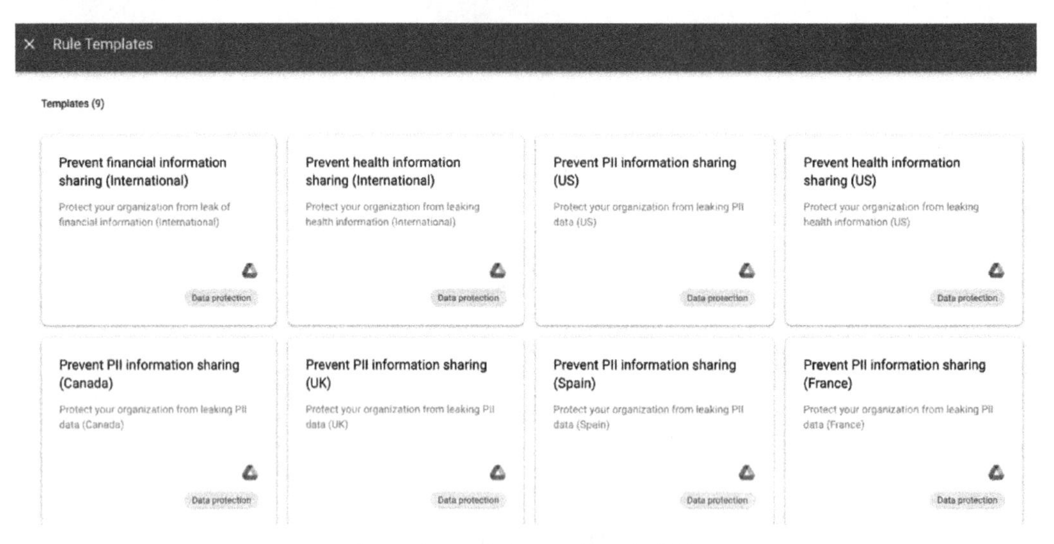


Figure 4.12 – Rule templates in DLP

Follow these steps to create a new rule from scratch without the help of a template:

1. Log in to the Google **Admin** console.
2. Click on **Security** from the left-hand side panel.
3. Select **Data Protection** and click on **Manage Rules**.
4. To get started with a new rule, click on **Add a Rule** and select **New Rule** or **New Rule from Template**.
5. Select the OUs or groups this rule will apply to:
    - Selecting the top-level OU will cascade this rule to all nested OUs.
    - Specific OUs can be included or excluded:

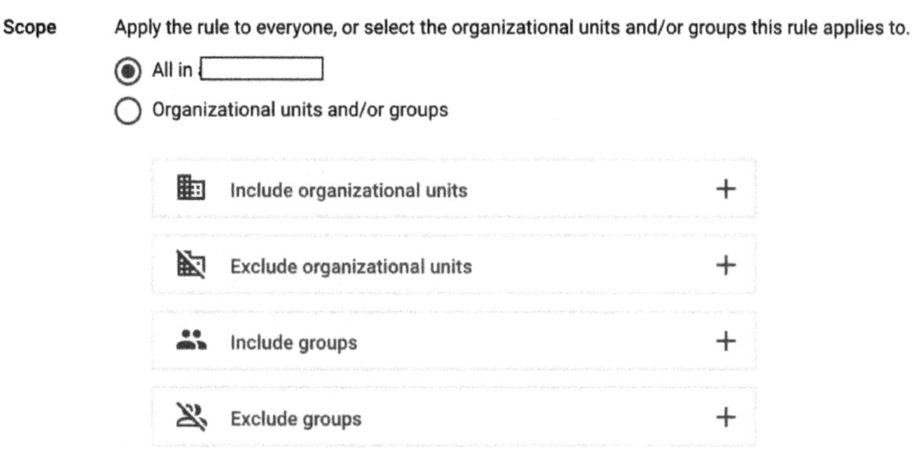


Figure 4.13 – Scope of rule application in DLP

6. Click **Next** and select **Trigger Conditions**.
7. Select the detectors that will trigger this rule execution. Two variables will help trigger the rule:
   - **Threshold**: Likeliness of sensitive data occurring
   - **Minimum match count**: Frequency of sensitive data occurring:

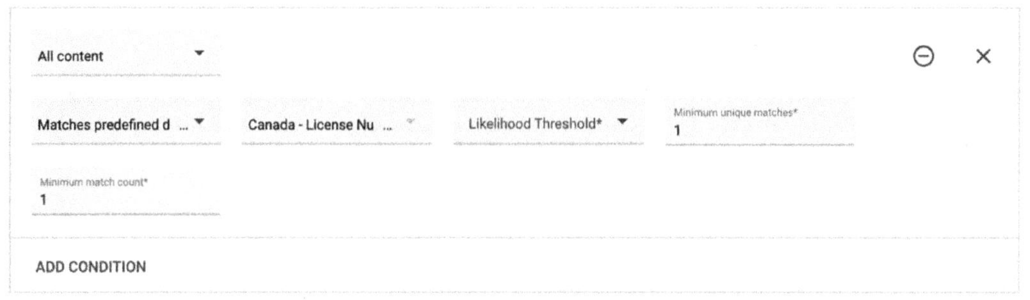


Figure 4.14 – Conditions for triggering a DLP detector

8. Click **Next** and select the actions you wish to execute (under **Actions**) if the conditions have been met.

   The typical actions for a detector include the following:
   - Warn the user.
   - Block external sharing.
   - Disable the ability to download, print, and copy this content.

9. Finally, click **Save** and **Activate** the rule.

The detectors can also be configured with multiple and varying actions for DLP incidents and can be applied across various OUs/groups.

While DLP is a great feature, it alone cannot prevent all data leaks and losses. Organizations should typically augment DLP capabilities with a trained workforce that organizes data in a way that will not be susceptible to losses. For instance, a DLP-friendly Drive structure would be a good start. Business processes should be established to remove employee data as soon as they leave the company. Also, you should set up alerts so that administrators can be notified of risky behavior by users.

With that said, it's time to look at security alerts that notify administrators and summon them to action.

# Alert center

**The alert center** is a central place that lets administrators review all actionable alerts coming in from different services.

In the previous sections, we learned about defining security policies, validating the domain's current security posture, and reviewing security audit reports in a dashboard. If an administrator wants to proactively be notified about any incident or suspicious activity within the domain, these notifications should be configured as security alerts within the alert center:

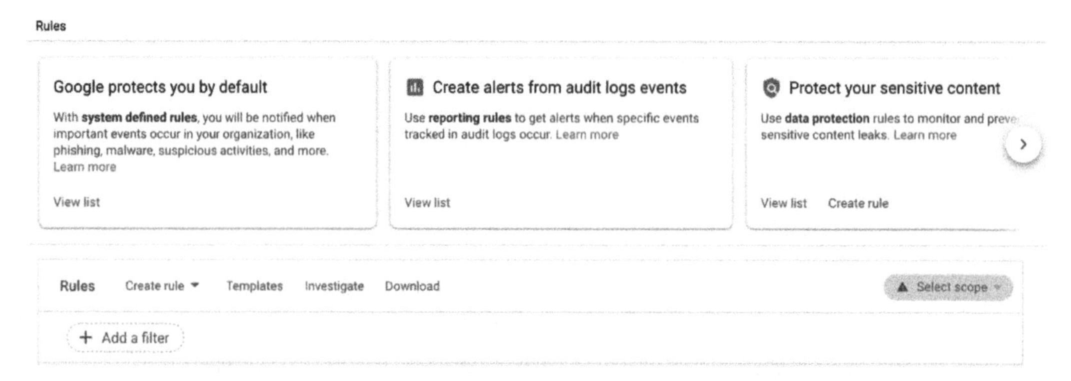


Figure 4.15 – Creating alerts in the alert center based on templates

These notifications keep the administrators informed about potential issues within the domain that require them to take necessary action in response to these alerts.

The alert center also provides an additional layer of detailed reports. It should also be noted that the alert center is included with all Google Workspace editions:

Here is how to get to the alert center:

1. Log in to the **Admin** console.
2. Select **Security** from the left-hand side panel and click on **Alert Center**.

Once selected, the alert center will display a list of alerts with a filtered view. The alert center triggers alerts based on rules that are defined. There are multiple ways to receive alerts:

- Using system-defined rules that notify administrators upon predefined triggers provided by Google
- Using activity-based alerts
- Using DLP-based alerts
- Using reporting-based alerts when a specific activity occurs

Clicking on **Manage Alerts** in the alert center UI will display various alerts based on the source of the events. Alerts are initiated sequentially based on actions or rules:

Actions Alerts **Rule type**

**System defined**

Google provided rules that notify you about specific activity or information related to your domain.

Learn more

**Activity**

Allows you to be notified and take automated actions when defined activity thresholds are met. These can also be created using the security investigation tool.

Learn more

**Data protection**

Allows you to protect your sensitive content and prevent data leaks to unauthorized users.

Learn more

**Reporting**

Allows you to be notified when specific activity occurs.

Learn more

*Some features are only available in specific licenses and may require delegated admin privileges.* Learn more

Figure 4.16 – Types of rules in the alert center

The interface enables administrators to perform *one-click recommended* actions that result in quick remediation when an alert is received:

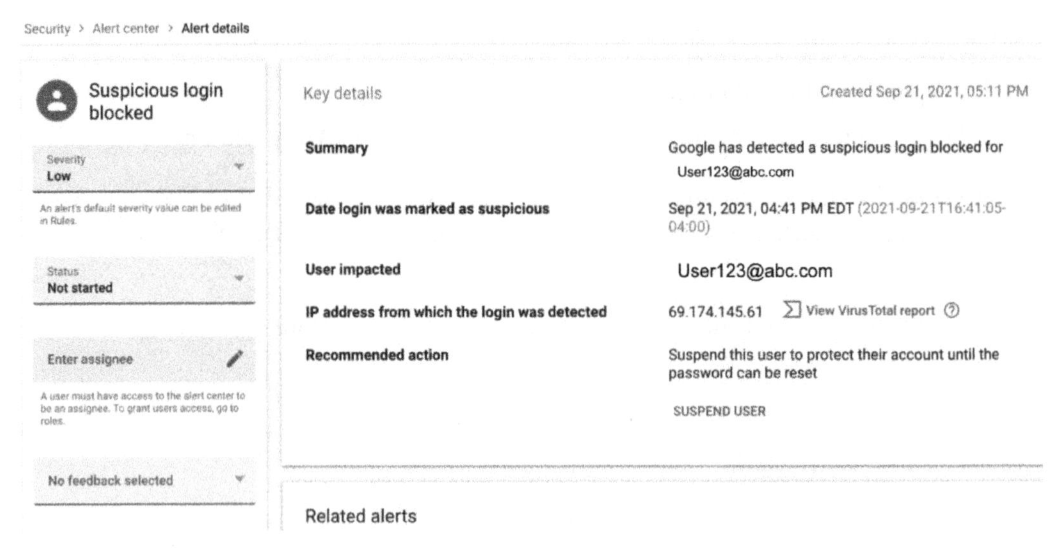


Figure 4.17 – Details of an alert in the alert center

Administrators can also share their workload by adding other recipients as *assignees* for receiving these alerts:

1. Log in to the **Admin** console.
2. Click on **Security** from the left-hand side panel and select **Alert Center**.
3. Select the alert you'd like to update.
4. In the left-hand side panel, add other email addresses in the **Assignee** section.

Let's look at some examples where the alert center can help manage several day-to-day activities for administrators:

- If users in a domain are prone to receiving spam or phishing emails, administrators can set up alerts for these users. Upon the arrival of these emails, the alert center will notify you of these incidents, along with recommended actions, such as moving the message to the Spam folder or deleting the email message.
- If companies want to audit users when downloading Drive files, that can be set up as a rule. For instance, alerts can be raised when users are downloading more than 10 files within an hour.

## VirusTotal

**VirusTotal** is a new addition to the security toolset that's integrated inot the alert center in Google Workspace. It provides contextual data on threats to help analyze suspicious files, domains, links, and IP addresses to detect security threats. VirusTotal reports are available from the **Alert details** page; these reports are relevant to a specific alert. The reputation data can be insightful and administrators can choose to use that crowd-sourced information for additional insights:

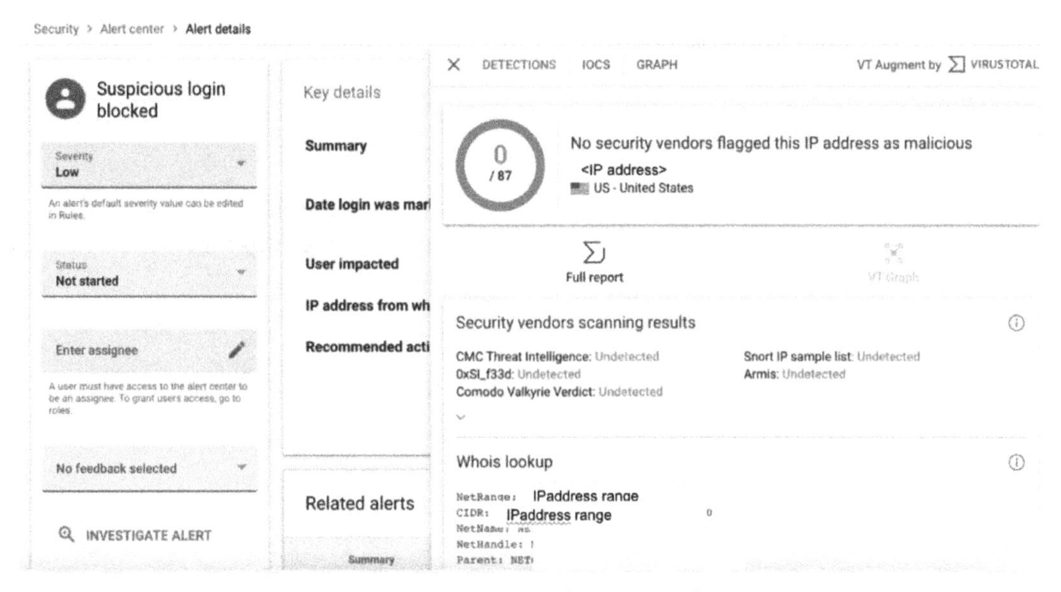


Figure 4.18 – VirusTotal reputation data

Within the alert center, admins can now directly access VirusTotal reports for suspicious content. It is worth noting that VirusTotal is not used for generating alerts; however, it provides additional insights with additional context around the reputation of the source of malicious content. VirusTotal is a product of the Alphabet company and uses data across 70+ security vendors to provide detailed assessments of security threats.

So far, we have seen several tools and features that Google Workspace offers to protect data in the cloud. However, often, governments of sovereign nations and unions enact rules that dictate where data should be stored physically and accessed. One such well-known compliance regulation is **General Data Protection Regulation** (**GDPR**), which dictates how PII from individuals who live in the European Union should be handled in terms of collection and processing. For enterprises with strict compliance policies, Google Workspace offers a nifty way to segregate user data and store it in different geographic regions.

# Segregation of data by regions

As we saw in *Chapter 1*, *Introducing Google Workspace*, Google Workspace uses a distributed architecture to store data across multiple data centers. Enterprises typically have specific compliance policies that require that the data be saved in a specific data region. Google Workspace addresses these requirements through **data regions** by allowing administrators to select the destination data region where Google Workspace data will be saved.

There are two editions of data regions:

- Fundamental
- Enterprise

While **Fundamental data regions** lets you set a region for all the users within the organization, **Enterprise data regions** lets you configure various regions for each OU:

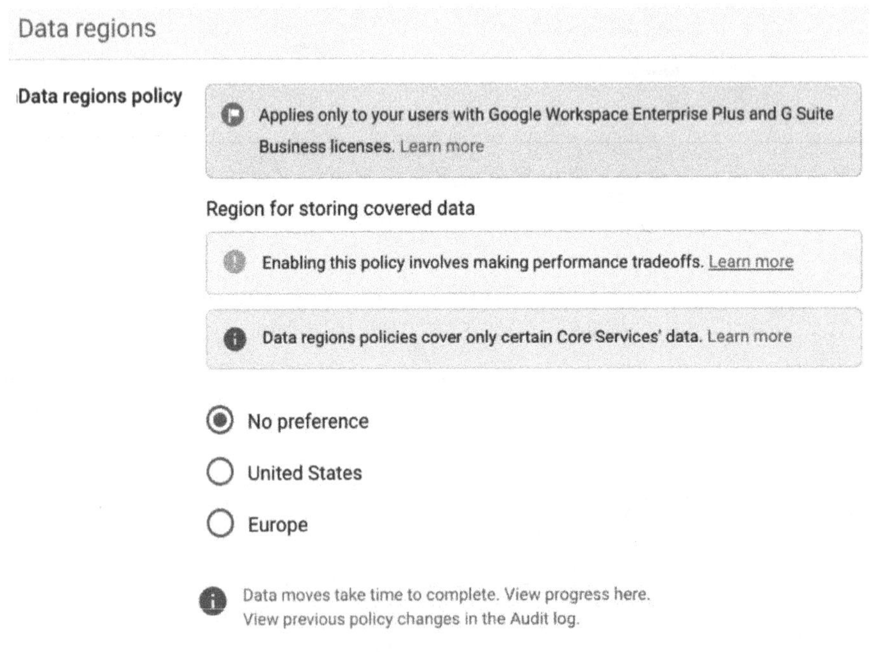


Figure 4.19 – Configuring a data regions policy

Please note that when **data regions** is enabled for a user and if the user is physically located outside of the region, performance delays may be observed when accessing data. A classic example is when a user in the United States tries to access their data from a server in Australia. The user's request must travel halfway across the world before the request is fulfilled. The response then has to travel halfway again to reach the user. There would be high latency because of the geographic distance.

**Data regions** covers content that's created in the following Google Workspace core services:

- Calendar
- Gmail
- Drive
- Chat
- Meet
- Keep
- Vault
- New Sites

It's not just the data that is bound to the data region policy. For instance, indices that are created on that data to speed up search queries must also be co-located with data and must be bound to the policies covered under **data regions**.

When administrators select **data regions**, a progress dashboard is provided to indicate the percentage of data being moved from various locations to the destination region.

The power of the cloud is realized when applications and data can be accessed from anywhere and on any device. Google Workspace provides a secure way to manage devices that access data that complements the broader security initiatives and tooling we have seen thus far. Let's segue into talking about the **endpoint management** system, which provides a comprehensive way to manage user devices.

# Endpoint management

The primary value of Google Workspace is the ability to connect to your work data from anywhere on any device. Users typically use a laptop or a mobile device to access their respective Google Workspace content, such as emails, files within Drive, and messages in Google Chat; connect to video calls in Google Meet; and access their checklists in Google Keep.

While Google Workspace lets users connect from anywhere, it also comes with the added responsibility of keeping the domain data secure. Google Workspace's endpoint management system solves this conundrum and helps keep an organization's data safe.

The endpoint management system covers the following:

- Mobile devices
- Chrome browsers
- Windows 10 device endpoints
- Google Meet hardware that's used in conference rooms
- Jamboard devices that are used with whiteboards
- Chromebook laptops

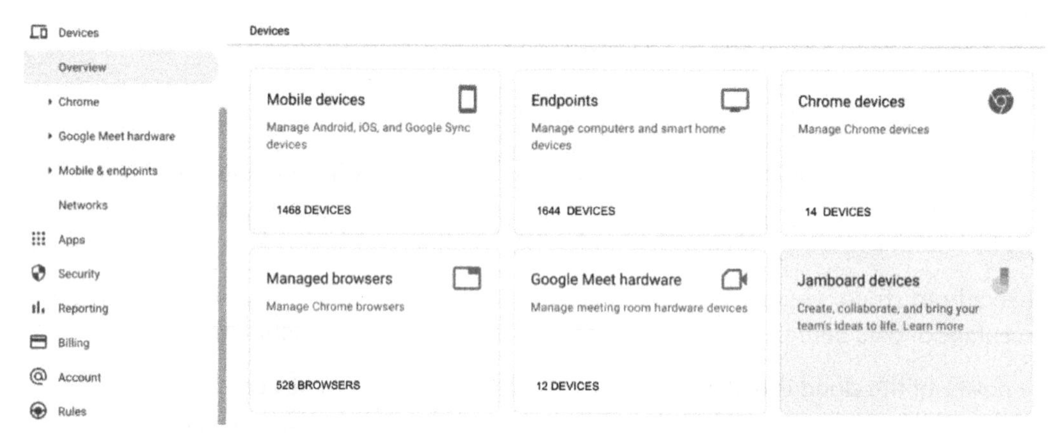


Figure 4.20 – Managing different devices using the endpoint management UI

Let's briefly talk about mobile management.

## Mobile management

There are two types of mobile device management options available:

- **Basic**: Using this type of management, administrators can keep track of device inventory, wipe account data from the device in a remote manner, enforce the use of a passcode, run device audit reports, and block devices, which will prevent the device from accessing this domain in the future.
- **Advanced**: In addition to all the basic management features, Google Workspace provides additional options to manage apps and OS security for mobile devices, standardize device approvals for enrollment, set device security policies, and more. These ensure an enterprise organization can control data exfiltration across all endpoints.

Like Google Workspace apps, these management options can be enabled for a smaller subset of users within an OU or access group. Here's how you turn on the **basic and advanced** mobile management options:

1. Log in to the **Admin** console.
2. Select **Devices** from the left-hand side panel.
3. Click on **Mobile & Endpoints | Settings | Universal Settings**.
4. Click on **General | Mobile Management**.
5. Here, admins can select **Basic** or **Advanced**.

> **Note**
>
> If you wish to enable advanced mobile management on iOS devices, an Apple Push certificate is required.

Once you've configured this selection, other detailed management options are made available:

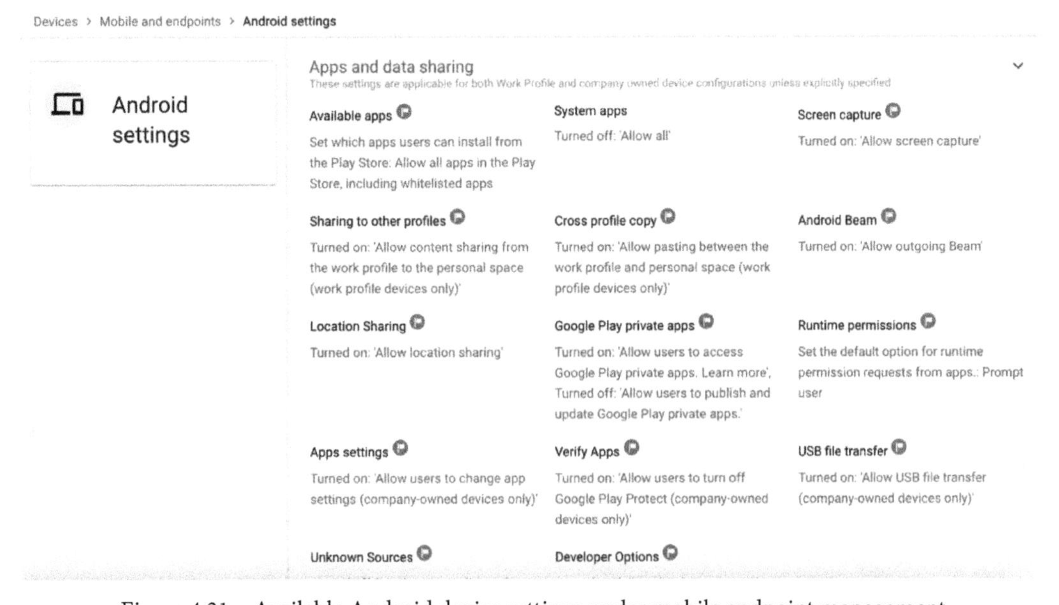


Figure 4.21 – Available Android device settings under mobile endpoint management

Mobile endpoint management makes it easy for organizations to import employee device data in bulk to track company-owned inventory.

Here is the workflow:

1. Log in to the **Admin** console.
2. Select **Devices** from the left-hand side panel.
3. Click on **Mobile & Endpoints | Company Owned Inventory**.
4. Click on + from the top left.
5. Select the OS of the device.
6. Download the format of the asset.
7. Populate the device's details and upload this file.

   Once you've done this, a notification is sent to admins indicating the result:

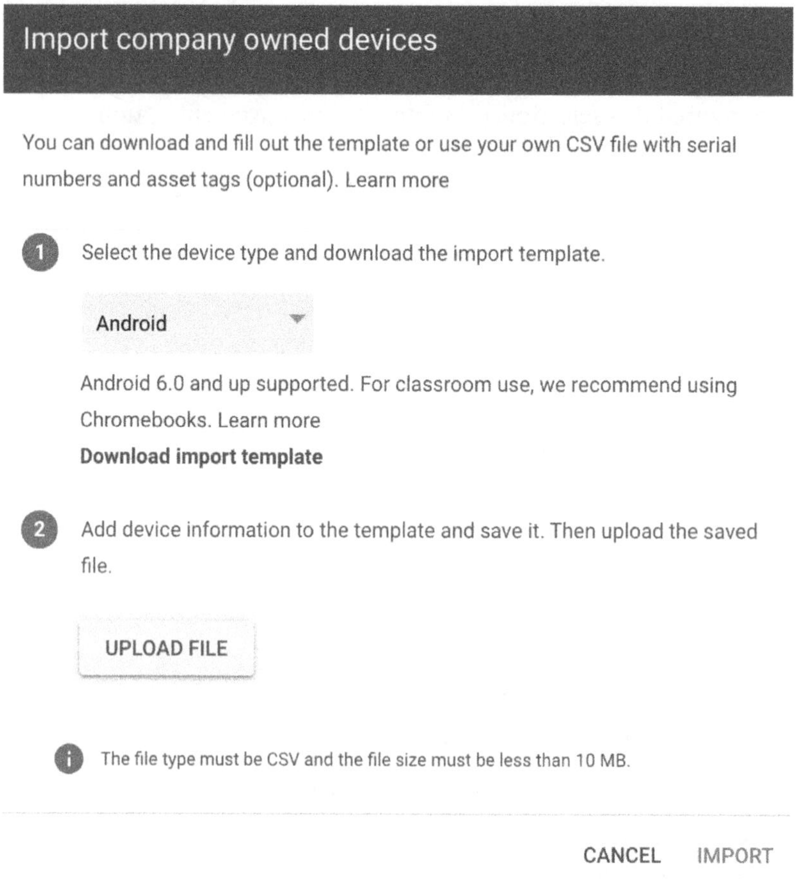

Import company owned devices

You can download and fill out the template or use your own CSV file with serial numbers and asset tags (optional). Learn more

1 Select the device type and download the import template.

Android

Android 6.0 and up supported. For classroom use, we recommend using Chromebooks. Learn more

**Download import template**

2 Add device information to the template and save it. Then upload the saved file.

UPLOAD FILE

The file type must be CSV and the file size must be less than 10 MB.

CANCEL IMPORT

Figure 4.22 – Bulk import company-owned devices

When a user receives a company-owned device and turns it on, the device checks for any enterprise device configuration that's been assigned to this device. If the configuration is found, it automatically downloads a Device Policy app. This Device Policy app controls the apps that are used on this device and enforces security policies.

Similarly, if a user tries their own personal device and logs into their Google Workspace app, the device configurations that have been assigned to the user's OU take effect. The login process through the app will redirect the user to the Device Policy app.

With this understanding of how endpoint management allows devices and data to be kept secure, let's build on this capability with automated device management.

# Automated device management

In the previous section, we learned about security alerts, which are triggered based on certain actions. We also noted that they are configured through rules. Google Workspace allows admins to automate device management through similar rules. An event on the device triggers these rules based on the conditions defined, and actions are executed sequentially.

For example, when unlocking a device, if a user enters an incorrect password more than five times, this could mean that the device is with an unauthorized person. A rule could be configured to automatically wipe the account from the device without anyone's intervention.

To create such rules, follow these steps:

1. Log in to the **Admin** console.
2. Select **Security** from the left-hand side panel.
3. Click on **Rules**.
4. Select **Device Management Rules**.

5. Select **Add a rule from template** or **Create a new rule**.

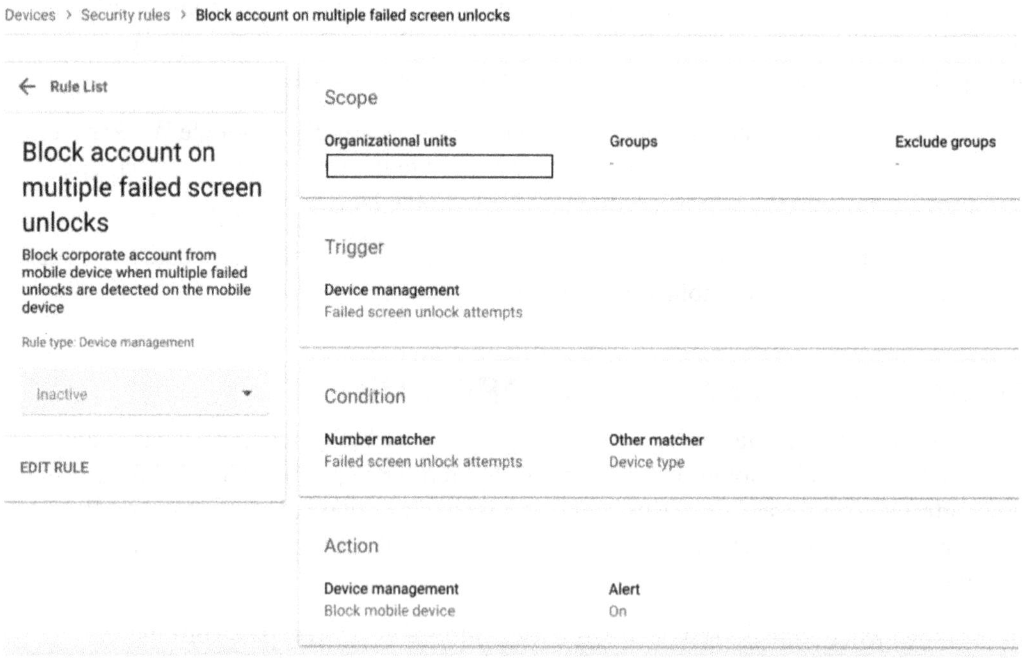

Figure 4.23 – Rule to block an account on multiple failed screen unlocks on a mobile device

Another popular use case where the endpoint management system comes into play is dealing with data and devices when a user leaves an organization. Once an employee leaves the organization, depending on whether the user used their personal device or a company-owned device, the user account could be blocked from the device.

If the employee used their personal device, their work profile and work data could be removed, leaving their personal data untouched:

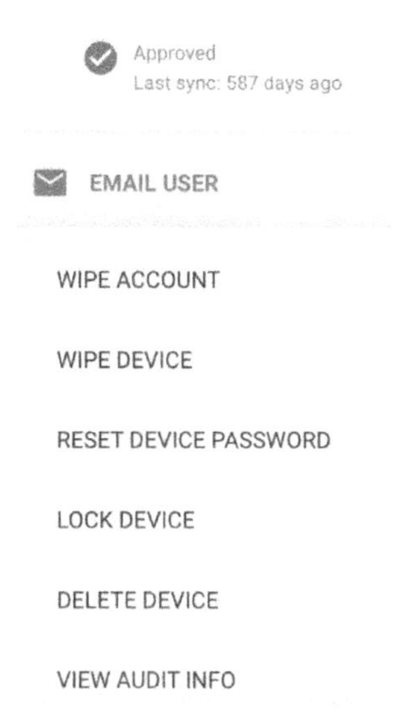


Figure 4.24 – Administrator options with device endpoint management

The endpoint management system can be powerful and offers several features to keep data and devices secure. Let's wrap this chapter up by looking at the reports that are available for administrators and users to get detailed insights into their accounts, data, and security incidents.

# Reports

Google Workspace intends to make administrating the domain intuitive and automated to lessen the burden on the IT team. With that in mind, there are pre-built reports available for monitoring data and user activity. Let's take a look at them:

- **Reporting Highlights**: This displays a list of reports showing various activities such as the status of accounts, storage being used, and files shared externally.
- **Reports**:
  - **Apps Reports**: Shows app-specific reporting data such as the total number of emails, the total number of files created in Drive, and active users in Meet across all the apps.
  - **User Reports**: Shows user activity reports such as apps usage and 2SV enrollment.

- **Device Reports**: This shows a list of mobile devices and Chrome devices, as well as reports on OS-specific devices:

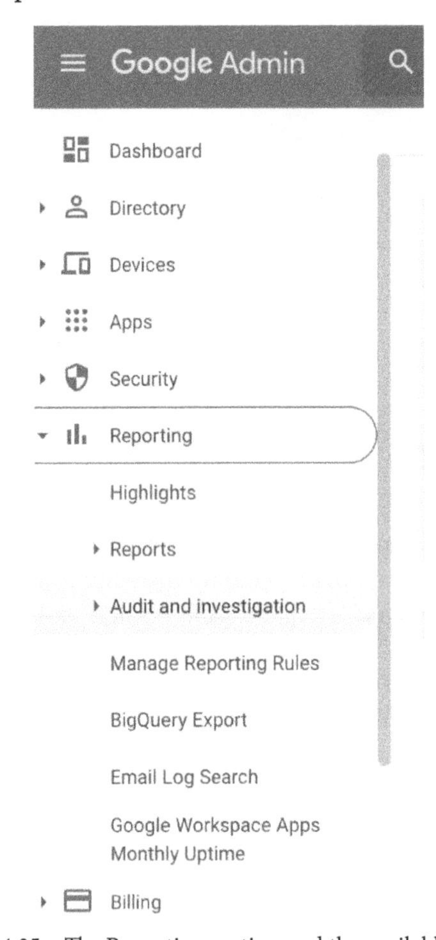


Figure 4.25 – The Reporting section and the available options

Beyond these pre-built reports, there are detailed audit activity reports available, such as the following:

- **Admin Audit Activity**: All configuration changes that are made within the Admin console are logged as an activity, with the time and username of the user specified.
- **Login Audit Log**: List of logins across all users.
- **OAuth token audit log**: List of OAuth-based app authorizations granted by users.

- User activities within the following apps are also listed in the audit logs:
    - Calendar
    - Drive
    - Chat

These logs are available for 6 months historically and mostly are not real time. The reports may have a certain lag based on whether it is a user audit log or an app usage log.

For example, if a user creates a Drive file, the information does not immediately get reflected in the Drive usage or Highlights report. Sometimes, it takes a day or two. The following is the typical lag across report types:

Lag time: 1-3 days:

- Highlights
- Security Reports
- Aggregate Reports
- Apps Usage Activity reports

Real time:

- Admin Audit activity
- Access Transparency
- Calendar Audit
- Groups Audit
- Meet Audit
- Meet Quality Tool

Reports can also be connected to a BigQuery table for storing usage and activity data over a longer duration and can also be used to analyze trends in data. Additional storage and query costs for BigQuery will be applicable.

The Google Workspace API offers a nifty way to automate reporting data; however, we will look at that in the next chapter.

# Summary

This chapter laid bare the security tooling infrastructure with Google Workspace and how it empowers administrators with improved auditability and observability functions. We started by looking at the security center, which offers a comprehensive single-pane view of *all things security*. We deep-dived into the security health checklist, which is the one-stop shop for all security-related events. The security dashboard allows administrators to slice and dice data and look at events, both past and present, and be able to find patterns.

DLP gave a glimpse of what the future of preventing data leaks could look like. With powerful detections built into it, which are augmented by custom detectors, DLP leads the way in improving the security posture for organizations.

We moved on from DLP to look at segregating data by geographic regions for compliance needs. Google's global infrastructure makes this easy and enables it with the click of a button. Endpoint management offers several options for administrators to deal with company-owned devices and data, as well as when users bring their own devices.

This comprehensive set of security tools reiterates how Google has woven security into all its layers, never leaving it as an afterthought. With a good understanding of security options in Google Workspace, let's look at extending Workspace's functionality via third-party apps in the next chapter. We will also look at Google Classroom and how it enables the future generations to thrive.

# Part 3: Data Integrations

The objective of this part is to familiarize readers with data and how to integrate it with different platforms. This part will provide a high-level overview of the core services available in Google Workspace, using Google Apps Script, Google App Sheet, or Google Cloud Platform.

This part comprises the following chapters:


- *Chapter 5, Beyond Workspace*
- *Chapter 6, Designing Custom Applications*

# 5
# Beyond Workspace

In the previous chapters, we extensively covered Google Workspace's core services and several add-on services in depth. This chapter will shed light on some of the non-core services and configuration options that extend Google Workspace's functionality via third-party apps and help reach a global audience of different categories and sizes.

Google is committed to making the world a better place, and true to its commitment, Google Workspace has products that target the younger generation and help them learn and comprehend the world around them. Google Classroom is one such product that integrates several core Workspace services into a seamlessly integrated platform, to enable student and teacher communication and collaboration.

In this chapter, we will cover the following topics:

- Google Classroom
- Google Marketplace apps and add-ons
- Google Assistant for Google Workspace
- Using third-party clients
- Accessibility settings

# Google Classroom

Google Classroom has been around for a few years now (since 2014, to be precise). However, the recent pandemic has accelerated the adoption of Classroom globally and pushed this service to more enterprise customers. Classroom has been traditionally used in educational institutions for teacher/student collaboration, but companies are now starting to use the platform for training employees and enabling their professional growth. Through native integrations with other services, such as Drive, YouTube, Slides, and Forms, Classroom allows content creators to make training sessions fun and interactive.

Google Classroom allows two sets of users to access content on the platform:

- **Teachers**: These users create classes, training material, and quizzes. They can grade answers and keep track of enrolled users' progress.
- **Students**: Those users who have enrolled in a course or class can access the material.

Google Classroom is bundled with Google Workspace for Education, which is a suite of easy-to-use tools that foster collaboration.

Google Workspace for Education is now available in four editions and depending on the needs and size of the organization, administrators can pick the edition that is right for them. The four editions of Google Workspace for Education, at the time of writing this book, are as follows:

- Google Workspace for Education Fundamentals
- Google Workspace for Education Standard
- Teaching and Learning Upgrade
- Google Workspace for Education Plus

> **Old versus New**
>
> If you are familiar with G Suite offerings, then you will know that Google Workspace for Education Fundamentals was known as G Suite for Education and that Google Workspace for Education Plus was known as G Suite Enterprise for Education.

Google Education for Classroom Fundamentals edition is available globally to all qualifying educational institutions for free. To qualify for this free licensing, typically, educational institutions must be government-recognized and formally accredited. Once an application has been filed by the institution, Google determines the organization's eligibility to participate in the program and approves the application if all criteria are met successfully.

A comparison of the capabilities and features that are offered by the different Google Workspace for Education offerings can be found here: `https://edu.google.com/intl/ALL_us/products/workspace-for-education/editions/`.

Now, let's move on to learning how to enable Google Classroom to take advantage of its great features, such as teacher and student classifications, setting up classes, enrolling students, managing grades and rosters, and unenrolling students.

# Enabling Google Classroom

Similar to the app configurations we saw in *Chapter 3*, *Application Security*, Google Classroom can be enabled for the entire domain or partially for a smaller subset of users. To enable Google Classroom as an administrator, follow these steps:

1. Log into the Google **Admin** console.
2. Click on **Apps** from the left-hand side panel.
3. Click on **Overview** to access **Additional Google services**.

   The following screenshot shows the **Additional Google services** section in the **Apps** list:

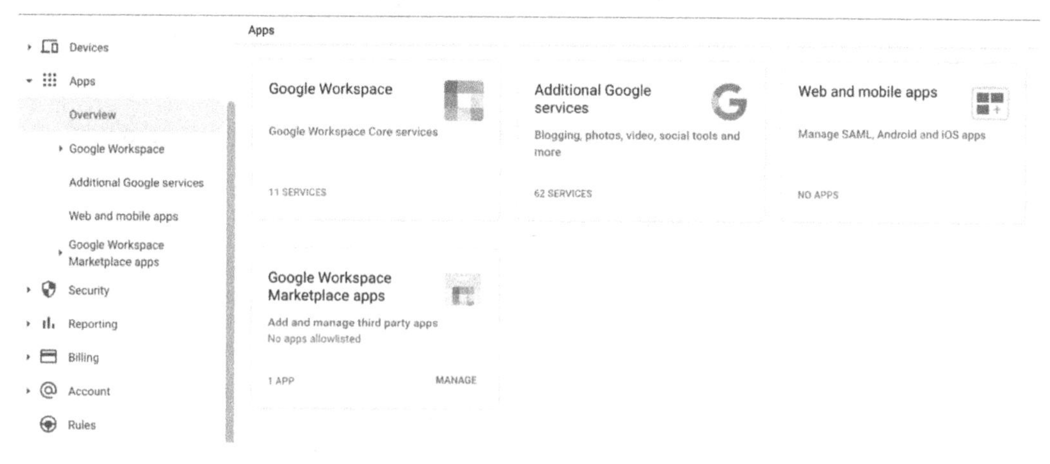


Figure 5.1 – Additional Google services in the Apps list

4. Enable **Google Classroom** for the intended OUs or groups of users.

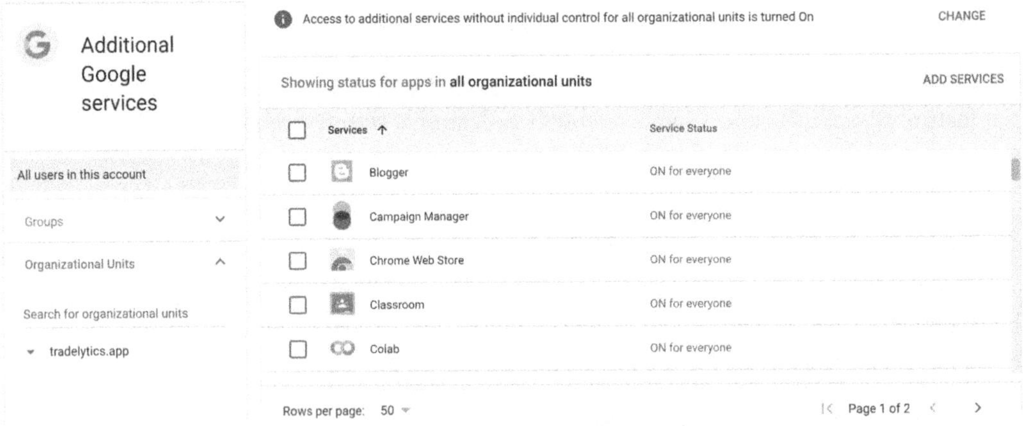

Figure 5.2 – Classroom in the list of Additional Google services

Once these entities have been enabled, users and trainers can access Google Classroom at `classroom.google.com` or from the **App Launcher** grid.

# Managing Google Classroom settings

The Google **Admin** console gives administrators several ways to configure and manage Google Classroom.

Users can typically sign into Google Classroom with one of the following user account types:

- School account
- Personal Google account
- Google Workspace account

Depending on the Google Workspace edition, users may be restricted to accessing content that is hosted in other domains, which would mean that not all users can join a class. Users' cross-domain access control policies typically determine whether they can access the content.

Google Classroom also controls access to certain services based on the age of the users. If users are under the age of eighteen, certain services will be disabled for those users.

The following screenshot shows the access settings that can be used to restrict or allow users from sharing their classes with users in other domains:

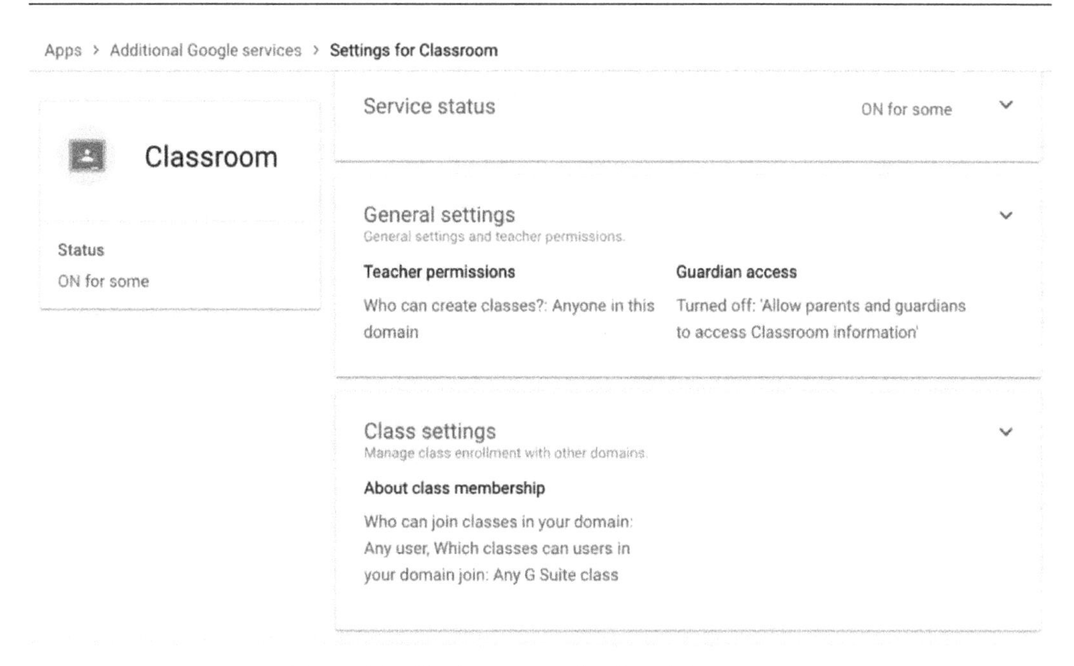


Figure 5.3 – Sharing settings for Google Classroom

We will look at each of these settings in the next few sub-sections.

## Teacher permissions

Google Classroom provides an intuitive way to classify users as teachers and students. When users sign into Google Classroom for the first time, they identify their role as either a **Teacher** or **Student**. When the user identifies themselves as a teacher, they are added to the **Teachers** group. Administrators can validate and give specific access to teachers, which allows them to create classes and view and manage guardians. The following screenshot shows what the **Teacher permissions** settings page looks like:

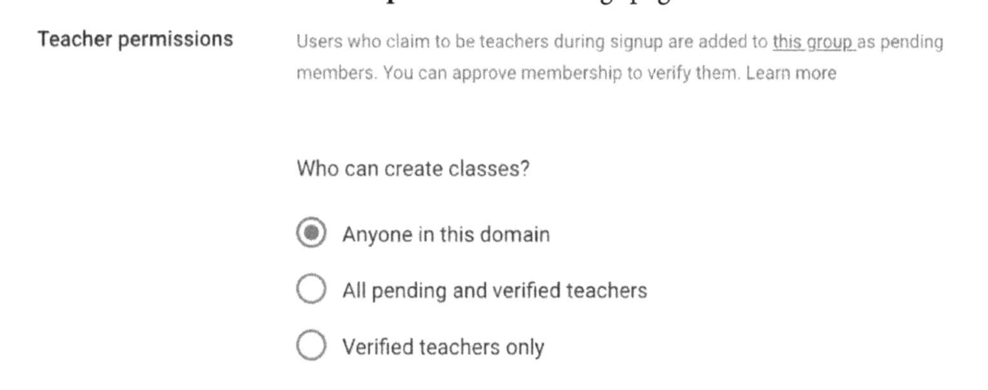


Figure 5.4 – Teacher permissions available in Google Classroom

> **Important Note**
>
> Once a teacher has created classes, caution should be exercised before deleting the teacher's account. Deleting a teacher's account before transferring ownership of classes to another teacher would limit functionality and would make the classes inaccessible.

## Guardian access

For educational institutions, parents or guardians can be added to a class so that they can receive a class summary about the student.

This setting controls whether a parent or guardian can be granted access to a class and controls the elevated access granted to teachers. The following screenshot shows what the **Guardian access** settings page looks like:

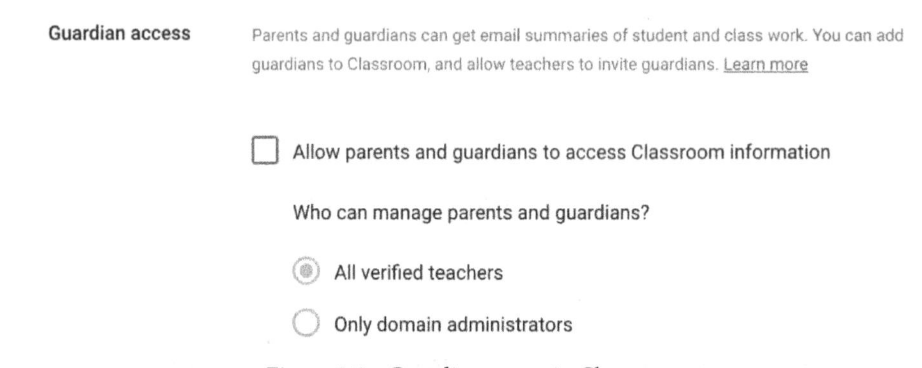


Figure 5.5 – Guardian access in Classroom

As you can imagine, with a large enrollment of students in a class, there would be a lot of guardians to invite or remove. Classroom makes it easy to invite guardians in bulk by importing a `.csv` file and manage them via the **Google Apps Manager** (**GAM**) tool.

> **GAM**
>
> GAM is a command-line tool for Google Workspace administrators to manage domain and user settings quickly and easily using the Workspace API. GAM requires a special service account that is authorized to act on behalf of the users to modify user-specific settings. More details on GAM can be found here: `https://github.com/jay0lee/GAM`.

## Class settings

When the teachers are creating classes, students can be directly invited to join the class, or a class code is shared with the students who wish to enroll.

If organizations wish to keep this content secure, administrators can restrict who can join the class in Google Classroom. The following image shows the different options that are available for administrators:

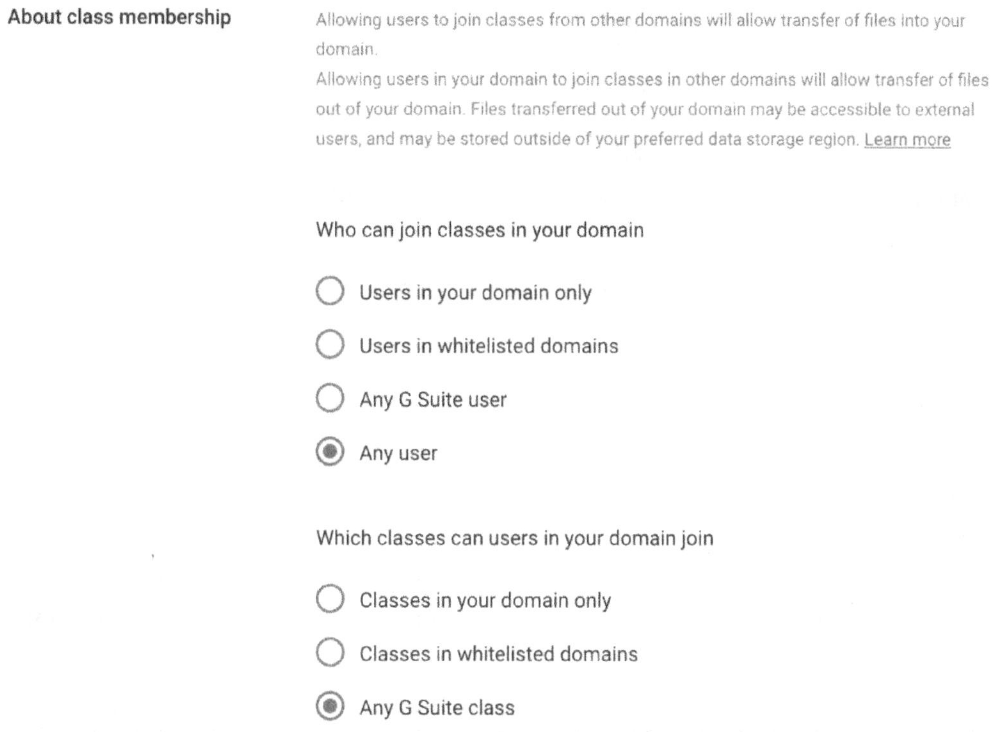

**About class membership**

Allowing users to join classes from other domains will allow transfer of files into your domain.
Allowing users in your domain to join classes in other domains will allow transfer of files out of your domain. Files transferred out of your domain may be accessible to external users, and may be stored outside of your preferred data storage region. Learn more

Who can join classes in your domain

- Users in your domain only
- Users in whitelisted domains
- Any G Suite user
- Any user (selected)

Which classes can users in your domain join

- Classes in your domain only
- Classes in whitelisted domains
- Any G Suite class (selected)

Figure 5.6 – Class settings in Classroom

Trusted domains that frequently collaborate with the organization are added as whitelisted domains. You can either allow or restrict users from joining classes created by external domains. To allow users to join classes that have been created by trusted domains, you will have to whitelist them.

Since Google Classroom is well integrated with Google Drive and Meet, the content created in Classroom is stored in Google Drive. Access settings for Classroom determine if the content stored in Google Drive is accessible to external users.

Google Meet enables teachers to handle distance learning effectively. Teachers can create a unique Meet link for each class in Classroom. To help teachers manage meeting attendees, Meet links that are created in Classroom can be nicknamed. A teacher can control access to the video meeting, mute participants, prevent students from sharing their screen, and more.

> **Nicknaming Links**
> Nicknaming links with Google Meet helps ensure that students don't rejoin a class meeting after the last participant has left the meeting. Typically, the last participant could be the teacher, and this prevents students from accessing Meet without a teacher present. Google Meet has more host controls for the education domain than other domains. The facility to nickname links is only available with Google Workspace for Education.

All editions of Google Workspace for Education, except for Google Workspace for Education Fundamentals, allow teachers to generate an attendance report at the end of a meeting.

Grades and rosters are essential functions in any classroom setup, so let's look at them in the next section.

# Grades and rosters

Grades for quizzes and assignments can be exported for all the students in a class. This information can then be imported into **School Information Systems** (**SISs**) to reflect in respective educational tracking systems.

Educational institutions can enable classroom roster information to sync to the SIS, called **Clever**. To navigate to **Roster import**, go to **Google Admin Console | Settings for Classroom | Roster import**.

The **Roster import** option must be turned on before data can be integrated with Clever. However, educational institutions that need this integration would need to have a Google Workspace for Education Plus license.

More details on Clever and how it handles rostering can be found here: `https://support.clever.com/s/articles/000001463?language=en_US`.

# Student unenrollment

Just like students can enroll in a class, administrators can configure who can unenroll students from a class. Typically, educational institutions may not want students to unenroll themselves to avoid problems with the class roster. Further, students may unenroll themselves for fun. So, it would be better if teachers could control the unenrollment process. This can be achieved via the **Student unenrollment** setting in the Google **Admin** console.

To access this setting as an administrator, Navigate to **Student unenrollment** using the following path: log into the Google **Admin** console | **Apps** | **Google Workspace** | **Setting for Classroom** | **Student enrollment**:

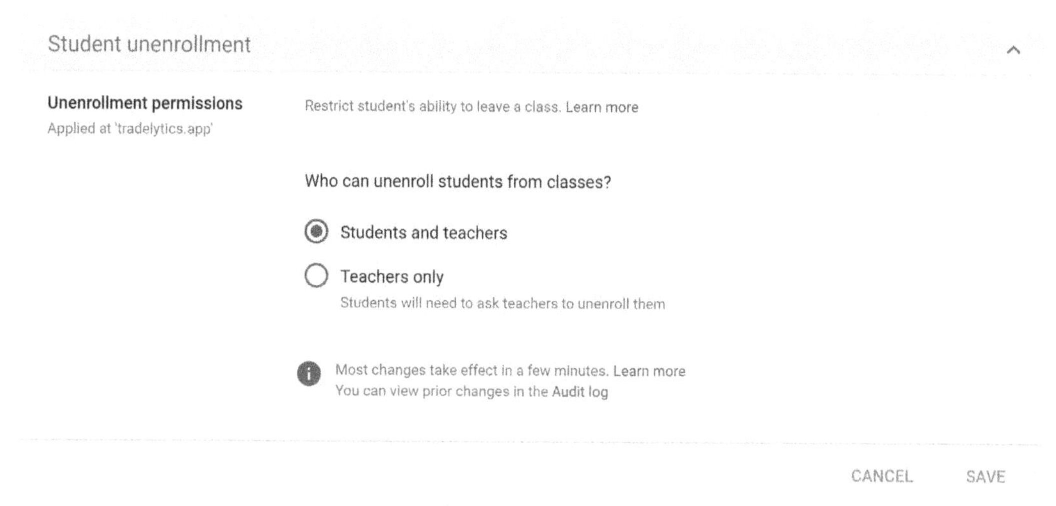


Figure 5.7 – The Student unenrollment setting

Under **Who can unenroll students from classes?**, select **Students and teachers**. After this step, students will not be able to unenroll themselves and only teachers or administrators will be able to perform the action

As we can see, Google Workspace is feature-rich, secure, easy to use, and seamless when it comes to collaboration in educational institutions. Its popularity is always increasing, and the free version has made it easier for people in different regions of the world to take advantage of these features. With Google Classroom taken care of, let's move on and talk about Marketplace apps in detail.

# Google Workspace Marketplace apps

We gave a brief introduction to Marketplace apps in *Chapter 2, Configuring Users and Apps*, where we covered the intent behind these apps and some of the popular Marketplace apps. In this section, we will talk about how to install and manage Marketplace apps across the userbase as an administrator. We will also talk about add-ons and how they integrate with some of the core services. This will be followed by a deeper look at access control for third-party applications, which enables administrators to keep Workspace data and users secure.

> **Important Note**
>
> As you may recall, Marketplace apps are applications developed by aspiring developers or product owners trying to integrate their product with Google Workspace and help extend the tool set's functionality beyond Google Workspace.

As an organization with multiple functional groups, there may be several business needs and workflows to solve daily. While Google Workspace tries to solve several of them, Marketplace apps fill in the gaps where Google Workspace services are not available just yet. To make it easy to work with and integrate Marketplace apps, **Security Assertion Markup Language** (**SAML**) authentication is supported within Google Workspace, making Google Cloud Identity the primary identity provider.

There are several notable workflows that Marketplace apps help with. For instance, users can use an e-signature app with Drive to initiate a document for an e-signature workflow.

Another example would be users opening a support ticket notification email to see relevant support ticket information populating the side panel within the Gmail page. This information will be fetched from the case management app hosted in Google Marketplace.

Based on whether the application is developed by your organization or by a third-party developer, it can be published internally within the organization or added to the allowed list of apps that users can install.

To add a Marketplace app to a list of approved apps that users can install, follow these steps:

1. Log into the Google **Admin** console.
2. Click on **Apps** from the left-hand side panel and select **Google Workspace Marketplace Apps**.
3. Click on **Add app to Domain Install list**.
4. Use the **Browse** option to select relevant apps for installation.
5. Install the app using one of the following options:
    - **Individual Install**: This installs the app just for the logged-in user's account.
    - **Domain Install**: This option installs the app for all the users in the domain.

Once the app has been installed, users can start using the app right away. Sometimes, app owners may choose to enforce licenses when using an app. Administrators may have to procure licenses for app usage.

The following screenshot shows the section in the Google **Admin** console where apps could be added to the **Domain Install** list:

Figure 5.8 – Adding third-party applications to the Domain Install list

Installed Marketplace apps can surface on multiple locations within Google Workspace. Here are some examples of where the apps can surface:

- In the **Google Docs/Sheets/Slides** page via the **Add-Ons** menu:

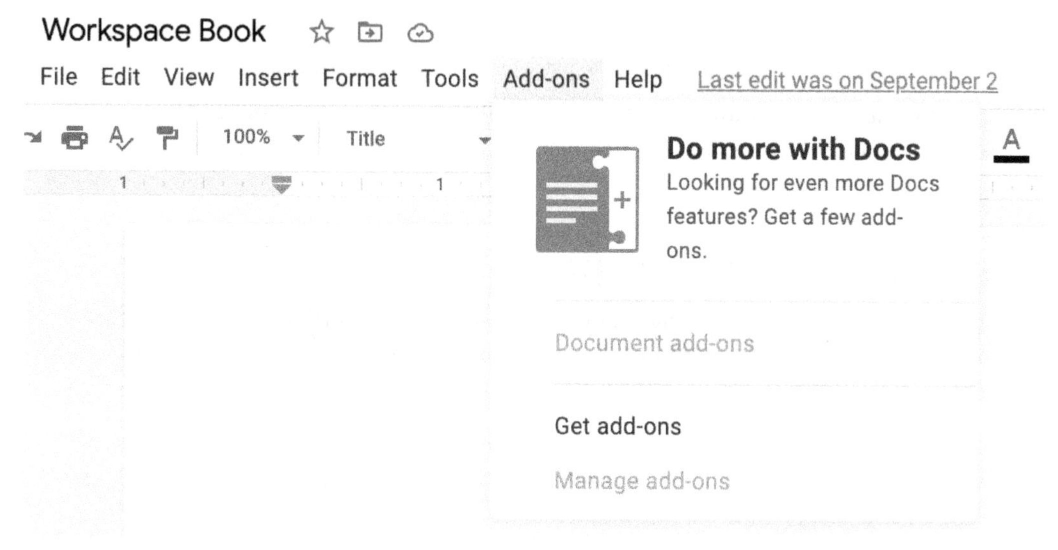


Figure 5.9 – Marketplace apps via Add-ons with Google Docs

- In the Google Drive home page through the **File** menu option.

- Through the **App Launcher** icon, you need to scroll past listed core services to get to the Marketplace apps listed there:

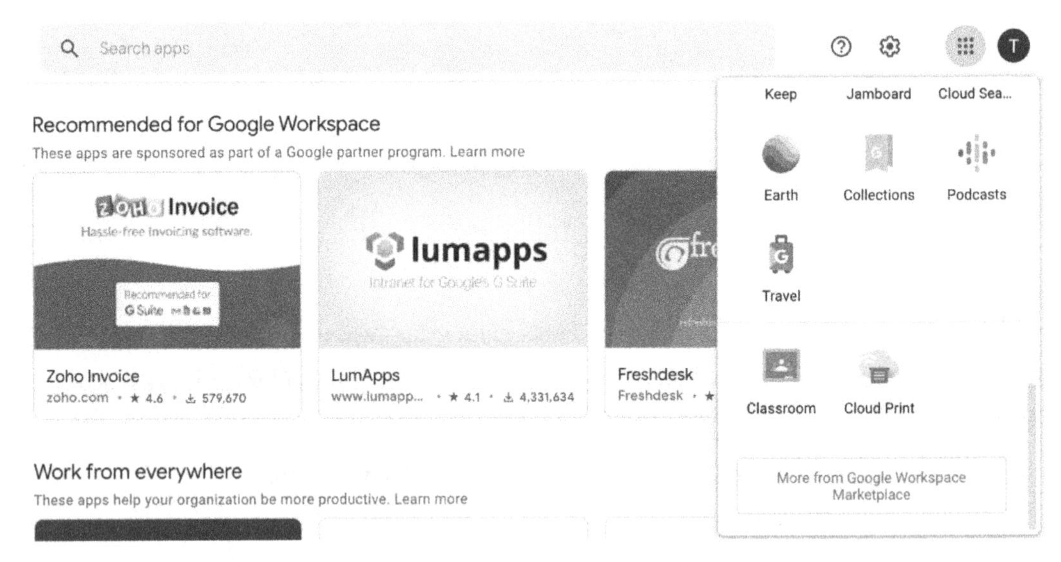


Figure 5.10 – Navigating to Marketplace apps using the App launcher icon

The ability to restrict the installation of Marketplace apps improves a domain's security posture tremendously by not allowing installation of non-curated applications that may be harmful.

## Managing Marketplace apps

While the installation of a Marketplace app sounds straightforward, organizations may want to restrict users from installing multiple apps in their domain. Google Workspace provides the option of completely restricting users from installing any app.

If users are restricted from installing any app, administrators can create a curated list of apps that are allowed for installation within the domain. Users can only pick apps from this list for their use.

You can navigate to the **Marketplace Settings** page to make these adjustments by following these steps:

1. Log into the Google **Admin** console.
2. Click on **Apps** from the left-hand side panel and select **Google Workspace Marketplace Apps**.

3. Click on **Settings**. From here, you can choose whichever setting you want:

Apps > Settings for Google Workspace Marketplace apps
Google Workspace Marketplace Settings
Manage access to apps
Allow Install
Settings to install third-party Google Workspace Marketplace apps:
Allow users to install any app from Google Workspace Marketplace
Block users from installing any app from Google Workspace Marketplace
Previously-installed apps will not be uninstalled.
Allow users to install only allowed applications from Google Workspace Marketplace
Manage allowlist
Users in your organization can install apps in the allowlist. Apps no longer allowed will not be uninstalled.
Changes may take up to 24 hours to propagate to all users.
Prior changes can be seen in Audit log
CANCEL
SAVE

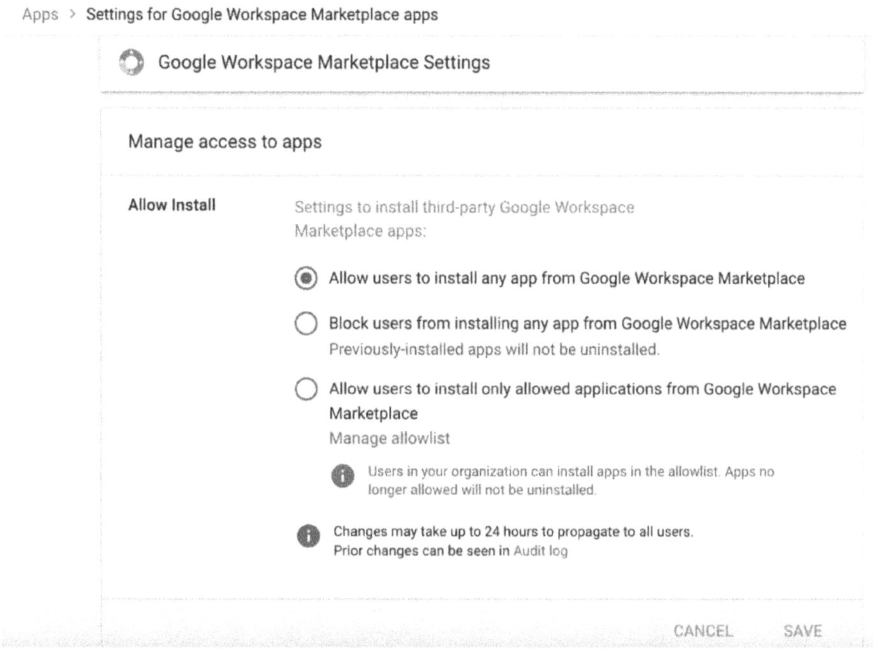

Figure 5.11 – Marketplace apps settings for administrators

Google Workspace also has add-ons, which are remarkably similar to third-party Marketplace applications, the purpose of which is to augment the capabilities core Google Workspace services already offer.

Add-ons differ from third-party applications in terms of how they are discovered and installed. Add-ons can be browsed directly from Google Workspace services by clicking the **Add-ons** tab on each service. Service-specific add-ons show up across these core services. Many of these add-ons are developed by third parties but they are seamlessly integrated with Workspace services. We'll learn how to enable and work with these add-ons in the next section.

# Add-ons for Google Workspace services

In this section, we will look at add-ons and some representative examples of using them across Google Workspace core services such as Drive, Docs, Sheets, and Calendar.

Users can use the add-ons that have been installed by an administrator from their Google Drive. Furthermore, there is an option for users to install add-ons individually via the Google Docs editor.

This can be allowed or restricted from the Google **Admin** console, as follows:

1. Log into the Google **Admin** console.
2. Click on **Apps** from the left-hand side panel and select **Google Workspace | Drive and Docs | Features and Applications | Add-ons.**

This setting allows you to enable or disable add-on installation, as per the OU:

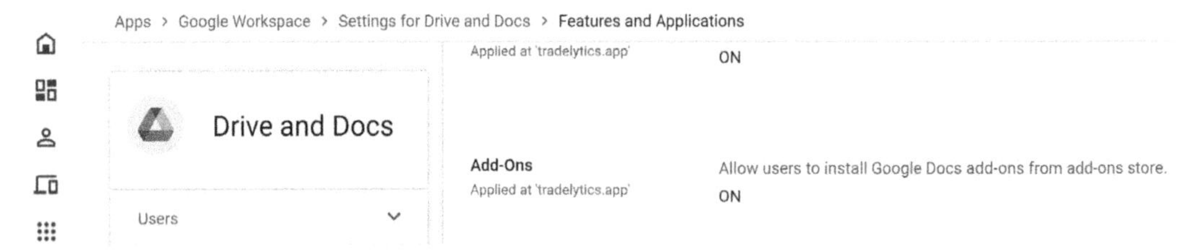


Figure 5.12 – Enabling/disabling add-ons

Once enabled, add-ons can be accessed from the Drive, Gmail, and Calendar home pages through the right-hand side panel using the + icon:

Figure 5.13 – The + icon in Docs, which helps install add-ons

When add-on installation is allowed, users can use the **Add-ons** menu from the Document editor and use the **Get Add-ons** option to browse the available and compatible add-ons for their business needs.

Due to how seamlessly add-ons can be integrated with Workspace services, add-ons can be used to surface contextual information that's specific to the application you are working on. Let's look at a couple of representative examples of how add-ons can be beneficial across some popular Workspace services.

The following image shows the add-ons that are available for Google Docs:

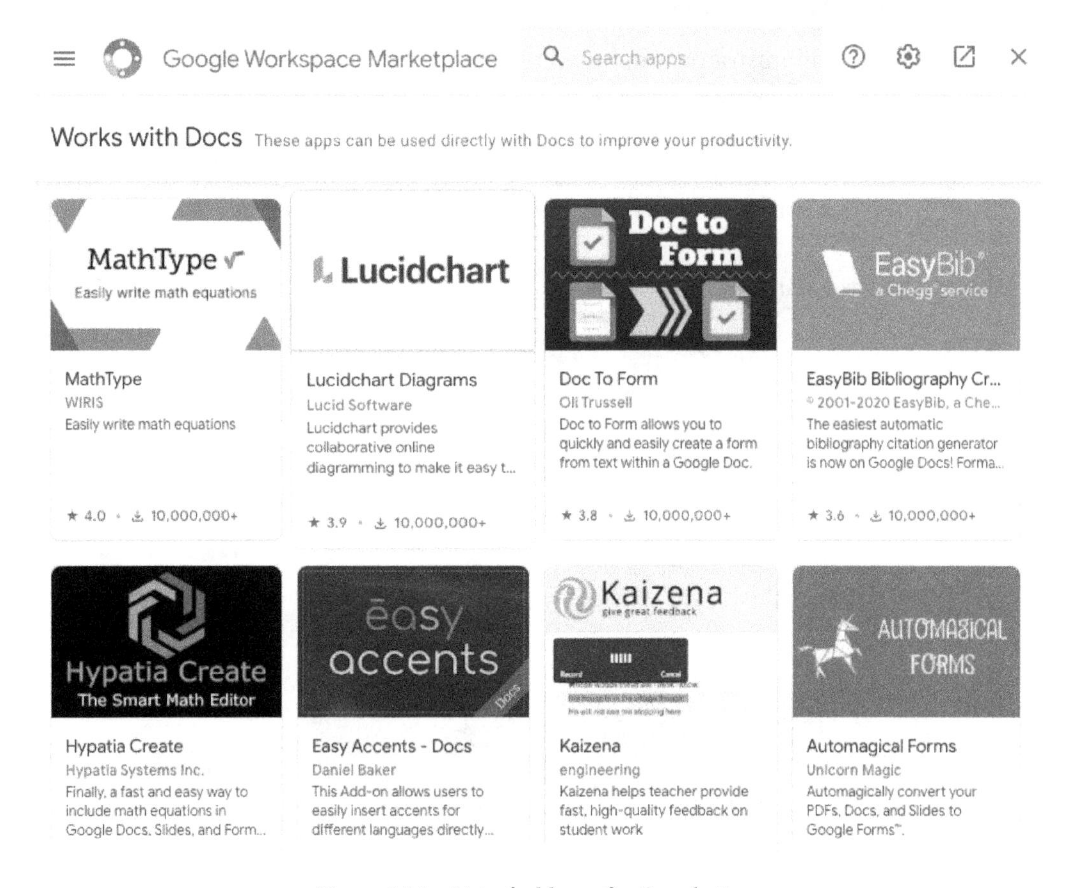


Figure 5.14 – List of add-ons for Google Docs

Let's look at an example of using add-ons from Google Sheets using the *Salesforce* add-on. By installing the **Salesforce** add-on, users can start using the data integration capability across Salesforce and Google Sheets. To make this happen, administrators should enable add-on installation for users or add the Salesforce app to the allowlist. Users can then install the add-on.

Then, users can open a Google Sheet and use the **Extensions** option to create a data connector for Salesforce. This connector can be used to import a report from Salesforce into Google Sheets or to write a query to pull data from Salesforce into Google Sheets.

Google Sheets can help derive intelligence and insights on the data that's been pulled from Salesforce. In a bi-directional flow, when data in Google Sheets is updated, changes get reflected in Salesforce as well through this data connector.

Like Drive add-ons, administrators can install the relevant add-ons for Gmail and Calendar as well. The following screenshot shows some of the add-ons for Calendar:

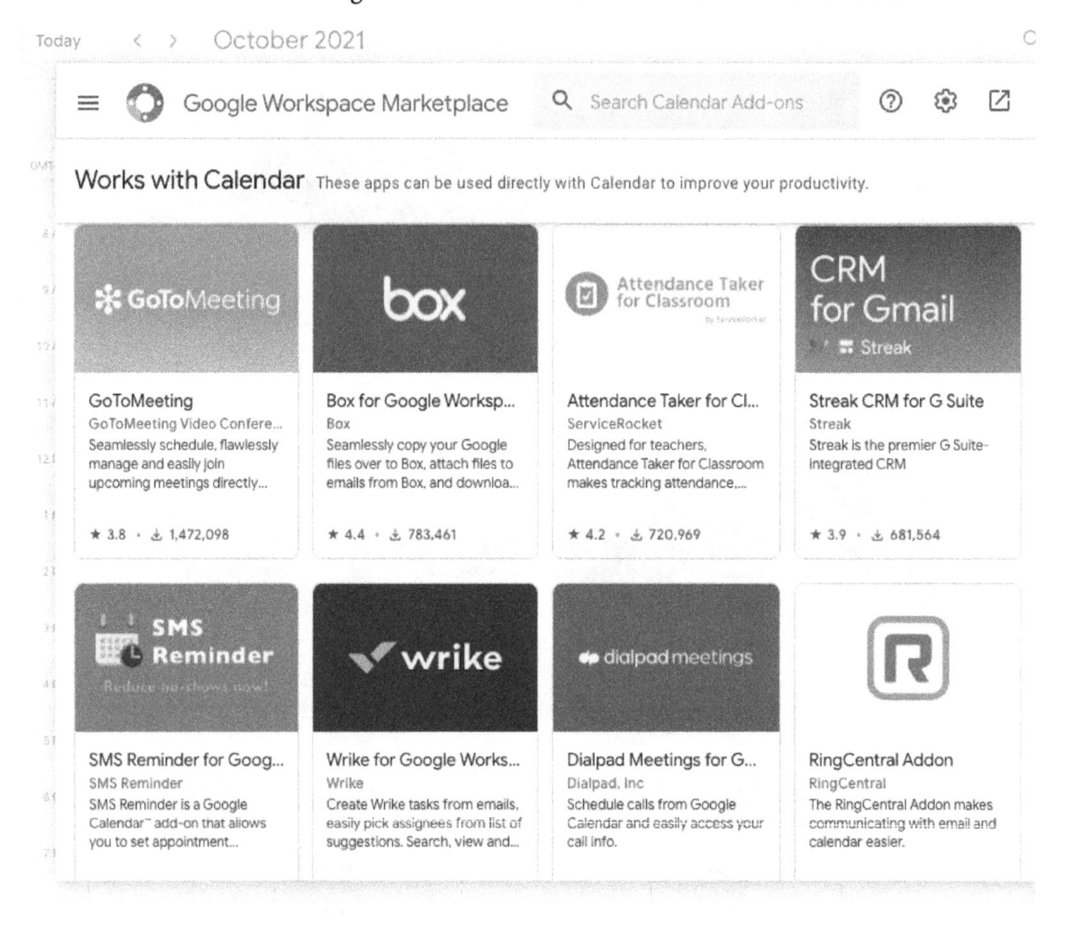


Figure 5.15 – List of add-ons for Calendar

For example, when users search for add-ons in the Calendar UI, Google Workspace Marketplace displays specific add-ons that are compatible with Calendar data. Add-ons such as **SMS Reminders**, **Dialpad Meetings**, and **GoToMeeting** will show up in the search results.

All these add-ons, which have been published on Google Workspace Marketplace, go through a detailed security review before being approved for usage across all domains. This security review is a very critical step as these add-ons seamlessly integrate and look like they are developed by Google, giving users a false sense of security. Caution must be exercised when users work with third-party apps and add-ons.

When a third-party application is installed, it will request several permissions for accessing your Google Workspace data. These may include the following:

- View and manage your contacts
- Share documents with others
- Connect to third-party services to read/write data
- Send emails on behalf of users

These are very sensitive and critical functions that users should not typically trust a third-party application with by default. Administrators and users should join forces to restrict application access to keep their Workspace data secure. The next section will describe how granular access can be granted to third-party applications using Auth scopes and the OAuth 2.0 protocol.

# Access control for third-party applications

Administrators can control which third-party applications can access Google Workspace data. Access control for applications is defined using the OAuth 2.0 protocol, which is a mechanism that controls an application's access to the user's account. Administrators can choose to do any of the following:

- Restrict access to Google Workspace services
- Give unrestricted access to Google Workspace services
- Trust specific applications with data
- Trust all domain-owned applications

Follow these steps to accomplish the preceding options:

1. Log into the Google **Admin** console.
2. Select **Security**, followed by **Access and data control**, and then **API Controls**.
3. Under **App Access Control**, select **MANAGE THIRD-PARTY APP ACCESS**:

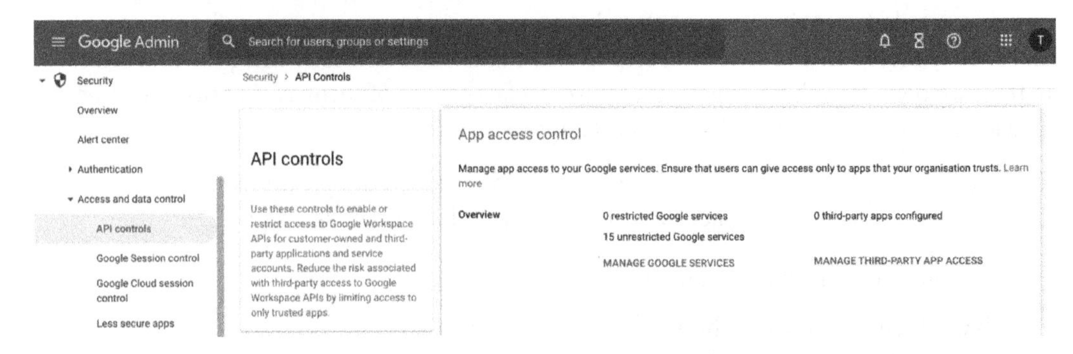


Figure 5.16 – Security option to set app access control for third-party apps

4. From the list of apps, Select applications to change accesses, then choose **Change access**:

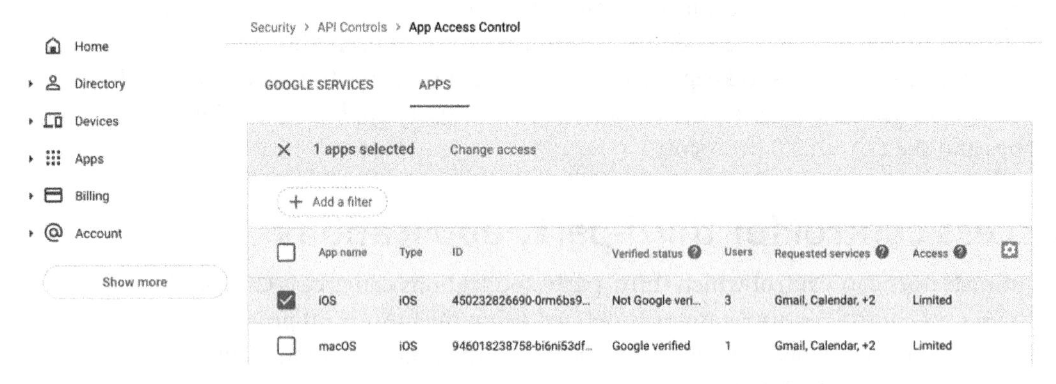


Figure 5.17 – The Change access option for third-party applications

5. Select either **Trusted, Limited**, or **Blocked**:

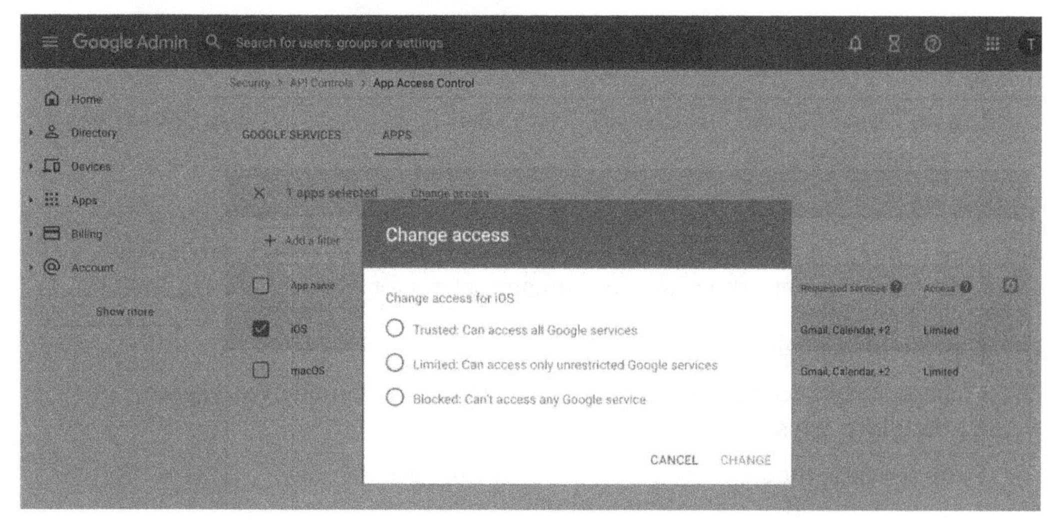


Figure 5.18 – Options for changing access for third-party applications

6. Click **CHANGE**.

**Trusted** third-party applications will be allowed to access all Google services, while **Blocked** applications cannot access any services at all. **Limited** third-party applications find common ground, which allows administrators to pick and choose between Google services that a Marketplace application will be allowed to access.

Several third-party applications typically request a lot of overarching permissions and will request access to data that may not be needed. Google Workspace provides a nifty way to handle such applications using APIs and OAuth scopes.

Using an **application programming interface** (**API**) is an intermediary option that allows programmable access to data sources. Developers use APIs to programmatically access data across Google Workspace. Auth scopes express the permissions you request to users to authorize your apps.

The following are some examples of Auth scopes:

- Use the Gmail API, `messages.list()`, to list all the messages for a particular user.
- Use the Drive API, `driveService.files().create()`, to create Drive files programmatically.

Third-party apps can integrate with Google Workspace using Google Workspace APIs. Using your app settings, the level of data access these apps can have is controlled via scopes. The following steps show how to configure scopes for Marketplace applications:

1. Log into the Google **Admin** console.
2. Click on **Apps** from the left-hand side panel and select **Google Workspace Marketplace Apps**.
3. Upon selecting the app, you will see the following page:

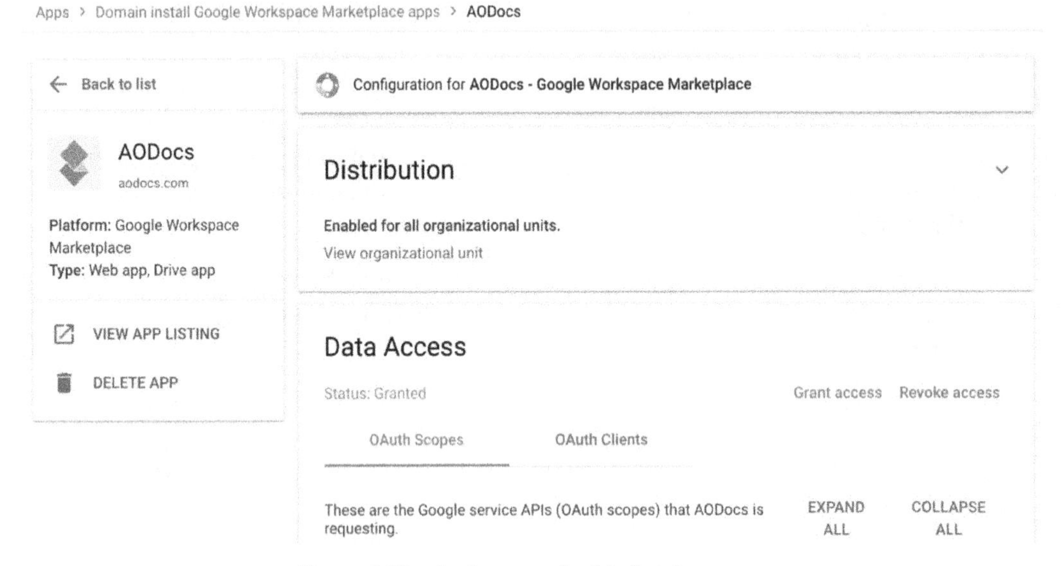


Figure 5.19 – Auth scopes for Marketplace apps

Here's what the options seen in the preceding screenshot control:

- **Distribution**: This controls whether the apps are enabled or disabled for the selected OU. Like any app settings, the controls are inherited from the parent/root OU. This can be overridden with a different setting for each nested sub-OU.
- **Data Access**: This controls the API scopes the app has access to.

Users must authorize access scopes for an app when they are run the first time. For example, an app may want permission to create events in a calendar. By selecting a specific granular scope, users can ensure that the app cannot do anything other than create events in your calendar.

At any point in the future, if an app is no longer required, it can be deleted. All associated licenses related to the app will also be removed.

Apps that have been created by internal employees of the domain or any external developers may interact with Google Workspace using an API. Administrators can evaluate an app to check what scope of access is required for this application to function. Developers generally follow best practices to use restricted scopes that are required for the application and do not use scopes that are not required for the application.

For instance, the following are some examples of Gmail scopes:

- `https://www.googleapis.com/auth/gmail.insert`
- `https://www.googleapis.com/auth/gmail.modify`
- `https://www.googleapis.com/auth/gmail.readonly`
- `https://www.googleapis.com/auth/gmail.send`

These scopes are very intuitive and give extremely specific access to Gmail data. Some scopes are categorized as **Recommended**, **Sensitive**, or **Restricted**.

The following steps will help administrators navigate and review the scope of each Marketplace application installed in the domain:

1. Log into the Google **Admin** console.
2. Click on **Security** from the left-hand side panel and select **API Controls**.
3. Click on **Manage Third-Party App Access**.

This lists the following details about the app:

- **App Name**
- **ID**
- **Verified Status**: Apps that are validated by the Google Security team are listed as verified.
- **Type**
- **Users**: This shows the number of users using this app.
- **Access** shows **Limited**, **Trusted**, or **Blocked**. The preceding steps are very similar to what was described in *Figure 5.15* and *Figure 5.16.*

4. Click on the app for more details on its scopes:

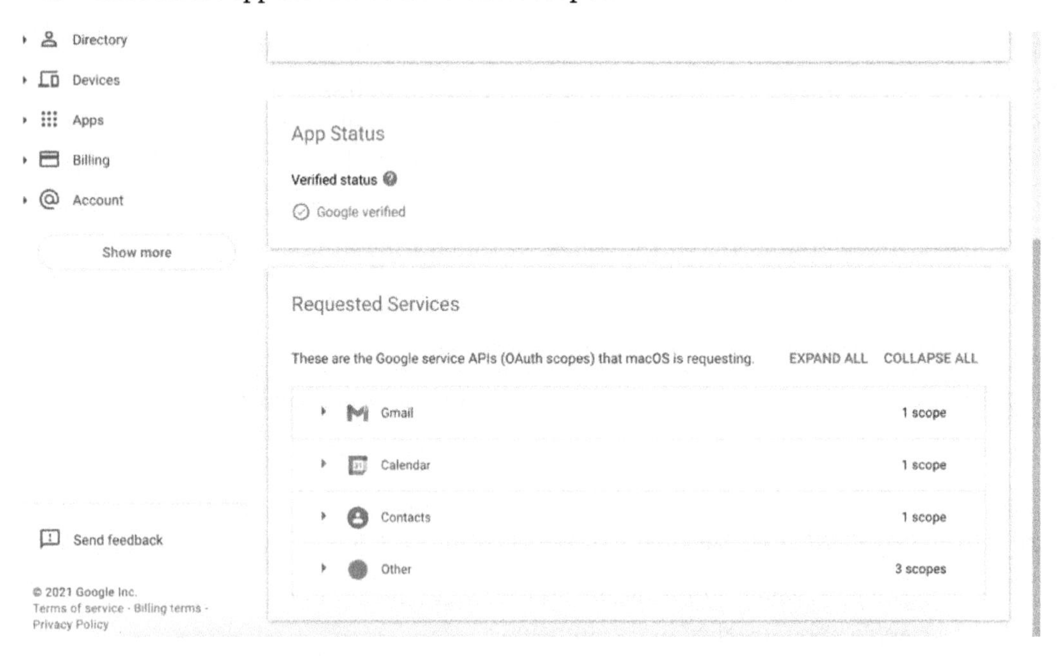


Figure 5.20 – The Google Admin console showing scopes for a Marketplace app in a collapsed view

5. From the **App details** page, review the API scopes that have been requested by the app.

6. Expand the scopes to see the detailed list:

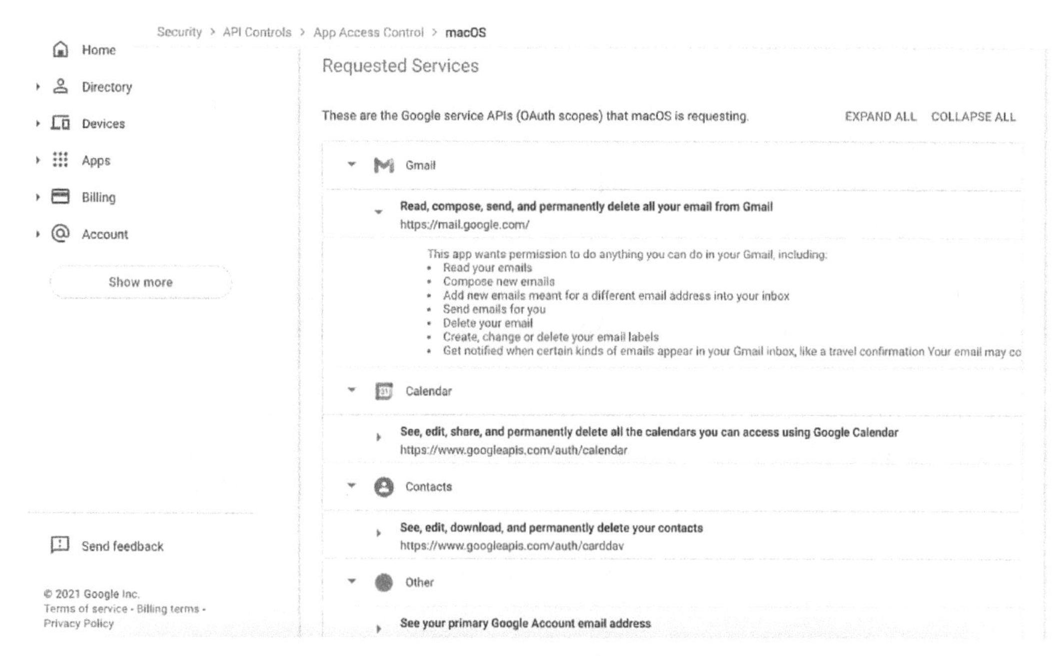


Figure 5.21 – The Google Admin console showing scopes for a Marketplace app in an expanded view

On the same page, after reviewing the list of OAuth API scopes, administrators can make an informed decision regarding whether to allow or restrict access to this application.

To change access to the scope of an application, administrators can follow these steps:

1. Click on **Manage Google Services** and look at the list of Google services that can be controlled from the Google **Admin** console.
2. Select the service that needs to be changed and click on **Change Access**.
3. Review the list of OAuth scopes and apply the changes.

Once the changes have been applied and the OAuth access level has been updated, users who are using the app will see the changes being reflected immediately. If an existing app is changed to have a "restricted" scope, then it will stop working for users using the app. Similarly, apps that are blocked can no longer be installed.

To make it easy for users to understand the changes that have been implemented, administrators can post a user-friendly error message when an app's access is changed. To accomplish this, the admin can do the following:

1. Navigate to the **App Access control** section within the Google **Admin** console and click on **Settings**.
2. Enter the customized error message in the text box provided.
3. Click **SAVE**.

In the next chapter, we will learn how to create customized third-party applications using developer tools such as Apps Script and AppSheet, which can interact with the Google Workspace API.

We covered a lot of ground in this section by talking about how to limit or grant access to third-party applications using OAuth scopes for more granular access control. These are powerful weapons in any administrator's arsenal and can help them defend a domain when a security war is raging.

Now, let's learn more about the friendly Google Assistant feature for Google Workspace.

# Google Assistant for Google Workspace

Most households have Google Assistant devices for voice-controlled actions. It could be as simple as "Hey Google, what's the weather?" or "OK Google, what sound does a cat make?"

Google Workspace can integrate with Google Assistant devices for a better user experience, allowing users to perform business actions using those Google Assistant devices.

These actions can include the following:

- Hey Google, when is my first meeting for the day?
- Hey Google, join my meeting
- OK Google, create a meeting
- OK Google, send an email to cancel the meeting

Administrators need to turn on Google Assistant in the Google **Admin** console. Users who have it can use their accounts to see personal results and access additional features. When you turn on Google Assistant, it will want other features to be turned on as well, such as Google Search, Assistant services, and Web & App Activity.

Administrators can also manage voice match and face match for users. Admins must get parental consent for users under the age of 18 to link their Google Workspace for Education accounts to a Google Assistant-enabled device to enable voice match and face match. Turning off voice match would mean that users may lose core features such as personalized results. Let's talk about how Google Assistant is enabled and integrated with consumer devices.

## Nest Hub

One of the most popular Google Assistant-enabled devices is Nest Hub. It comes in different sizes and is marketed as Nest Hub, Nest Hub Max, and Nest Mini:

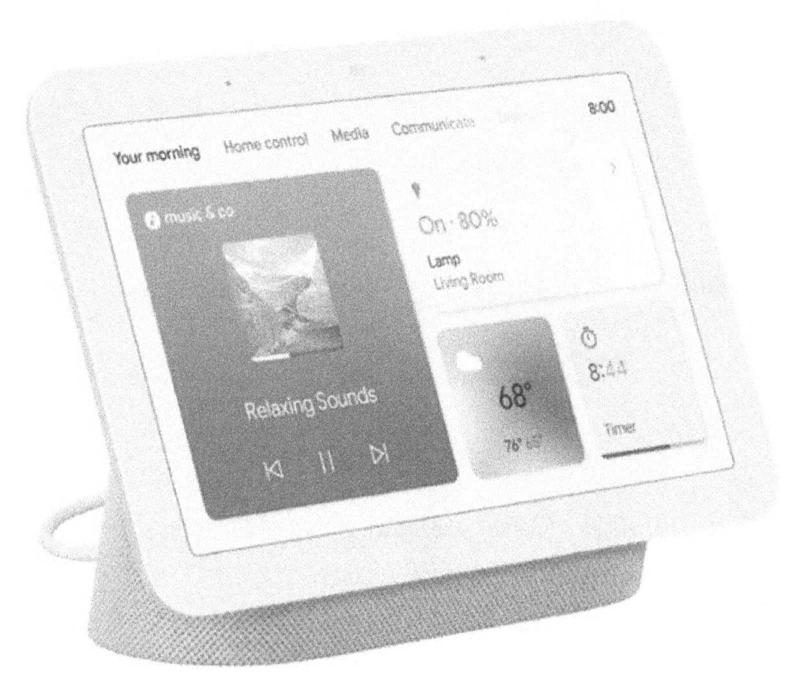


Figure 5.22 – Google Nest Hub

Nest Hub integrates with Google Workspace seamlessly using the Google Nest Hub app, which is available as an additional Google service. Admins can mark this app as **Trusted** and allow it to be installed for users across a domain.

## Enabling the Search and Assistant service

As the next step, the administrator will have to enable the Search and Assistant service so that devices can interact with Google Workspace data using Google Assistant. To accomplish this, follow these steps:

1. Log into the Google **Admin** console.
2. Click on **Apps** from the left-hand side panel and select **Additional Google** Services.
3. Select **Search and Assistant**.
4. Enable this service for the specific OU or access groups for the user.

Once the service has been enabled, users can start using search features for this Google Workspace account:

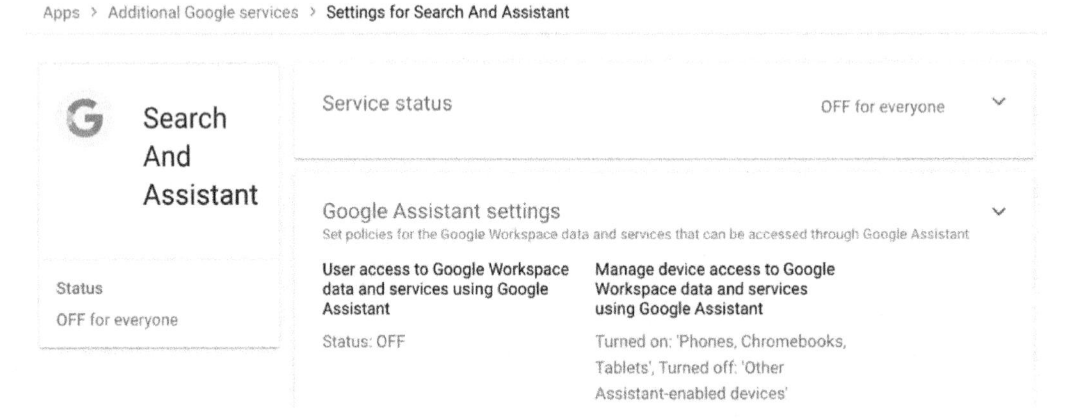


Figure 5.23 – Enabling the Search and Assistant feature

Furthermore, admins can also enable assistant devices to access Google Workspace data, as follows:

1. Log into the Google **Admin** console.
2. Click on **Apps** from the left-hand side panel and select **Additional Google Services**.
3. Select the **Search and Assistant** service.
4. Select **Google Assistant Settings**.
5. Enable the setting for **User access to Google Workspace data and services using Google Assistant**.
6. For the **Manage device access to Google Workspace data and services using Google Assistant** setting, select all the devices the organization wants to manage.
7. Click **Save**.

Now that searching across assistant devices has been enabled, administrators can enable **SafeSearch** for users to ensure that queries are indeed safe to use:

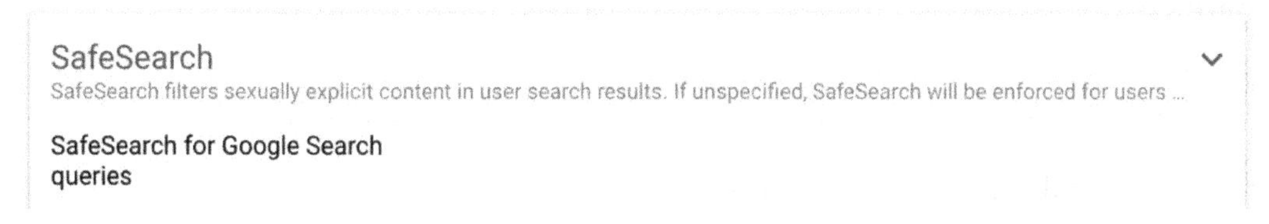
SafeSearch
SafeSearch filters sexually explicit content in user search results. If unspecified, SafeSearch will be enforced for users ...
SafeSearch for Google Search queries

Figure 5.24 – SafeSearch enablement in the Google Admin console

Google Assistant can be very helpful as we all move toward using voice as a primary input form. Assistant's natural language processing is top-notch and can understand several languages and dialects. Google Assistant makes Workspace a joy to use.

With Google Assistant spoken for, let's move on and look at some popular third-party client integrations with Google Workspace.

# Using third-party clients

Google Workspace can be used on the web or on mobile devices. Users have an agile experience when connecting to Google Workspace data from anywhere, on any device, at any time. Services such as Gmail and Drive have offline capabilities that allow users to access Workspace data when there is no network connectivity.

If users would like to avoid web browsers and use a native mail client such as Thunderbird, Kiwi, or Apple Mail, the IMAP/POP3 setting must be enabled.

**IMAP** stands for **Internet Message Access Protocol** and uses internet standards to extract email messages from servers and display them on a local client.

**POP** stands for **Post Office Protocol** and uses standardized RFC-compliant methods to sync email messages from mail servers to local clients, such as Thunderbird and Apple Mail.

All actions, such as composing an email, sending an email, organizing emails into folders, and more, can be performed within the client. The emails that are sent using the client are synchronized with mailing servers. In this section, we will learn how to enable access for third-party mail clients and focus on a popular third-party client that can be used to access Google Workspace data.

# Enabling access for mail clients

IMAP and POP can be enabled individually. Furthermore, administrators can create an allowlist of clients that users can use to access their Google Workspace data.

These settings can be enabled selectively for a specific OU or access group. Nested OUs will inherit this configuration as well. To configure this option, follow these steps:

1. Log in to the Google **Admin** console.
2. Click on **Apps** from the left-hand side panel and select **Gmail**.
3. Click on **End User access**.
4. Select **POP and IMAP access** and turn on POP, IMAP, or both as appropriate for the domain.
5. Click **Save**.

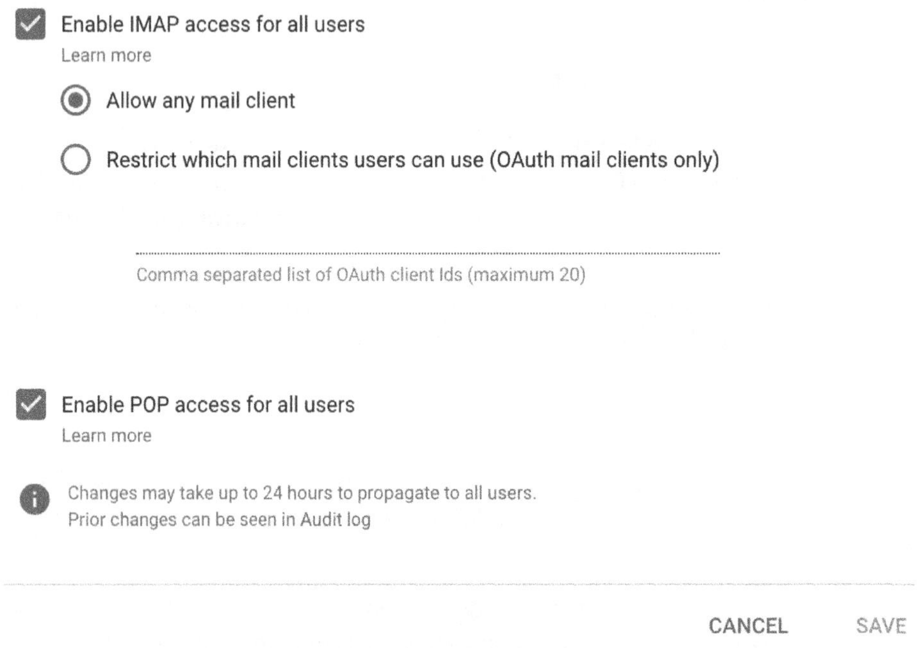

Enable IMAP access for all users
Learn more
Allow any mail client
Restrict which mail clients users can use (OAuth mail clients only)
Comma separated list of OAuth client Ids (maximum 20)
Enable POP access for all users
Learn more
Changes may take up to 24 hours to propagate to all users.
Prior changes can be seen in Audit log
CANCEL SAVE

Figure 5.25 – Enabling IMAP and POP access

If the administrator creates an allowed list of clients to be used, the list of OAuth client IDs will have to be mentioned as well.

Some mail client applications require the **Less Secure Apps** setting to be enabled for a successful mail client setup. To enable this setting, follow these steps:

1. Log into the Google **Admin** console.
2. Click on **Security** from the left-hand side panel.
3. Select the **Less Secure Apps** configuration to allow or disable the use of such apps.
4. Click **Save**.

Once these settings have been configured in the Google **Admin** console, users can individually download their choice of mail client and set it up to use Google Workspace.

The following screenshot shows how to enable the **Less secure apps** setting:

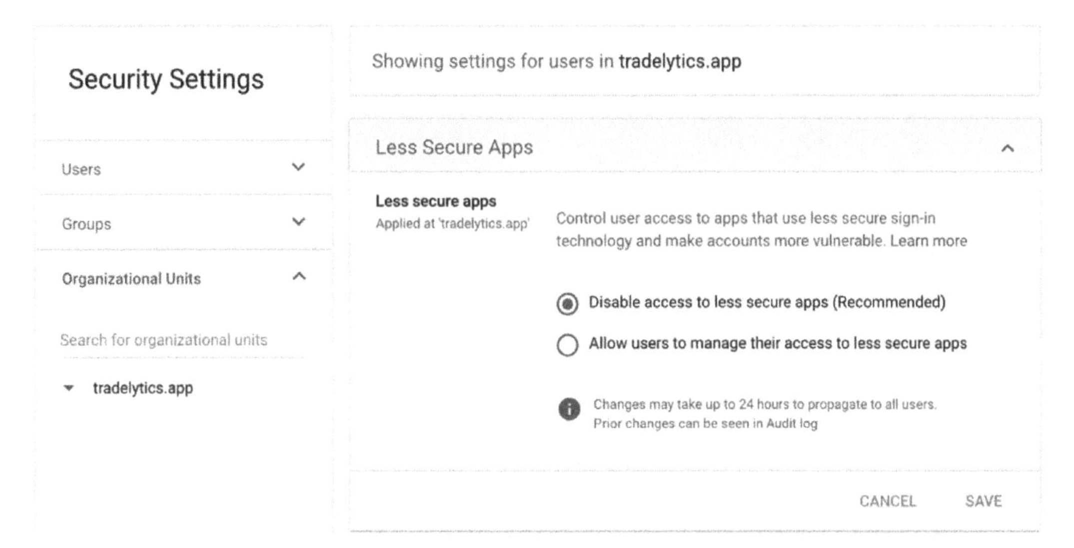


Figure 5.26 – Enabling the Less secure apps setting

> **Important Note**
>
> Caution must be exercised when enabling the **Less secure apps** setting as this can open a new attack vector and will make your Google Workspace settings less secure. Google's recommendation would be to switch to using a more secure authentication process for accessing apps, instead of turning this option on.

## Using Google Workspace Sync for Microsoft Outlook (GWSMO)

Now that we have reviewed the process of configuring various mail clients for accessing Google Workspace data, let's review the process of using Microsoft Outlook to access Google Workspace data:

1. Download and install GWSMO from `https://tools.google.com/dlpage/gssmo`.
2. Enter the appropriate username and password credentials to sign into the user's Google Workspace account.
3. Grant access for GWSMO to connect to this Google account.
4. Once GWSMO has been installed, import the data in one of the following ways:
    - From a PST file
    - Using an Outlook profile
    - Using a Microsoft Exchange profile

This will import Google Contacts, Calendar, and email messages from the connected Google Workspace account into the Microsoft Outlook client.

Once the import process is completed, users can use Google Workspace within Microsoft Outlook.

With third-party clients squared away, let's wrap this chapter up by looking at the accessibility features that are available in Google Workspace that makes this platform very inclusive.

# Accessibility for users

Google Workspace has been designed with users being the primary focus. The mission is to make the product accessible for all users, including people with disabilities, such as those with color vision deficiency and visual and hearing impairment. Google has been building accessibility into their products and Google Workspace is no exception.

To make it easier for organizations to comply with Accessibility standards, a **Voluntary Product Accessibility Template** (**VPAT**) is available for several Google Workspace services:

- Calendar VPAT: <https://static.googleusercontent.com/media/www.google.com/en//accessibility/static/pdf/google-calendar-vpat.pdf>
- Gmail VPAT: <https://services.google.com/fh/files/misc/gmail_vpat.pdf>

The accessibility features include screen reader compatibility, a larger font for the user interface, enabling IMAP/POP to allow users to use their choice of mail client, braille device compatibility, and more.

# Summary

This chapter provided you with a glimpse of how Google helps students and educational institutions with Google Classroom. Although various learning management and collaboration platforms exist, no one comes closer to offering services like Google at a global scale. More interestingly, to make Google Classroom more accessible, Google gives away its basic version for free, which is sufficient for a lot of educational institutions. While there are some negative reviews about the simplicity of the Google Classroom UI and its workflow, Classroom continues to evolve and will reshape the educational landscape across the globe.

We also saw how Google Workspace services can be extended beyond the services offered by Google, a true differentiator in the market with these Marketplace apps and add-on functionalities. Google Assistant and its integration with Google Workspace turns mundane activities such as setting up a calendar into a delight with voice inputs. Personalized search results for users means that every user gets an assistant, unleashing the full potential of voice-assisted services whose feature set continues to grow.

Google's commitment to making information available across all users is well etched into its accessibility capabilities. People with impairments can access almost all Workspace services and enjoy its benefits.

In the next chapter, we will dive into developing custom applications that will automate your unique business processes using Apps Script and Workspace API.

# 6
# Designing Custom Applications

In the previous chapters, we explored several Google Workspace services and their feature sets. We also looked at how to expand Google Workspace services using third-party applications and add-ons.

What if your organization has a unique scenario that needs to be automated, but none of the Workspace services can help solve this scenario? For instance, this could be a business process workflow that requires special integration with one of your custom-built home-grown applications. Typically, integrating with homegrown applications could require customizations that may not be readily packaged and be available for use.

As you think about this, several scenarios may crop up, such as generating reports, data consolidation, approval processes, or even paper forms. All these scenarios are time-consuming tasks that could be automated. Manual processes don't scale well, and it will prevent an organization from becoming more agile and nimble.

What if Google Workspace has an automation platform that will enable organizations to automate these unique scenarios tailored for their business?

Enter Apps Script.

Apps Script is a cloud-based JavaScript platform that lets you automate tasks across Google products. Apps Script integrates well with Google Workspace services and functions well within the construct and secure access mechanisms already established by these services. Apps Script is a true game-changer, which can help automate several scenarios and help you acquire a competitive advantage in running your business.

While Apps Script can do wonders, there is a new kid in the block named AppSheet. AppSheet is a low-code environment that enables users with non-programming backgrounds to efficiently build workflows and automation with very little code.

In this chapter, we will investigate concepts relating to building a custom application and integration beyond Workspace under the following topics:

- Apps Script
- AppSheet

# Apps Script

Apps Script is a development environment that helps extend the functionality of Google applications and build low-intensity cloud applications. The environment is well integrated with Google Workspace services that can be accessed from Google Drive, or editors such as Forms, Sheets, or Docs.

With a few lines of code, lengthy processes can be automated using Apps Script. There are templates and solutions posted in the Google Solution gallery that can be cloned and reused.

The Apps Script Solution gallery can be found here: `https://developers.google.com/workspace/solutions`.

Apps Script is automatically enabled for all users who are assigned a Google Workspace license. In this section, we will cover a lot of ground regarding Apps Script – the code editor, code and debugging, integration with Workspace services, security, and best practices.

However, before digging further into the capabilities of Apps Script and what it can do for us, let's look at a basic **Hello World!** example and define some jargon associated with Apps Script. It will help set the foundation for a deep dive later in this chapter.

# Hello World!

A basic *Hello World!* program in Apps Script would need a code editor, permission to run the program, and a command to actually run the program.

A code editor for Apps Script can be launched from several Google Workspace services, and in our example, let's invoke it from Google Sheets:

1. To launch the code editor, click on **Extensions | Apps Script** to open the code editor window:

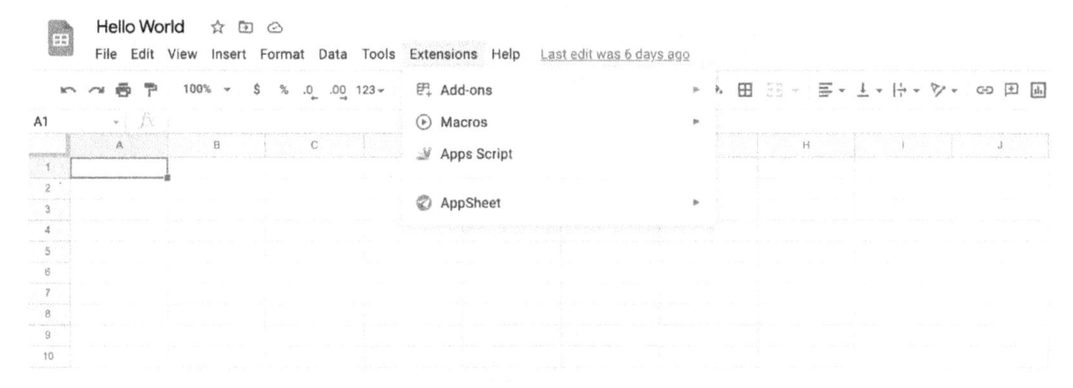


Figure 6.1 – Apps Script menu item in Sheets

The Apps Script code editor will launch in a new window with a default file named `code.gs`, prepopulated with a `myFunction()` function.

2. Let's rename the project to `Hello World`:

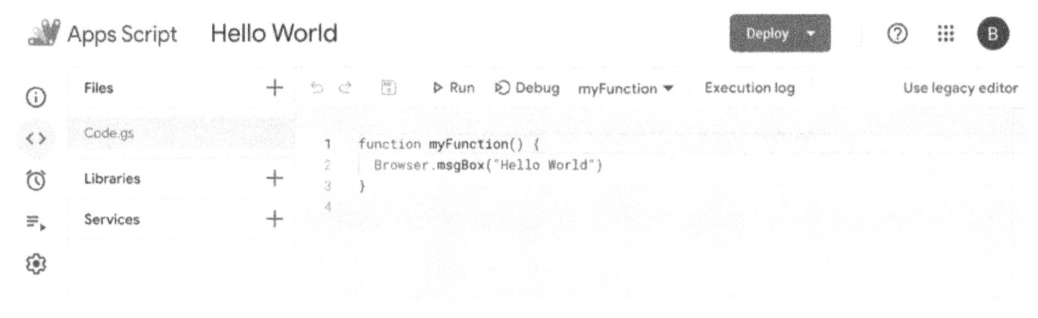


Figure 6.2 – Apps Script code editor with defaults

3. Then, let us write our first line of code within this default function:

```
function myFunction() {
 Browser.msgBox("Hello World")
}
```

4. Click on the **Save project** icon, followed by **Run**. In this function, we are asking Apps Script to display a message box in Sheets with the message `Hello World`.

When a script is executed for the first time against an application, Google will prompt for authorization to run the script. This is understandable as Apps Script can perform create, update, read, and delete operations on all entities.

In this example, since the script is run against Google Sheets, the authorization screen shown will be specific to permissions required for Sheets:

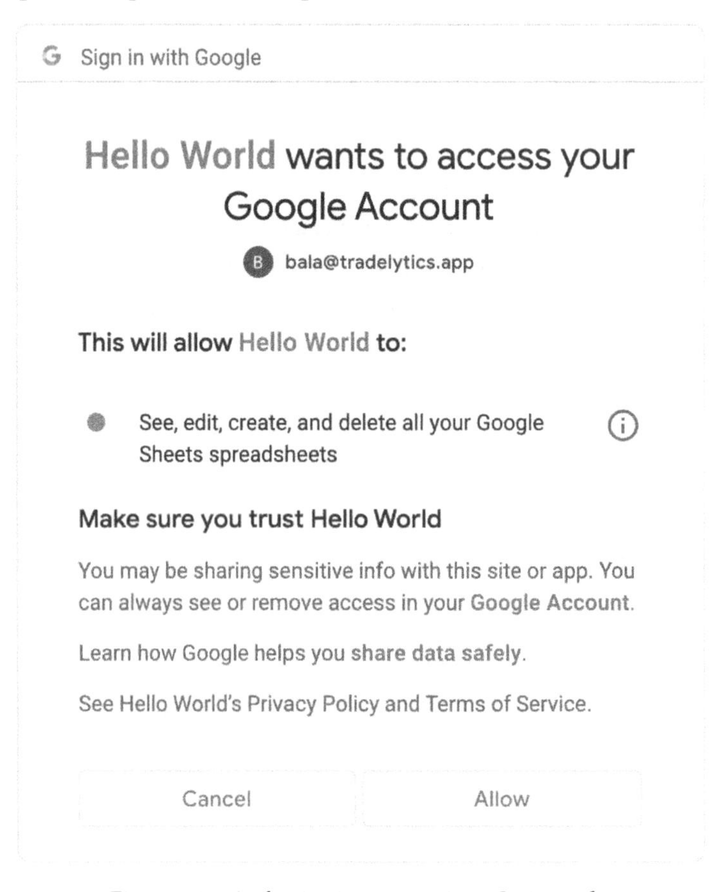


Figure 6.3 – Authorization to run Apps Script code

Once authorized, the code will execute, and in this case, a message box with the requested message will appear in Google Sheets as output:

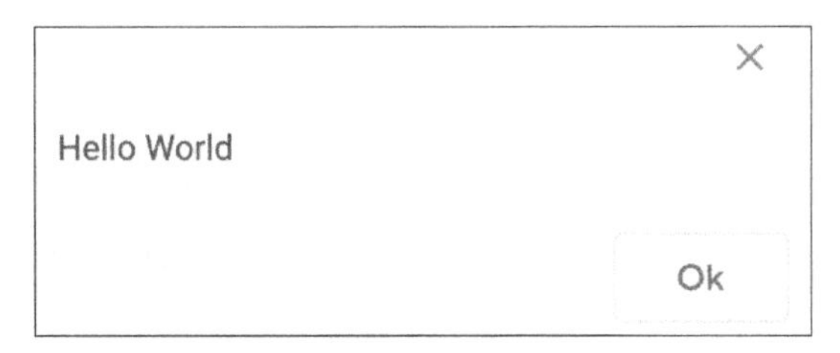


Figure 6.4 – Output from the Hello World program

Pretty fun, right?

> **Prerequisites**
> Working with Apps Script requires basic familiarity with JavaScript and Google Workspace APIs. For instance, being familiar with Google Sheets API would help manipulate adding, reading, updating, and deleting sheets, or data in sheets.

We are going to be looking at a lot of code examples in this chapter and it would be beneficial to understand the code editor a little bit better.

## Code editor

The code editor is simple and intuitive and packed with a lot of capabilities. The following figure shows the various functions of the code editor:

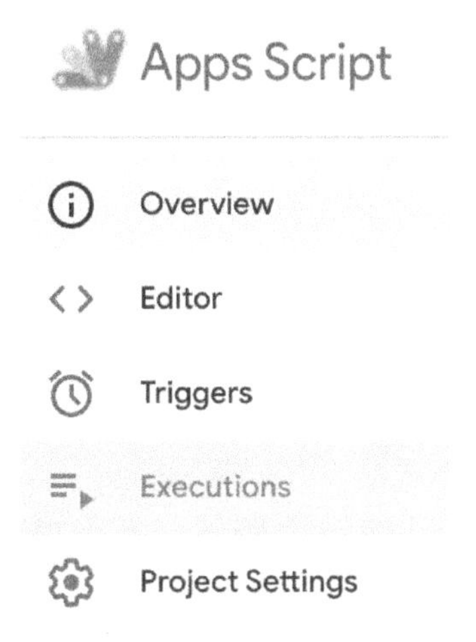


Figure 6.5 – Code editor functions

Here is a quick rundown of what the icons mean and do:

- **Overview**: This page gives a comprehensive overview of the project, its status, when it was last run, error details, and scopes.
- **Editor**: This is the code editor for Apps Script. This is used to write, edit, run, and debug code. This function is also a place to look at execution logs.
- **Triggers**: Triggers let Apps Script run a function automatically based on certain events, such as opening a document. This section allows users to create, edit, search, and manage triggers that are created.
- **Executions**: As the name indicates, this is a log of all executions that happened on a specific project. The function gives details regarding when the execution started and ended and the status of executions.
- **Project Settings**: A place where project-specific settings are managed, such as whether uncaught exceptions should be automatically logged to cloud logs.

Now that the stage has been set for diving deep into Apps Script, let's look at more practical examples that will help us solve everyday tasks in a typical work environment. First on that list is macros.

# Macros

A macro is a series of recorded actions within Google Sheets that are repeatable.

Google Sheets has the option to capture automated tasks once using the **Record Macro** feature and reuse it multiple times. The recorded macro can be scheduled to execute on a time-based trigger.

For example, users can select **Record Macro** to update formula, apply conditional formatting, add UI formats, and so on. This will automatically capture all the changes applied to the data and display the changes as Apps Script code. This code can be further improvised without having to write code from scratch.

When recording macros in Sheets, users can choose *absolute cell references* or *relative cell references* to dictate which cells should be targeted in the macros.

> **Absolute Cell References versus Relative Cell References**
>
> In the simplest terms, relative cell references change when a formula is copied to another cell. On the other hand, absolute references do not change and keep referencing the same cell regardless of where they are copied to.

The following figure shows how to access macros from the **Extensions** menu items in Sheets, to **Record macro**:

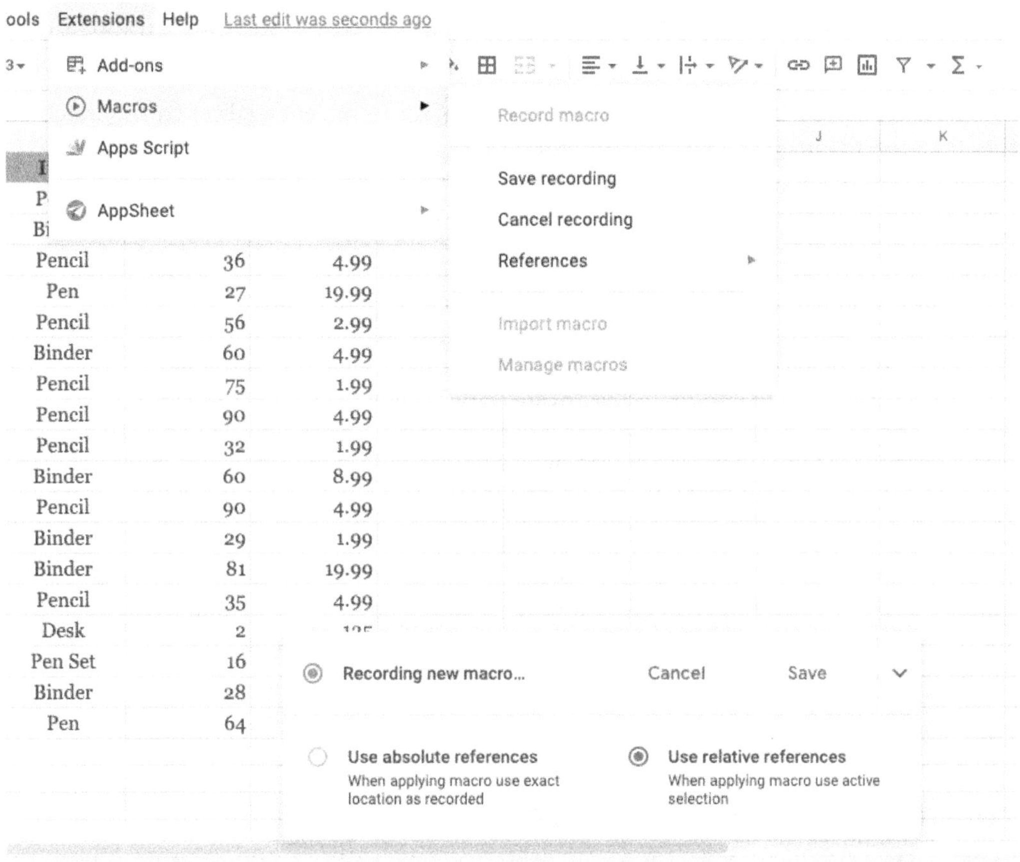

Figure 6.6 – Recording macros in Sheets

After the macro is recorded, it can be used to apply the same formula or UI formatting to other data within the same sheet. When the recorded macro is selected to apply this change to a different set of data, and if this is the first time the user is running this macro, an authorization page is displayed. Users must allow authorization to Apps Script to execute this macro successfully. All these actions will be captured in User Audit logs.

Administrators can revoke access or reduce the scope of macros from the Google **Admin** console at any time.

It is fascinating to look under the hood and figure out what happens when a macro is created. When a macro is created, Sheets automatically creates a function in Apps Script that replicates the macro steps. This function is enclosed in a project that is bound to the sheet. The function is added to a file called `macros.gs`. Users can then edit this function and customize it even more.

Power users of Apps Script typically like to create macros in the code editor from scratch rather than use the in-built recording function as it gives them greater flexibility to add existing code to macros.

> **Important Note**
>
> Macros are very powerful in what they can do; hence, caution must be exercised when wielding their power. The Apps Script platform has incorporated several restrictions to prevent malicious code executions and to keep data safe. For instance, macros are always bound to specific Google Sheets. Macro definitions are ignored if they are executed elsewhere. Also, macros as a feature are available only with Google Sheets. It is not available in Google Docs, Forms, or Slides.

Macros are best suited for automated manual tasks in Sheets that need to be repeated frequently with very minimal configuration. If the tasks that are being automated are complex and require additional configuration, creating a custom menu option would be more beneficial.

We will look at creating a custom menu item and its purpose in the next section.

# Creating a custom menu item

Macros can be tied to a keyboard shortcut and can be invoked by pressing a bunch of keys; however, users may like to invoke a custom action by clicking on something more intuitive than a random bunch of keys. A custom menu item can precisely guide users on a task that may be performed when invoked. Also, a menu item can come in handy if users want to automate tasks across other Google applications such as Docs and Forms, and not just Sheets. Recall that macros can only be associated with Sheets.

Let's look at an example of creating a custom menu in Google Docs:

1. Open Google Drive.
2. Click on **New | Google Docs** to create a new document.
3. Name the document and use the menu bar to select **Tools | Script editor**.

This opens the familiar Apps Script code editor. As you can see in *Figure 6.7*, all the default options are there, and no custom menu items are available in the menu bar. We are going to change that in a little bit.

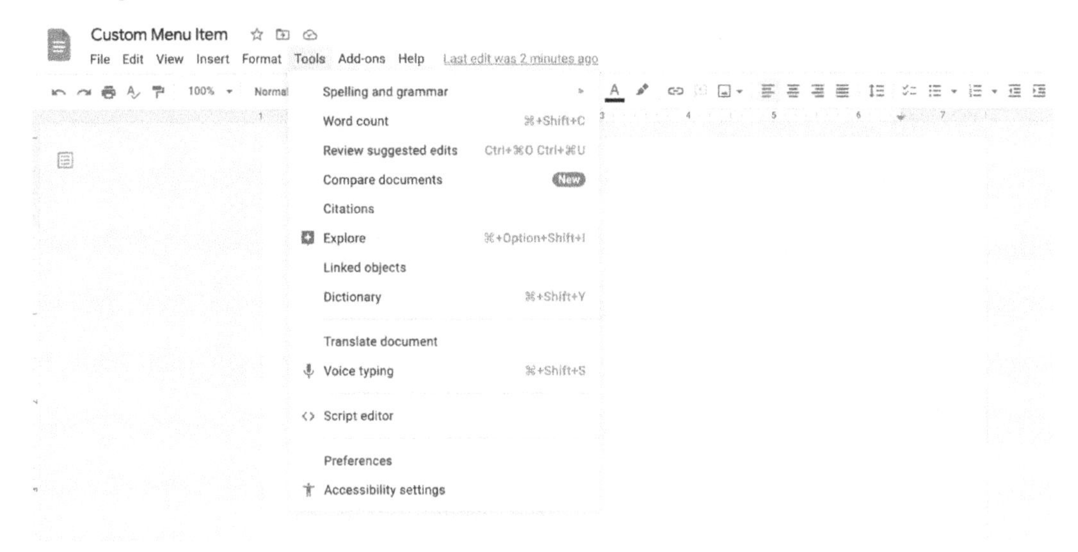


Figure 6.7 – Google Docs menu bar showing the Script editor

For our example, let's work with Star Wars characters. We want to create a top-level menu item called `Star Wars` and two sub-menu items named `Obiwan Kenobi` and `Darth Vader`. When the **Obiwan Kenobi** menu item is clicked, it should trigger an alert that displays Obi Wan's signature dialog. When **Darth Vader** is clicked, it should trigger a different dialog than Obi Wan's.

OK, let's start adding code to the code editor for creating a new top-level menu item named `Star Wars` and two sub-items named `Obiwan Kenobi` and `Darth Vader`.

The steps for accomplishing this are as follows:

1. In the `onOpen()` event of the document, create a top-level menu item and two sub-level menu items. This would mean that when the document is opened, these menu items would be created and be ready for user interaction.
2. As a menu item is defined, Apps Script can be wired up to know which custom function to call when the menu item is clicked.
3. Once defined, save the project by clicking on the floppy disk icon, and then click on **Run**.

> If this is your first time running a script with Google Docs, Google Workspace will surface an authorization screen prompting user action to grant permissions to run the script. This screen would be like the one shown in *Figure 6.3*.

Let's look at the Apps Script code that will make all that awesomeness possible:

```
function onOpen() {
  var ui = DocumentApp.getUi();
  ui.createMenu('Star Wars')
    .addItem('Obiwan Kenobi','mimicObiWan')
    .addItem('Darth Vader', 'mimicVader')
    .addToUi();
}

function mimicObiWan(){
    var ui = DocumentApp.getUi();
    ui.alert("Hello there!");
}

function mimicVader(){
  var ui = DocumentApp.getUi();
    ui.alert("I AM your father!");
}
```

This project would have three functions, one for adding the menu items during the `onOpen()` event, and one each for wiring up the behaviors when sub-level menu items are clicked.

The mimic functions are simple – they create a handle for the existing document through the `DocumentApp.getUI()` method and then display a message box via the `alert()` method. For more details on these objects and methods, please refer to the Google Workspace API documentation.

Let's see what happens when the program is run. When the code finishes execution, a new top-level menu item will be added to the menu bar, as you can see in the following screenshot:

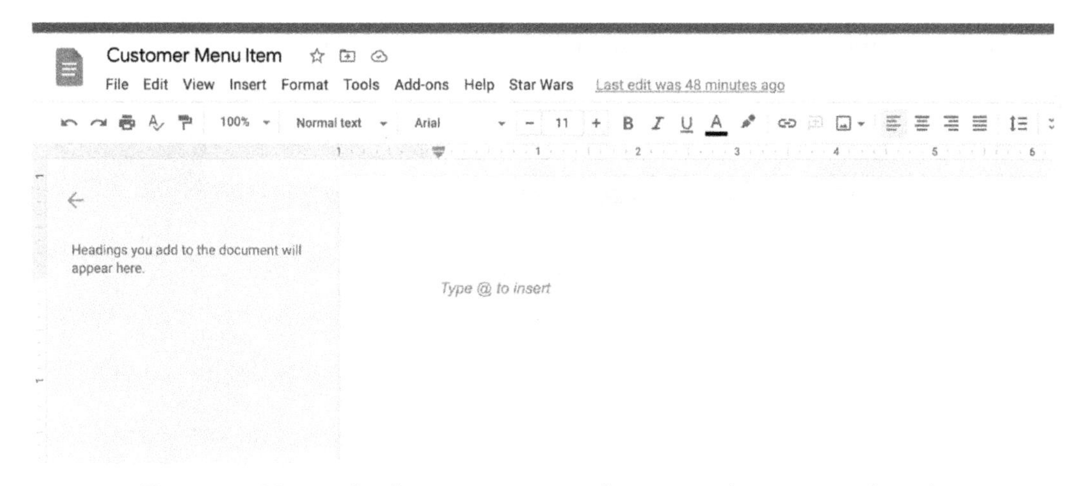


Figure 6.8 – New top-level custom menu item showing up after executing the code

Clicking on the **Star Wars** menu item brings up two sub-level menu items, as expected:

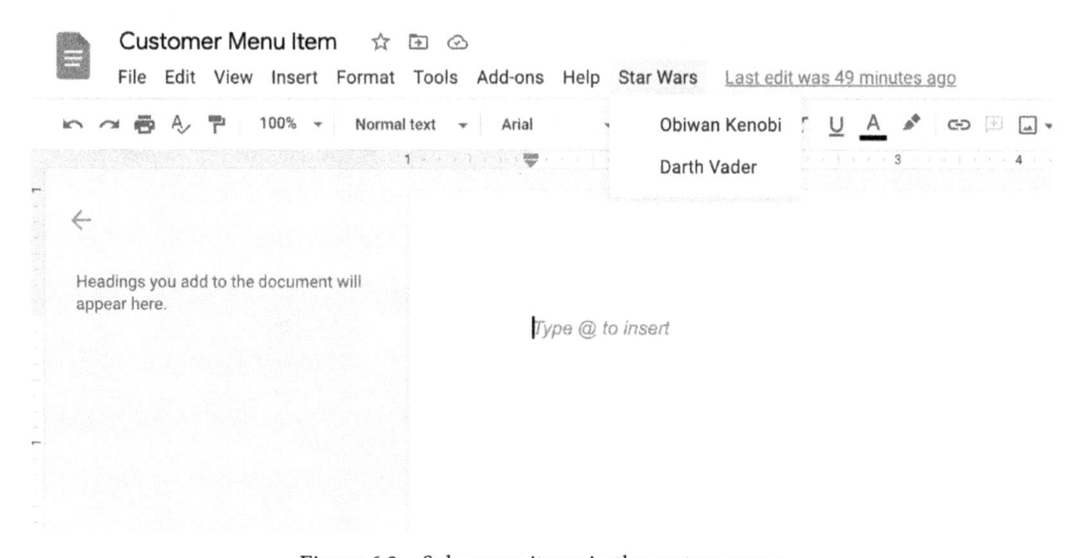


Figure 6.9 – Sub-menu items in the custom menu

Clicking on the **Obiwan Kenobi** menu item displays the following message:

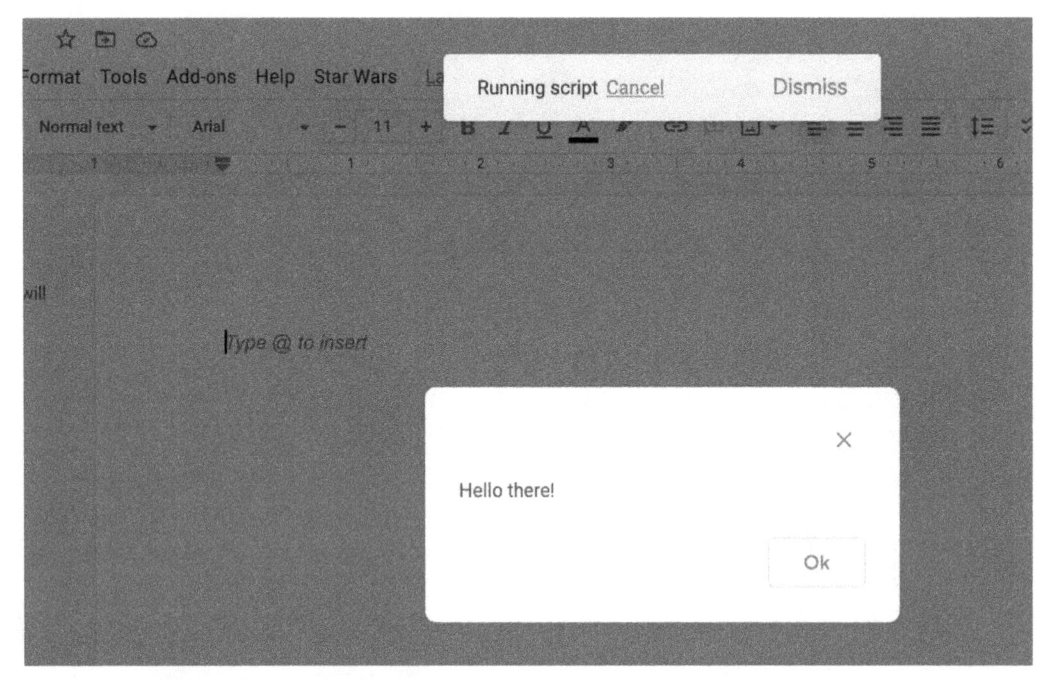


Figure 6.10 – Message displayed when the Obiwan Kenobi menu item is clicked

Clicking on the **Darth Vader** menu item displays the following message:

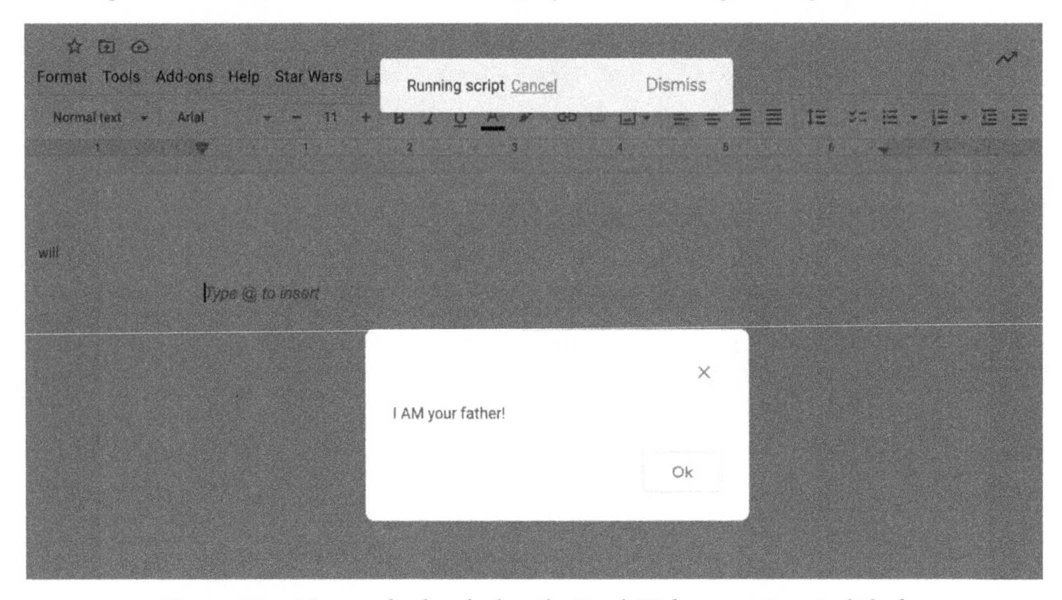


Figure 6.11 – Message displayed when the Darth Vader menu item is clicked

Voilà! We have managed to create custom menu items and wire up custom behavior when those items were clicked. This gives you a glimpse of how easy it is to add custom functionality with Apps Script.

That's our first foray into automating complex workflows and behavior in Apps Script. As you can imagine, combining the Workspace services API with Apps Script can give us infinite possibilities to interact with almost all the functions and capabilities of these services.

Let's motor on and explore a more complex example using the Sheets API in combination with the Gmail API to programmatically select, filter, and send emails.

## Interactions with the Gmail and Sheets APIs

For our next illustration, let's explore the relatively complex task of selecting data from a sheet and sending it via Gmail. Now that we are familiar with Apps Script, this exercise should not be complex at all. Let's dive into the details.

The following screenshot shows the sample data that will be used in our example:

File Edit View Insert Format Data Tools Extensions Help Last edit was seconds ago

100% $ % .0 .00 123 Default (Ari... 10 B I S A

F2

| | A | B | C | D | E | F |
|---|---|---|---|---|---|---|
| 1 | FirstName | LastName | EmailAddress | Enrollment id | Gender | Status |
| 2 | Joel | Warren | Joel.Warren@gr | 520788929 | Mr | |
| 3 | Sue | Elliott | Sue.Elliott@hotr | 687102986 | Ms | |
| 4 | Wilfred | Davidson | Wilfred.davidson | 3760959 | Mr | |
| 5 | Robin | Ramirez | Robin.Ramirez@ | 594197548 | Mr | |
| 6 | Heidi | Morton | Heidi.Morton@g | 648586412 | Mr | |
| 7 | Celia | Alvarez | Celia.alvarez@a | 437245027 | Ms | |
| 8 | Rosalie | Reynolds | Rosalie.Reynold | 647401167 | Ms | |
| 9 | Victoria | Frank | Victoria.Frank@ | 60106556 | Ms | |
| 10 | Helen | Mills | Helen.Mills@gm | 232823190 | Ms | |
| 11 | Thelma | Cox | Thelma.Cox@hc | 396258672 | Ms | |
| 12 | | | | | | |
| 13 | | | | | | |

Figure 6.12 – Data and columns used in the representative example

The steps for this task are very simple:

1. Use the Sheets API to read and iterate through the data.
2. For each selected row in the active sheet, which indicates a signup, send an email to the user with an enrollment ID using the email address in the **EmailAddress** column.

3. Once an email has been successfully sent, fill the **Status** column in green.
4. Add a custom menu item to make sending emails a breeze.

We have used the Sheets API in our `Hello World!` example. The new API to explore for implementing this example would be the Gmail API.

To make this intuitive for users to send emails, let's create a custom menu item, named `Send Email`. Once this button is clicked, it will trigger the action to read through the rows one by one and send emails.

The following code will create a menu item called `Send Email` and bind the `SendEmail` function to it:

```
function onOpen() {
 var ui = SpreadsheetApp.getUi();
 ui.createMenu('Menu')
     .addItem('Send Email', 'SendEmail')
     .addToUi();

}
```

When the menu item is clicked, the `SendEmail` function will be triggered.

As we noted earlier, the bulk of the logic for reading data, composing the email, and sending it via Gmail will be in the `SendEmail()` function. Let's look at the code for that function and walk through the code.

Here's what the code looks like:

```
function SendEmail() {
  var signups = SpreadsheetApp.getActiveRange();
  Logger.log(signups);
  var lastrow = SpreadsheetApp.getActiveRange().getNumRows();
  Logger.log("number of rows " + lastrow);
  for(var rowcounter=0; rowcounter < lastrow; rowcounter++)
  {
    var enrollmentID = signups.getValues()[rowcounter][3];
    var user_firstname = signups.getValues()[rowcounter][0];
    var useremail = signups.getValues()[rowcounter][2];
```

```
    Logger.log(user_firstname);
    var body = "Hello User, Your Enrollment ID is : "+
enrollmentID;

    MailApp.sendEmail(useremail,
                     "Subject",
                     "Hello " + user_firstname.toString()+", A
new User account has been created.\n\n",body);

    signups.getCell(rowcounter+1,6).setBackground('#00B050').
setFontColor('#ffffff');
  }
}
```

Now, let's walk through the code:

1. First, using the Sheets API, the selected rows for which the email needs to be sent will be selected using the `GetActiveRange()` method.
2. Second, the number of rows selected is determined using the `GetActiveRange().getNumRows()` method. This will act as the upper bound for our iterating loop.
3. Third, a loop iterates through every selected row in the active sheet and reads the columns individually while constructing the email.
4. Fourth, once the email message is composed, the Gmail API is invoked, and an email is sent using the `MailApp.sendEmail()` method.
5. Finally, after sending an email, the row's status will be updated in green indicating this row has been processed successfully. The iterator moves to the next row.

This code also has logging peppered throughout to make it easier to debug if something goes wrong. Please note that this code is very basic and definitely could be improved in several ways — in terms of handling empty rows and data values, dealing with email failures, and so on. This is a demonstration to show the power of Apps Script in combination with Workspace APIs.

The following screenshot shows the **Status** column in green after the code has processed several rows:

| FirstName | LastName | EmailAddress | Enrollment id | Gender | Status |
|---|---|---|---|---|---|
| Joel | Warren | Joel.Warren@gmail.com | 520788929 | Mr | |
| Sue | Elliott | Sue.Elliott@hotmail.com | 687102986 | Ms | |
| Wilfred | Davidson | Wilfred.davidson@aol.com | 3760959 | Mr | |
| Robin | Ramirez | Robin.Ramirez@gmail.com | 594197548 | Mr | |
| Heidi | Morton | Heidi.Morton@gmail.com | 648586412 | Mr | |
| Celia | Alvarez | Celia.alvarez@alvarez.com | 437245027 | Ms | |
| Rosalie | Reynolds | Rosalie.Reynolds@abc.com | 647401167 | Ms | |
| Victoria | Frank | Victoria.Frank@frank.org | 60106556 | Ms | |
| Helen | Mills | Helen.Mills@gmail.com | 232823190 | Ms | |
| Thelma | Cox | Thelma.Cox@hotmail.com | 396258672 | Ms | |

Figure 6.13 – Status column populated in green following successful processing

The code uses `SpreadsheetApp` to access this sheet and its data. If there are additional API services required, those services can be enabled from the AppSheet Script properties.

Executions within the Apps Script settings will show all the executions along with any Logger statements added for checkpoint verifications to debug the code.

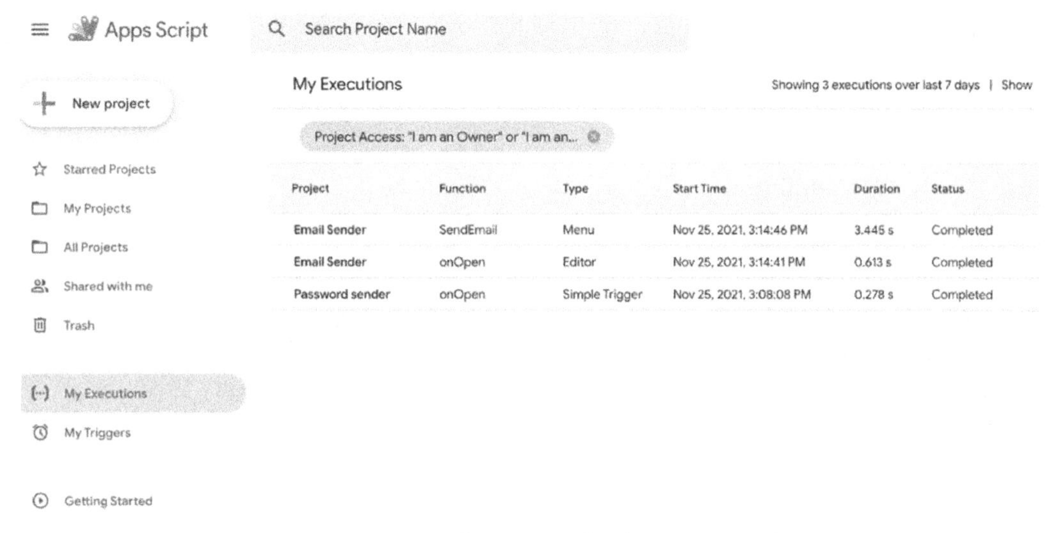


Figure 6.14 – List of executions for the example code

We had added `Logger.log(user_firstname);` to verify whether the **FirstName** column was being picked up as expected from the sheet, as the code was executing. These log statements are visible in the **My Executions** section for our debugging pleasure:

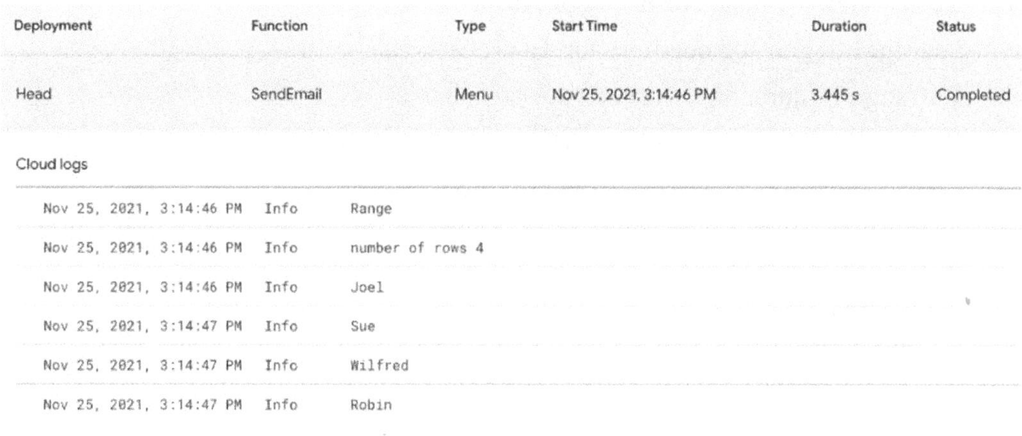

| Deployment | Function | Type | Start Time | Duration | Status |
|---|---|---|---|---|---|
| Head | SendEmail | Menu | Nov 25, 2021, 3:14:46 PM | 3.445 s | Completed |

Cloud logs

| | | |
|---|---|---|
| Nov 25, 2021, 3:14:46 PM | Info | Range |
| Nov 25, 2021, 3:14:46 PM | Info | number of rows 4 |
| Nov 25, 2021, 3:14:46 PM | Info | Joel |
| Nov 25, 2021, 3:14:47 PM | Info | Sue |
| Nov 25, 2021, 3:14:47 PM | Info | Wilfred |
| Nov 25, 2021, 3:14:47 PM | Info | Robin |

Figure 6.15 – Logger statements and output from the example

The preceding integration with the Sheets API and the Gmail API is probably one of the most widely used combinations used to automate mundane tasks, such as sending out internal communications and email confirmations, and running mail merge operations.

Let's continue our conversation on Apps Script integration with Workspace services by exploring Google Forms and Google Docs next.

## Using Google Forms with Apps Script

Google Forms is a nifty scalable service included with Google Workspace that lets users create an online form for surveys and analyze the responses.

As you may have guessed by now, Apps Script can be integrated with Google Forms for functions that can be triggered, such as when a user submits a form. These custom functions can be useful for validating data that is being submitted or routing the data to different destinations based on certain criterion.

A common place for introducing this custom logic in Google Forms is when users submit a form. Let's look at a non-glorified example of accessing user responses when a form is submitted.

To begin, let's create a Google form the same way as we would normally do:

1. Open Google Drive.
2. Click on **New | Google Forms | Blank form**.
3. Enter the title and add questions for data collection.
4. Rearrange the questions based on your preferences.
5. Click the **Preview** button to check its appearance for users.
6. Click on the kebab menu (3 dots) and select **Script Editor**.

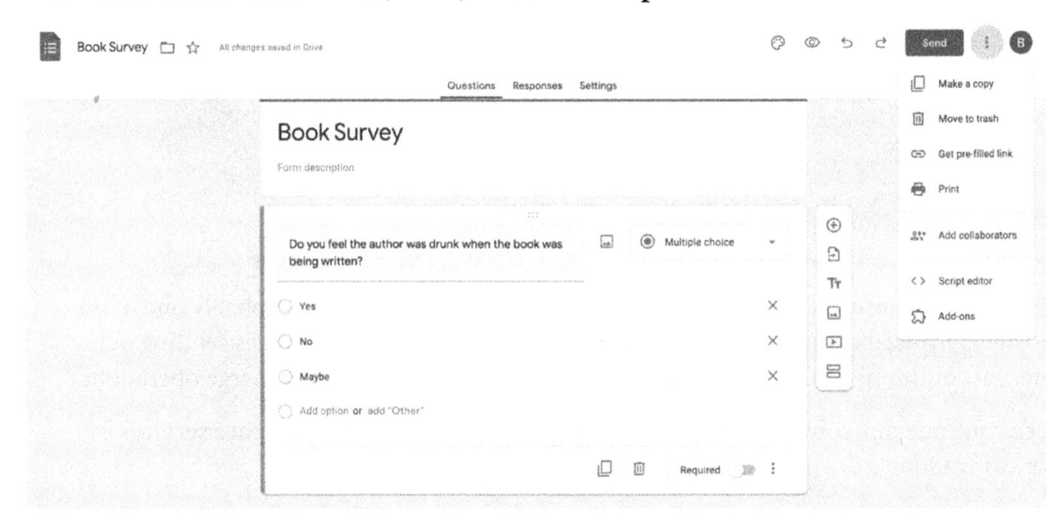


Figure 6.16 – Google Forms survey example

Here is a sample code to access the related sheet for responses. Based on the data entered, add some code logic:

```
function onSubmit() {
var form = FormApp.openById('1PHREyS5Dnsc-ejAbA2SuPY4l12lqXuQam
4gwdrCYA2s');
var formResponses = form.getResponses();
var totalreplies = formResponses.length;
var latest_formResponse = formResponses[totalreplies-1];
Logger.log(latest_formResponse.getItemResponses());
var itemResponses = latest_formResponse.getItemResponses();
```

```
    var itemResponse = itemResponses[0];
    Logger.log('Response  to the question "%s" was "%s"',
        itemResponse.getItem(),
        itemResponse.getResponse());
}
```

The preceding code accesses the form and its responses. Based on the response to a certain question, a sequential action can be initiated. To improve debugging capabilities, `Logger.log` is used to verify whether the correct row of the answer is being picked up as expected.

To trigger this code every time someone submits this form, an action-based trigger can be set up in the Apps Script editor interface. To achieve this, follow these steps:

1. Click on **Triggers** from the left-side pane on the **Apps Script** interface:

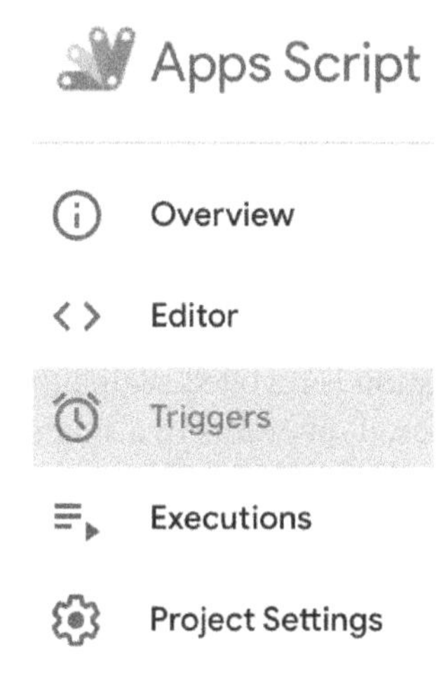


Figure 6.17 – Apps Script triggers

2. Click on **Add a Trigger**.
3. Select the function to execute and make sure that **On form submit** is selected under the **Select event type** option.

4. Click **Save**.

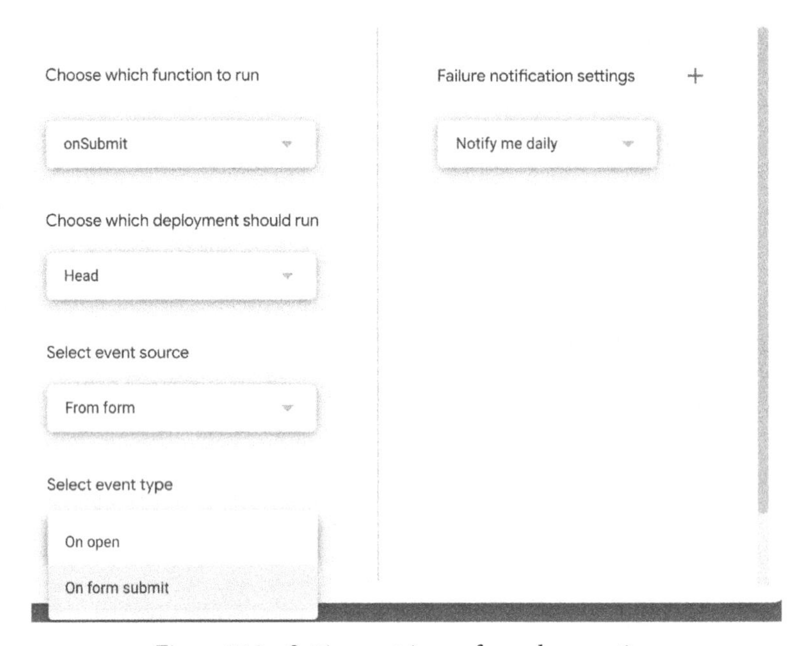


Figure 6.18 – Setting up triggers for code execution

The trigger will ensure that automation is invoked sequentially for incoming data. Multiple triggers could be added based on events in a single form, thus giving greater control to users for automation. The possibilities for using a Google Form are endless.

So far, we have covered Apps Script integration and its automation capabilities across multiple Workspace services such as Sheets and Forms, in the form of macros, custom menu items, and event-based automation. Continuing our theme on Apps Script integration with Workspace services, let's move on to Docs.

# Adding Apps Script for Google Docs

Apps Script can be added to Google Docs to add automation based on the content in the document. For example, an invoice can be designed in a Google Doc with specific key fields that can be swapped out or filled in for each recipient. This invoice can be automated using Apps Script to fetch data from various sources, and an email could be sent using the Gmail API. *Figure 6.19* shows a typical invoice that has the customer's details on top, company information and product information in the header, and pricing information in the body. A template could be created, and all the information could be populated based on customer information and their specific pricing details.

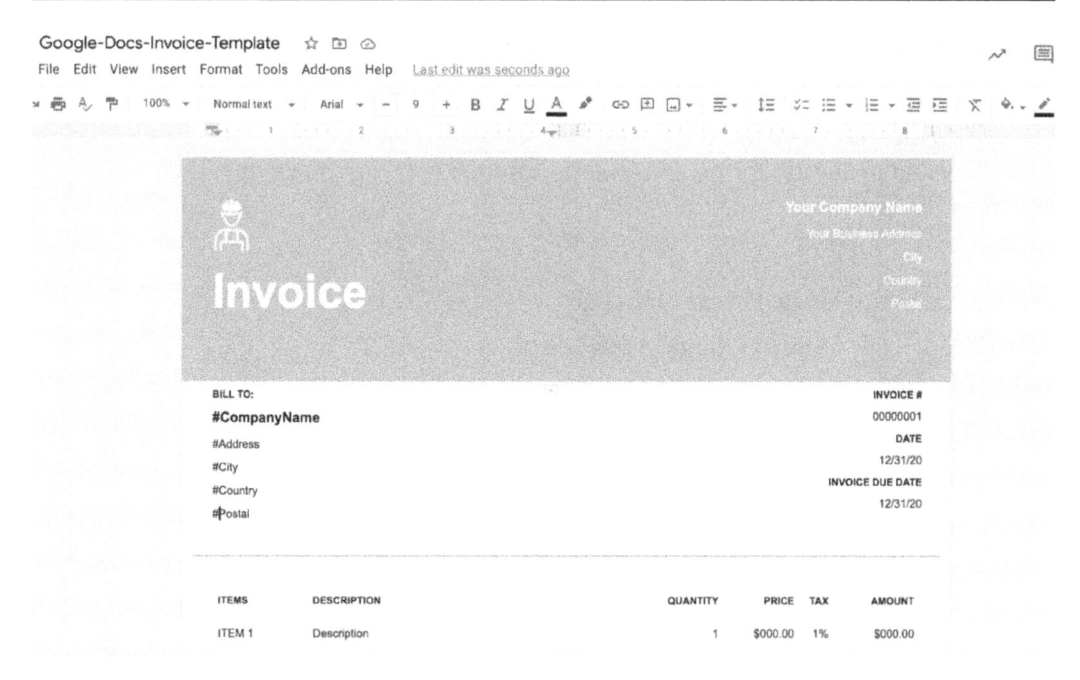


Figure 6.19 – Sample invoice in Google Docs

Fields that need to be populated with relevant data are marked and can be programmatically identified and replaced for generating an invoice.

The data can be accessed from other sources such as Google Sheets using the ID of the sheet. Using the `SpreadsheetApp()` function, specific rows and cells of data can be picked and used in conditional processing and replacement of data in the document.

If this code could be helpful for more users, the Apps Script code can be published as an add-on so that other users in the domain can install this add-on locally in their Drive account. This enables businesses to solve their problems faster.

I will spare the Apps Script code for this invoicing example and let you use your learning and creativity to come up with a solution. Given the past examples, a solution can be put together really quickly.

With that said, it's time to move past Apps Script integration with Workspace services and look at how Apps Script can help us build micro web applications.

## Creating a web application using Apps Script

In previous examples, we have seen Apps Script associated with Google Sheets, Google Forms, and Docs. Let's look at an example for creating a standalone web application that is unrelated to Sheets, Forms, or Docs. In this example, you will get the flexibility of designing the frontend user interface using HTML or any frontend markup language of your choice. The following steps detail how to create a standalone web application:

1. Log in to the Google Drive home page.
2. Click on **New | More | Google Apps Script**.

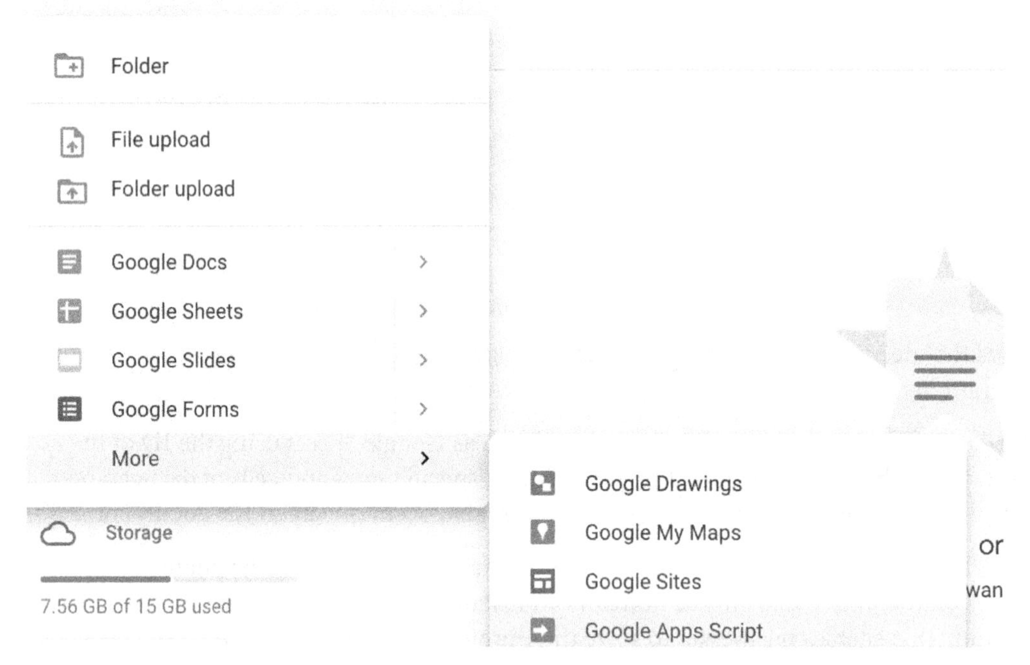


Figure 6.20 – Menu items showing how to invoke the Apps Script editor to build web applications

This will initiate the Apps Script editor, which can host HTML pages and backend code as a script.

3. Click on the + button near the **Files** section to add an HTML file. The HTML file can be customized heavily and has the option to use style sheets.

The script will connect with the HTML UI to invoke respective functional methods for each user action. For example, if you need to validate a user's input in a field, then the respective `Validation` function can be invoked, or if the user clicks on a button posted on the HTML page, then appropriate functions could be invoked as needed.

Using the <Script> tag, JavaScript actions can also be included in HTML. You can see some sample HTML code in the following screenshot:

Figure 6.21 – HTML code in the sample web application

Once the appearance is designed using HTML, CSS, and various styling options, the code for actions is invoked and finally, the entire web application is deployed using the **Deploy** button.

Deployment in Apps Script helps you track each version of your updated code, and each deployment generates a URL for accessing the Apps Script application.

It looks like this: https://script.google.com/macros/s/<alpha_numeric code to identify the application.

Deployment of this code can be configured to execute as the logged-in user or by using service accounts. We'll learn about service accounts in the upcoming sections of this chapter.

The deployed project can be shared with other users so that they can access this code and use it as a library repository. Any obsolete versions of old code are archived to help track the active version.

If there is a need to use Google Cloud Platform API for advanced cloud computing functionality, it can be accessed using the **Services** section in the left-side panel:

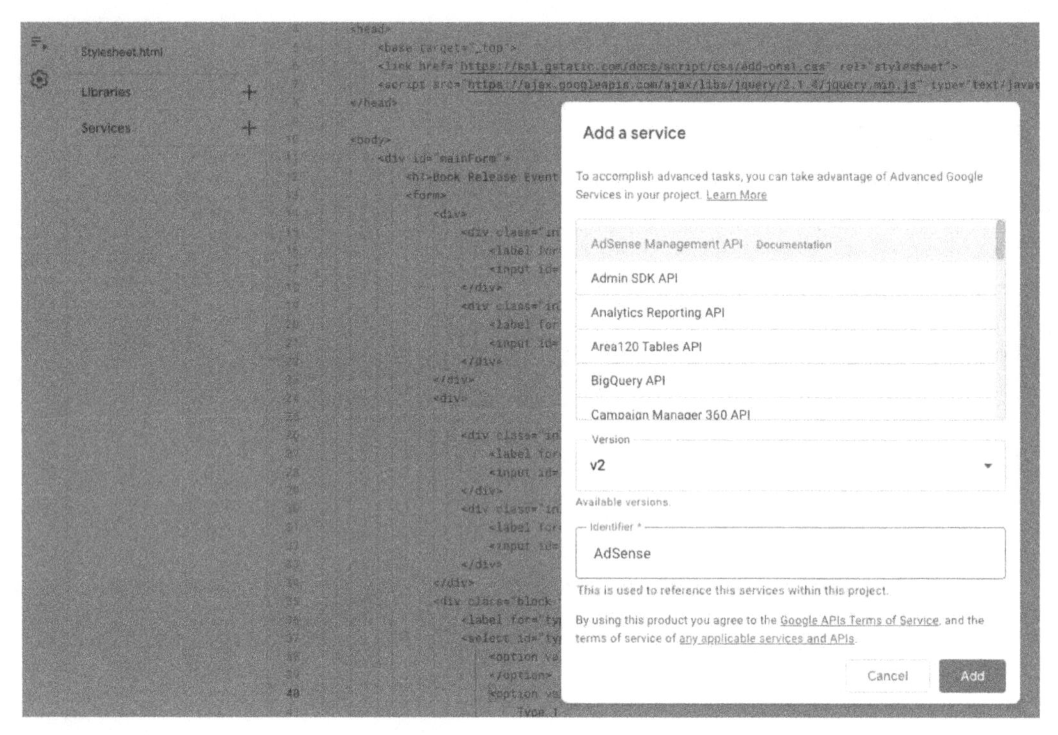


Figure 6.22 – Integrating advanced GCP capabilities in a web application built using Apps Script

Once the service, such as Admin SDK API or Analytics API, is added, relevant methods within that API can be used to automate several application functions.

As we have seen so far, Apps Script can make lives easier for Workspace users with added automation capabilities. The power resides in the hands of users to use Apps Script sensibly and responsibly in a multi-tenant architecture such as Workspace. To prevent abuse, Google has implemented several throttles that will automatically trigger and curtail code execution when the Workspace platform detects that a program run using Apps Script, goes over the defined threshold. In the next section, let's investigate the security paradigms and constraints under which Apps Script code executes.

## Apps Script security and best practices

Apps Script can programmatically access content and process it based on the logic defined by the user. However, this ability is a double-edged sword, as sometimes script execution can take forever to run, hogging shared compute and network resources. For example, long-running executions could occur because of data size or faulty logic in the code that results in an infinite loop. Bad actors could also trigger a denial-of-service attack by executing a script that takes forever to run.

In a SaaS environment such as Workspace, which is a multi-tenanted environment, the execution containers for multiple users reside on the same host, sharing the underlying hardware. One script hogging computer and networking resource would slow the platform for everyone, resulting in a poor user experience.

To encourage responsible coding, the Workspace platform has execution limits imposed on Apps Script. For example, a user can only create 50 Apps Script projects per day and the execution logic of an Apps Script is limited to 6 minutes per execution. After 6 minutes have elapsed, the script times out.

The full list of current quotas and limits are explained here: `https://developers.google.com/apps-script/guides/services/quotas`.

The 6-minute script execution time limit might pose some challenges for users who are working with large amounts of data. To overcome this limitation, developers can get creative and process the data in batches. Another way to overcome this limitation would be to make use of status fields to capture the current state of progress and resume processing from that point on during subsequent executions.

Continuing with the theme of protecting the Workspace platform, Apps Script code is encouraged to be run under a service account, rather than a user account.

> **Service Account**
>
> A service account is a special type of account that is intended to represent a non-human user that can authenticate and be authorized to run scripts. Service accounts are very helpful as they can be created with granular permissions and can perform specialized tasks. If scripts are running user service accounts, a user leaving a domain won't impact its execution.

In this section, we have covered a ton of stuff on Apps Script – from the introduction of setting up a `Hello World` program, to investigating its integration across various services, before wrapping it up with security and best practices. Apps Script is a powerful weapon in the Workspace arsenal and mastering it will make working with Workspace a breeze.

Let's now move on to explore another automation/low-code environment in the Workspace platform: AppSheet.

# AppSheet

AppSheet is a low-code platform for creating applications that can integrate with Google Workspace or cloud storage services. These applications can work both on the web browser and on mobile devices. Google acquired AppSheet in 2020 and has integrated it within its cloud portfolio.

> **Low-Code Platform**
>
> A low-code development platform provides a quick way to create application software through a drag/drop UI instead of the traditional hand-coded programming techniques.

The AppSheet application can use logical, conditional workflows to automate sequential tasks. It can be used for any kind of application, such as surfacing information to users, filling out a form, initiating an action, or updating data sources based on user actions.

AppSheet is available in four editions:

- **Starter**: Allows app creation with available Google Workspace connectors, and manages apps based on individual users or according to the domain.
- **Core**: Includes advanced features such as natural language processing and scheduling automation, and advanced security features such as managing apps based on user roles.
- **Enterprise Standard**: Includes advanced authentication and data features such as connectors to cloud data storage services, shared data sources, and shared authentication sources.
- **Enterprise Plus**: Includes advanced connectors and governance reports for auditing.

All these editions include support services provided by AppSheet.

As part of Google's acquisition of AppSheet, Google Workspace Enterprise Plus domains get the AppSheet Core edition at no additional cost. All other Google Workspace editions will get the free tier of AppSheet. All Google Workspace domains are eligible to purchase higher tiers of AppSheet.

In this section, we will first see how to enable AppSheet from the Google **Admin** console and then we will build an application using AppSheet.

# Enabling AppSheet

Depending on the Google Workspace edition being used, users can either use the AppSheet free tier or purchase an AppSheet subscription.

Once the subscription is confirmed, the service can be enabled for users from the Google **Admin** console by following these steps:

1. Log in to the Google **Admin** console.
2. Click on **Apps** on the left-hand side panel.
3. Select **Additional Google Services**.
4. Select **AppSheet** and enable it for the intended OU or group of users.
5. Click **Save**.

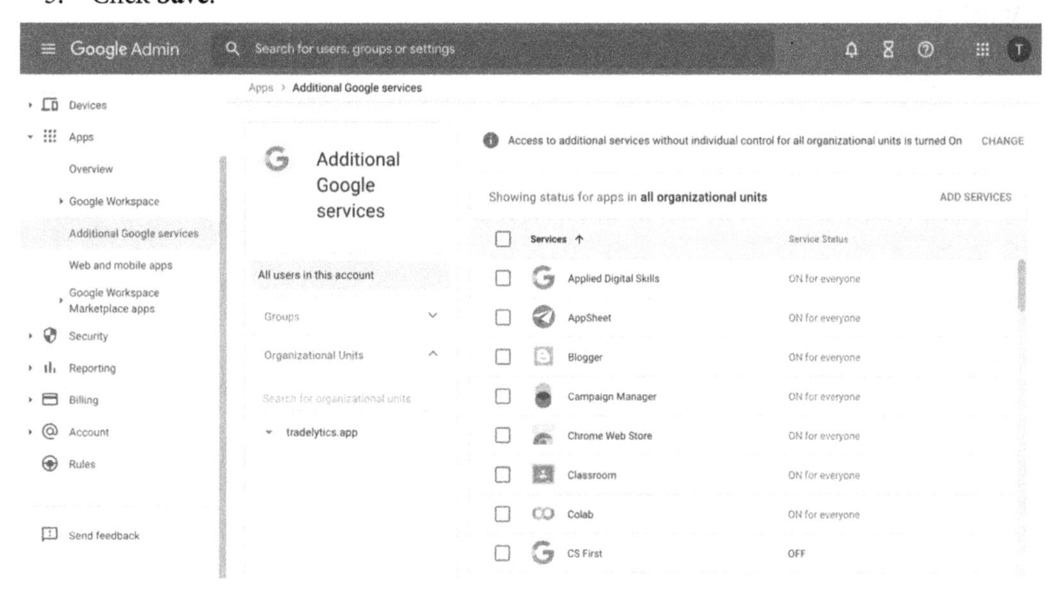


Figure 6.23 – AppSheet enablement in the Google Admin console

Once enabled, it's time to assign AppSheet licenses to the users. We have covered the process of assigning licenses to individual users in *Chapter 2, Configuring Users and Apps*. The same process applies to the AppSheet subscription as well:

1. Log in to the Google **Admin** console.
2. Click on **Users** from the left-hand side panel.
3. Select the users to whom you would like to assign licenses.
4. Click **More** and assign and select an AppSheet license from the list of subscriptions.
5. Click **Save**.

Similarly, all users within an org unit can be assigned AppSheet licenses using the auto-assign feature. For initial use, if a lot of users need to be assigned licenses, administrators can tap into the bulk user assignment feature as discussed in *Chapter 2, Configuring Users and Apps.*

With the foundation laid on AppSheet, it's time to look at how to build a simple application by taking advantage of the rich feature set that AppSheet provides.

## Build an app using AppSheet

AppSheet is a SaaS platform and can be accessed by visiting `https://www.appsheet.com/`. AppSheet supports authentication with different providers, and we will choose and log in using Google authentication. Users can use their Google Workspace email to log in to AppSheet.

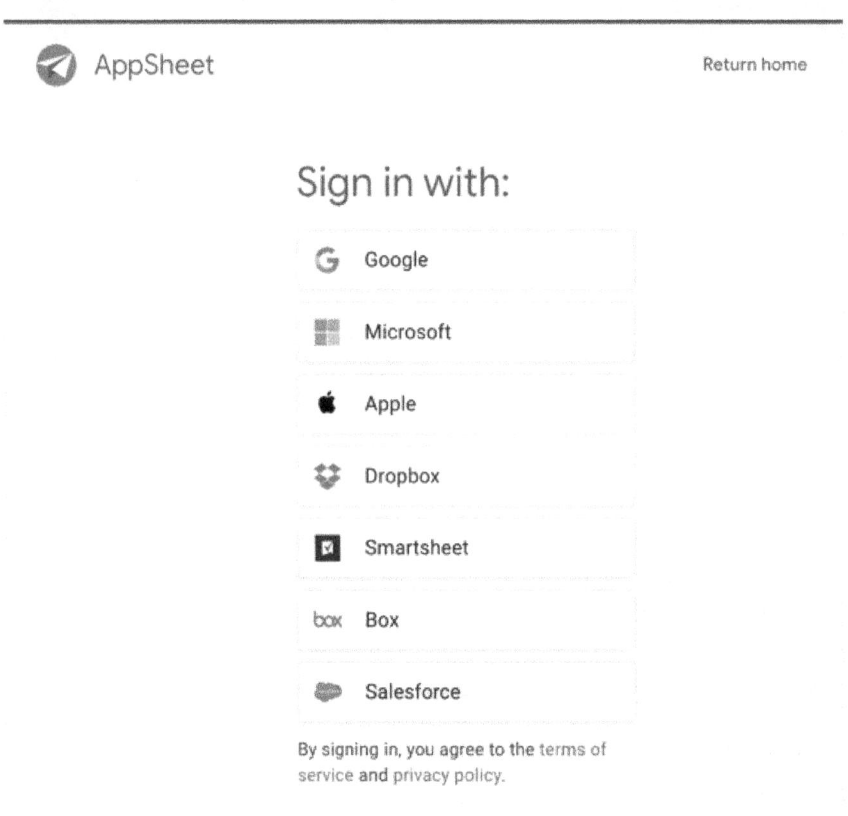


Figure 6.24 – Different authentication providers to choose from in AppSheet

When you log in to AppSheet for the first time, you will be prompted to provide authorization to AppSheet to read, edit, and delete files in Google Drive. Once you allow proper access, you are all set to create your first application with AppSheet. Here's what the AppSheet **Quick Start** page looks like:

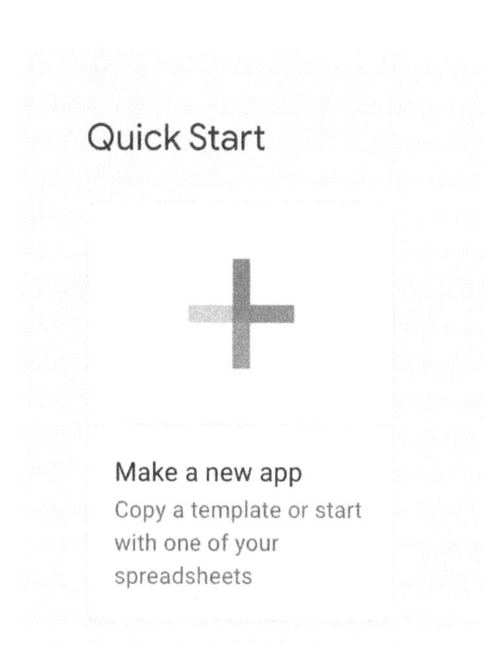


Figure 6.25 – AppSheet Quick Start page

For this example, we are going to build an application to allow users to register for a book release event. Since we have an idea, in the following screen, go ahead and select **Start with an idea**:

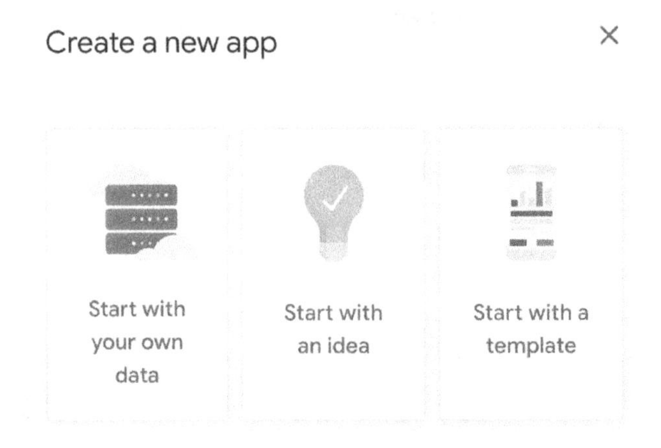


Figure 6.26 – Project types with AppSheet

Once AppSheet knows the type of project you are working on, it prompts the user for context-sensitive questions for it to build the database to store application data.

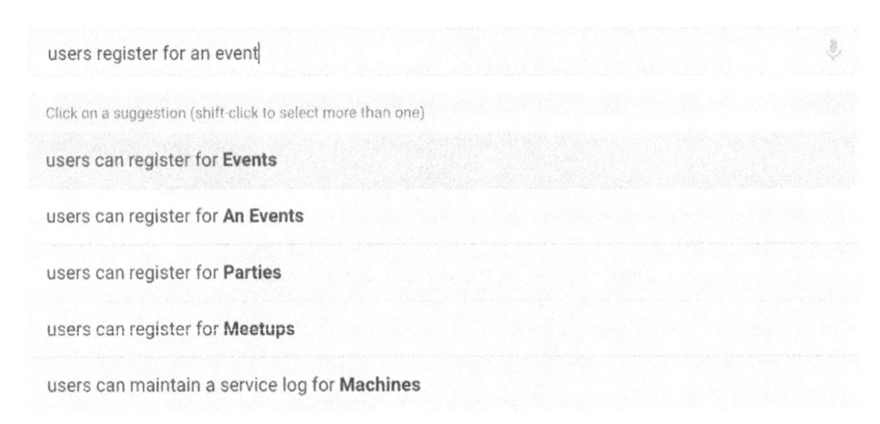


Figure 6.27 – Context-sensitive questions to guide users in AppSheet

Once the idea has been entered, the preview of the app is displayed on the right-side panel. The idea can further be developed by selecting whether users can **edit** their registration or **delete** their registration, and so on.

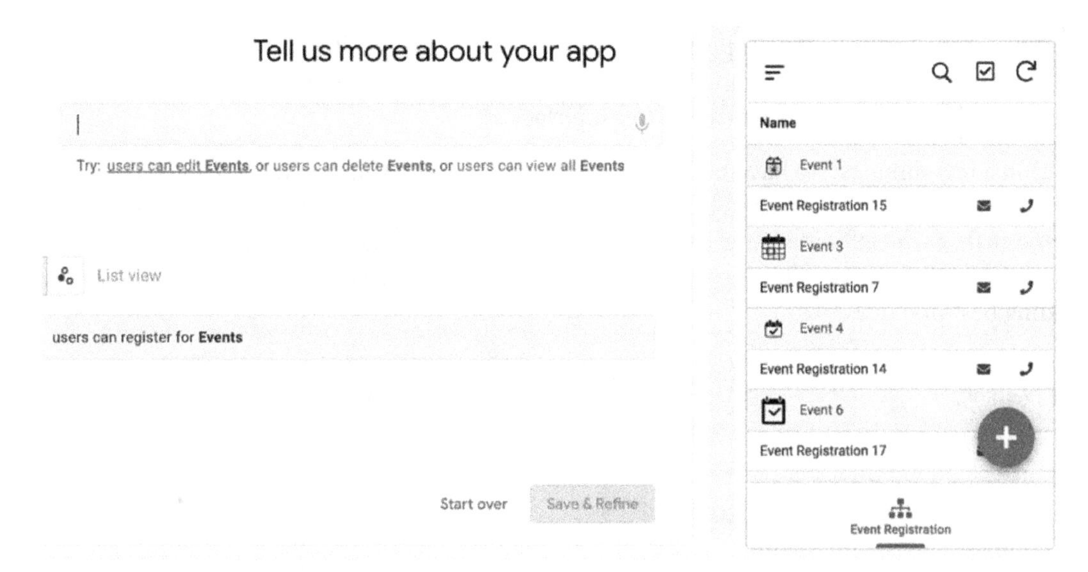


Figure 6.28 – App preview on the right-side panel

The preview can be updated to show the app on a web user interface or on a mobile device. After selecting all user actions, such as **Edit**, **Delete**, **View** events, and **View** charts, click on the **Save & Refine** button to enter the customization view for this app.

This customization view has more options for adjusting the data source, logical behavior, the user view for various roles, security, and so on, as you can see in the following screenshot:

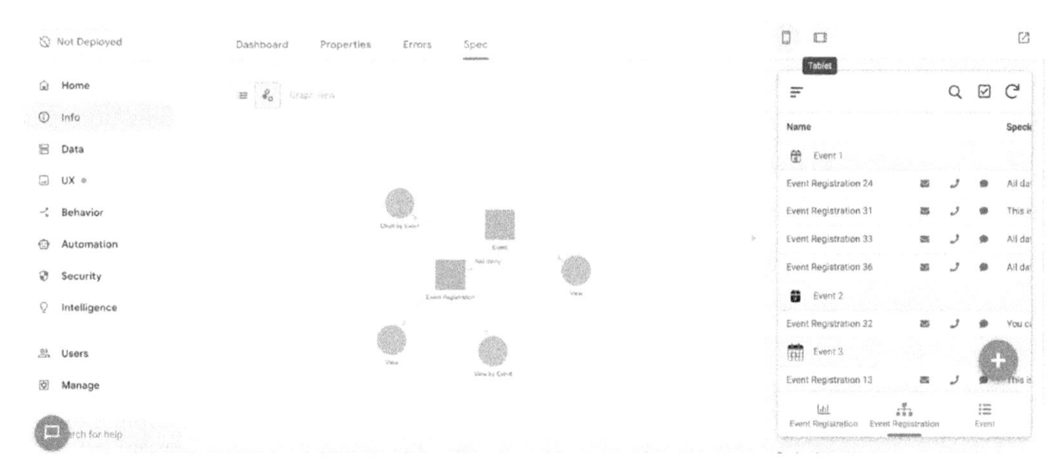


Figure 6.29 – AppSheet UI for app customization

Making each change to the properties on the left-hand side will alter the preview displayed on the right-side panel. Switching to tablet mode on the top of the preview section will display the preview for a tablet-sized user interface.

Within a few minutes, we have built an app and are ready for this app to be deployed for wider use. Now that all changes are complete and ready for deployment, click on **Manage** from the left-side panel and select the **Deploy** tab. This executes a deployment check to verify whether all information required for this app is configured according to coding best practices:

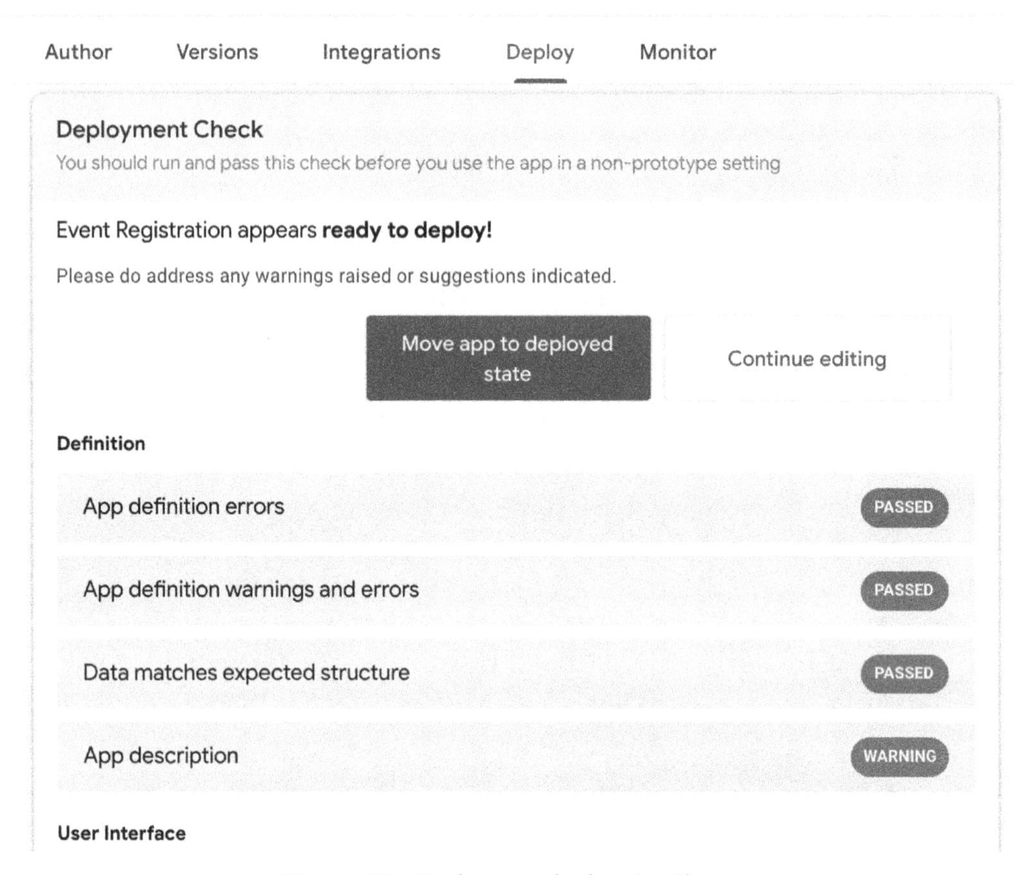


Figure 6.30 – Deployment check in AppSheet

When you run the deployment check feature in AppSheet against your sample application, you will see the feature is highlighting the fact that **App description** is missing in the interface. We can focus on fixing this and other recommended fixes prior to deployment.

Once these are fixed, the app is ready to be moved to a deployed state. This generates an app URL that can be distributed to users for them to start using this app.

As we have seen, it's very simple to put together simple applications that solve everyday, non-complex use cases. Instead of building an application from scratch, there are templates available for use as well. This facility helps administrators build applications on the go in an agile, fast-paced manner to meet immediate requirements emerging for the organization. AppSheet and other low-code platforms will revolutionize how applications are built in the future.

# Summary

In this chapter, we extensively investigated the capabilities provided by the Google Workspace Platform to design and build custom applications using Apps Script and AppSheet. Apps Script has a powerful API and is easy to work with since it is based on well-defined and widely popular JavaScript constructs. Apps Script's tight integration with Workspace services such as Sheets, Docs, and Forms makes it very useful for solving mundane manual tasks. We also touched upon the limitations of Apps Script and the security guardrails that the Workspace platform has put in place. Apps Script is not just limited to integration with Workspace services; it can also be used to build simple standalone web applications that can be hosted on the Google Cloud Platform.

We then moved on to look at AppSheet, which is a low-code platform that Google recently acquired and integrated with this cloud portfolio. AppSheet makes building simple applications even more elegant with its hand-off approach to coding and by putting an app together using its intuitive graphical user interface. We believe that we have set the foundation for Apps Script and AppSheet and encourage readers to go explore and build applications that would make their life simpler.

In the next chapter, we will look at how to move data in and out of Google Workspace using the data migration services at our disposal.

# Part 4: Migrating Data

The objective of this part is to show how organizations are adopting Google Cloud. This part will provide how you can migrate your data from mail servers to the cloud.

This part comprises the following chapter:

- *Chapter 7, Data Migration*

# 7
# Data Migration

In the previous chapters, we have extensively talked about Google Workspace features and some of the unique capabilities that they bring to consumer and enterprise markets for collaboration. And invariably, you may have asked the questions, *"How would I move to Google Workspace?"* and *"How would I move all the data from my environments to Google Workspace to take advantage of all the goodness?"*

If you have been working with cloud-hosted applications for a while, you may have noticed that it is relatively easy to move data to a new platform, rather than extracting data from an old platform. Dubbed "vendor lock-in," it becomes challenging to move data to a different service due to proprietary technology, unique protocols, data formats, and so on. As you navigate through tooling and platform choices, it is very important to keep this in mind.

In this chapter, we will take an extensive look at the data migration capabilities and tools that are at our disposal. Google makes it easier to move data into Google Workspace via a set of data migration tools tailored for specific applications. In most cases, data migration may not necessarily need to be from an external system; it can be between systems on the same platform or just the reclassification of data based on user life cycle changes.

With that context, let's break this chapter down into two sections – one that talks about data transfers within Google Workspace services, and one that talks about data migration from external platforms such as Microsoft 365.

We will be covering the following topics in this chapter:

- Data transfers within Google Workspace
- Transferring user data
- Data migration from external sources
- Migrating a large amount of user data

# Data transfers within Google Workspace

Data movement and reclassification are triggered across multiple services inside Google Worskspace primarily due to user life cycle changes. One of the common use cases that trigger this data migration and movement is terminating a user and the decision that goes with handling the terminated user's data. In this section, we'll look at user life cycle changes and the data transfer decisions that go along with them.

## User life cycle changes

Organizations go through employee churn on a regular basis. When an employee leaves the organization, invariably this question gets asked: *"What do we do with a terminated employee's data?"* As simple as it sounds, if we lay out the possible scenarios, data handling and retention decisions become complicated.

For instance, think of the following scenarios:

- When a user's account is deleted, should all of the user's data be deleted as well?
- What if the user was working on an important project and the files are needed?
- What if not all the data from that user is needed but only data from specific services?
- What if there is a need to resurrect a user account and their data in the future?

Every organization is unique, and there could be more scenarios that arise in addition to those listed. As you can see, data retention and handling policies became complicated and murkier very quickly.

Google Workspace obviously has thought this through and provides capabilities to change the state of a user's account, along with smart data transfer options that let administrators handle data the way they would like.

Here are a few options that are available:

- Delete or remove a user and remove all data.
- Delete or remove a user and transfer all data.
- Delete or remove a user and transfer data only from selected services.
- Suspend a user temporarily with no impact on their data.
- Restore a recently deleted user.
- Keep your organization secure once a user leaves.

We talked about deleting users and transferring data from specific services in *Chapter 2, Configuring Users and Apps*, in the *Cloud Identity* section.

In the following sections, we will discuss suspending a user account and archiving a user.

## Suspending users

When a user is suspended, they cannot access an organization's Google services; however, their data isn't deleted:

- Email and documents (including shared ones) are not deleted.
- Shared documents are accessible by collaborators.

A suspended user can be restored anytime, and things can get back to normal quickly, since there is no data restoration needed.

The following steps show how to suspend a user:

1. Log in to the Google **Admin** console.
2. Select the **Users** tab on the left.
3. From the list of users, hover over the user that needs to be suspended.
4. Click on **More**, followed by **Suspend user**.

5. To confirm, click **SUSPEND**.

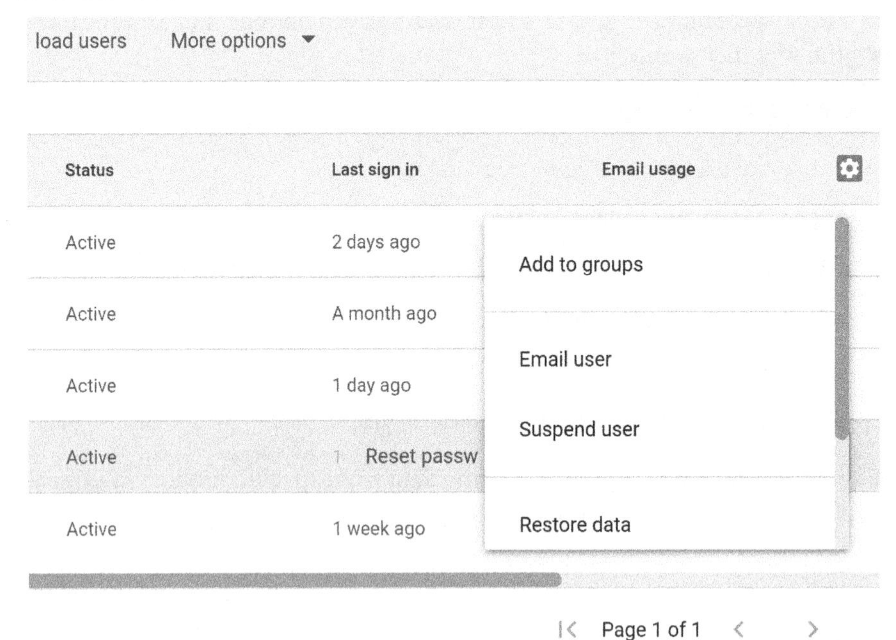


Figure 7.1 – The Suspend user option in the Google Admin console

When you suspend the user, Google Workspace explicitly states what happens to the data, license, and access to the suspended users.

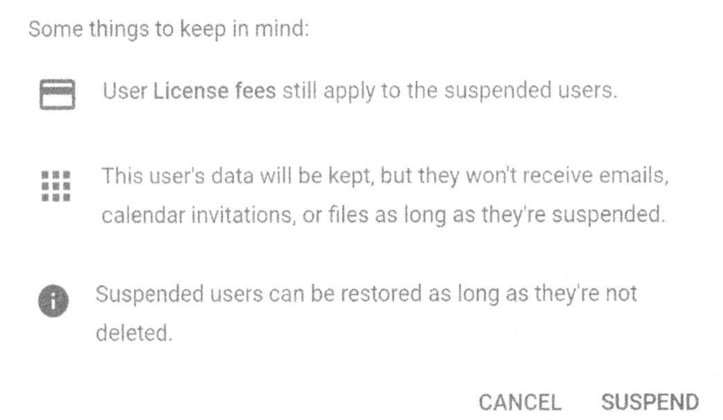


Figure 7.2 – Considerations when suspending a user

Users can also be suspended in bulk, using the CSV bulk upload feature, as discussed in *Chapter 2, Configuring Users and Apps*, in the *Adding users to Cloud Identity* section. Here, to suspend users, you need to mark the **New Status** column in the CSV file to **Suspended**.

## Archiving users

Although suspending a user account works well in preserving data, doing this consumes a user license. Paying for a full license when the user is not active might be prohibitive in some organizations.

If there is a need for retaining data, Google provides a license edition called **Archived User** (**AU**). When this license is assigned to a user, the data is retained in Google Vault while still keeping the user in a suspended state and hiding the user from the global address list.

Assigning an AU license will automatically free up the previously assigned Google Workspace license, thereby making it available for reassignment to a new employee.

The following steps indicate how to archive a user:

1. Log in to the Google **Admin** console.
2. Select **Users** from the left navigation bar.
3. Once the user list shows up, hover over the user you would like to archive and select **More** | **Archive user**:

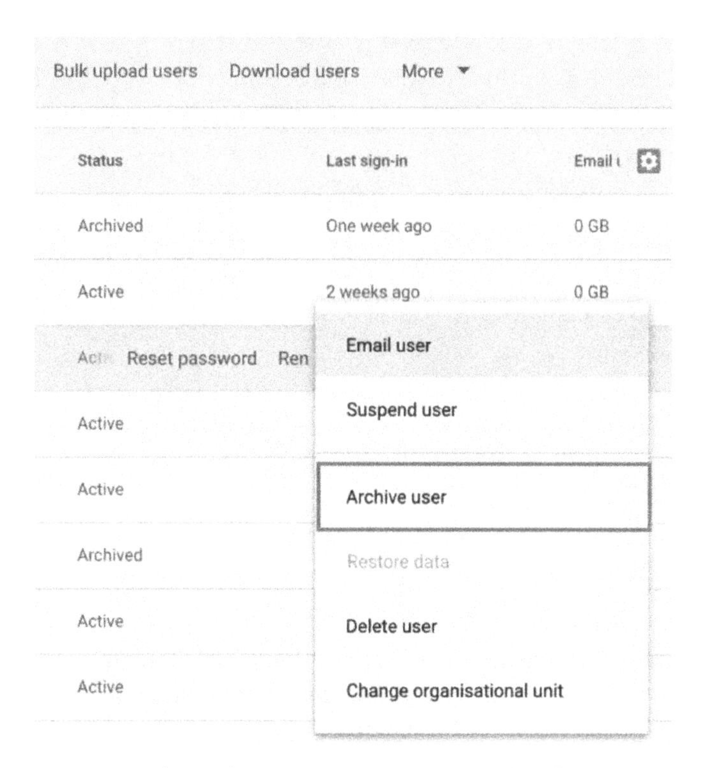


Figure 7.3 – The Archive user option in the Google Admin console

4. Select **ARCHIVE** to confirm.

This will automatically suspend and mark the user as **Archived**.

When the **Archive user** option is selected, Google Workspace shows the data, licensing, and access impacts for the user.

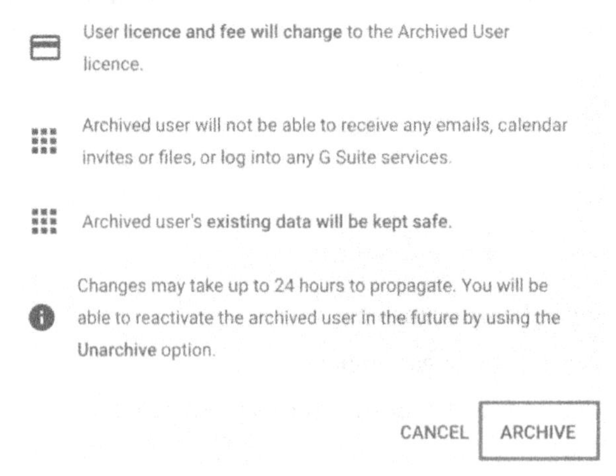


Figure 7.4 – Considerations when archiving a user

The archived user's data will continue to follow data region policies defined for the user's OU in the Google **Admin** console. This is important for organizations that need to follow certain mandated policies.

If the domain has certain **Data Loss Prevention** (**DLP**) rules defined for the OU, those rules will stay applicable and active against the archived user's data as well. There will not be any risk of accidentally sharing data with external collaborators.

> **The AU License**
> It must be noted that the AU license is available for the Enterprise Plus, Enterprise Standard, and Business Plus editions. It is not available in other editions.

An archived user cannot sign in to their Google account and cannot access any Google Workspace services. When a user is unarchived, they immediately regain access to all their previous data.

So far, we have talked about retaining a user's data even after their state is changed, such as suspension and archiving. In the next section, let's talk about how to transfer data from one user to another as part of user state changes.

# Transferring user data

In this section, we will look at options to transfer data from one user to another any time and also during user deletion. We will also have a peek at one of the lesser-known services – **Google Takeout**. We will be covering Google Takeout from both an administrator and a user's perspective.

First, we will look at transferring ownership of Google Drive contents between users.

## Transferring Google Drive content

Contents in Google Drive from a user can be transferred anytime, not necessarily only during the deletion of users. We will swiftly explore those two scenarios in the next two subsections.

### Transferring data any time

Administrators can transfer ownership of a user's file stored in Google Drive, including files in shared drives. The only caveat is that the target user must have enough storage to receive all the files from the user.

The following steps will transfer files in Google Drive:

1. Log in to the Google **Admin** console.
2. Click on **Apps** in the left-hand side menu, followed by **Google Workspace**.
3. Select **Drive and Docs**.
4. Click **Transfer ownership**:

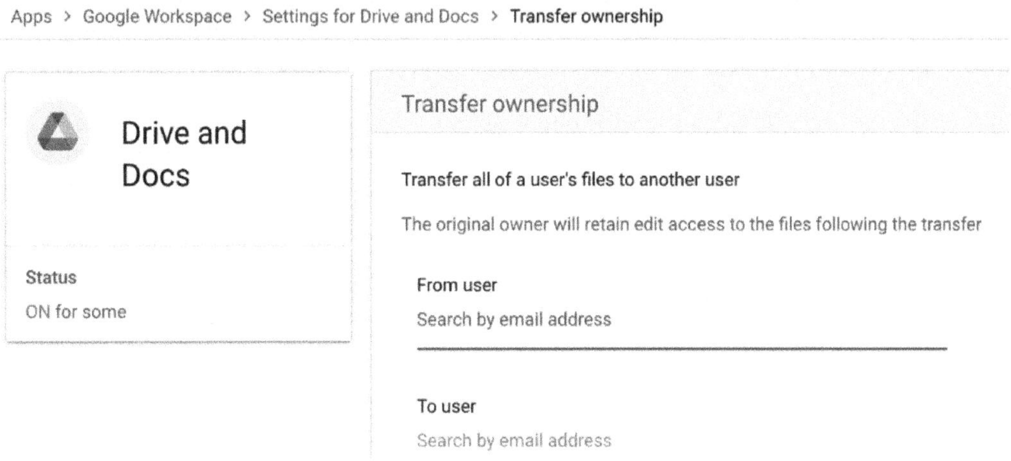

Apps > Google Workspace > Settings for Drive and Docs > Transfer ownership

Drive and Docs

Status

ON for some

Transfer ownership

Transfer all of a user's files to another user

The original owner will retain edit access to the files following the transfer

From user

Search by email address

To user

Search by email address

Figure 7.5 – Transfering ownership of Google Drive content

Transferring ownership of files in Google Drive will result in a new folder, with the source user's email address as the name of the folder. Within the folder, all transferred files will be placed for easy retrieval and better organization of content.

If the domain is using one of the Google Workspace Business editions that come with data allocation per user, then the administrator will have to be careful to not exceed the user's storage capacity.

> **A Better Alternative**
> Google Workspace recommends that moving all files of a user to a shared drive is a better alternative to transferring the ownership to an individual. Contents in a shared drive can still be accessed even when the user leaves the organization and their account gets deleted.

## Transferring data during the deletion of users

This is an option that we are familiar with and has been discussed in the *User deletion* section of *Chapter 2, Configuring Users and Apps.*

In that section, we reviewed the options available for retaining and managing data for business continuity with other employees when someone leaves the organization.

Continuing on the topic of data transfer from Google Workspace services, let's review a lesser-known data export option – Google Takeout.

# Google Takeout

Google Takeout allows administrators and users to download or transfer a copy of the data they store in a variety of industry-standard data formats. Google Takeout is also called a **download your data** service in certain geographic regions.

The Google Takeout service is an important outcome of the effort by Google's **Data Liberation Front** initiative. This initiative allows for better transparency of how users' data is being stored and used across different services, thus marching against proprietary vendor lock-in issues.

More details on the Data Liberation Front initiative can be found here: `https://en.wikipedia.org/wiki/Google_Data_Liberation_Front`.

## Using Google Takeout as an administrator

Administrators have the capability to download all of a user's data to a Google Cloud archive using the Google Takeout service. The following screenshot shows the requirements for using the service as an administrator:

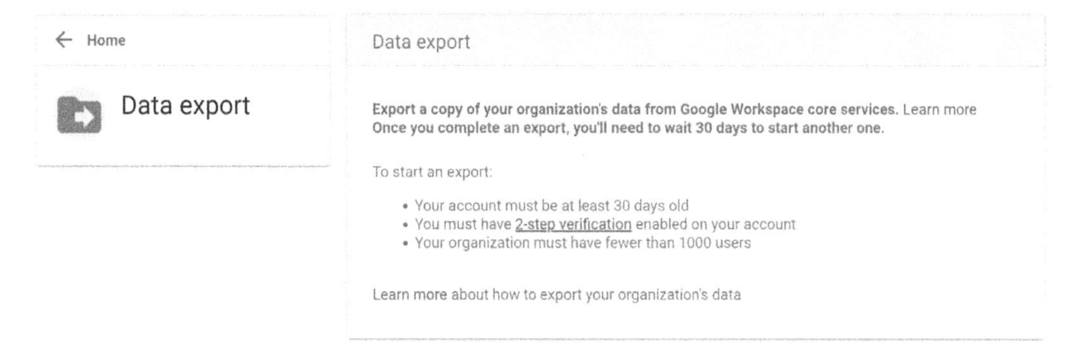


Figure 7.6 – The prerequisites for the Google Takeout service for administrators

Once the prerequisites are met, administrators can run data export to download all of the user's data, including any administrative data that is on these accounts. Takeout produces a comprehensive data export summary report once the export job has successfully finished running. The service also offers several ways to retry failed exports.

If users need to download their data, then administrators have to enable the Takeout service for them. This status can be verified by visiting **Apps** | **Additional Google Services** | **Settings for Google Takeout** in the Google **Admin** console:

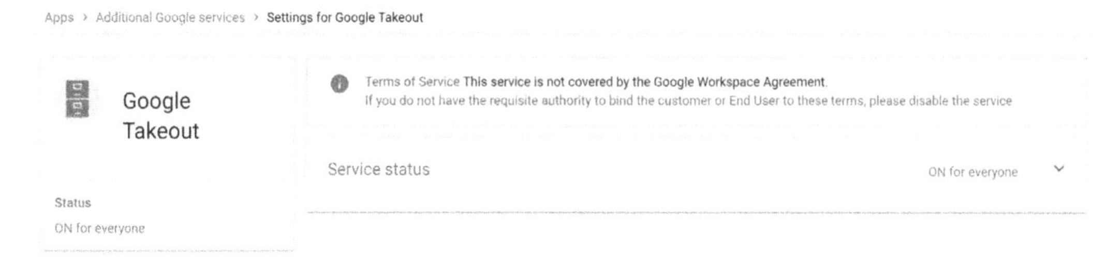


Figure 7.7 – The Google Takeout service enablement for users

Data export for users from individual Google services can be toggled on or off, as shown in the following screenshot:

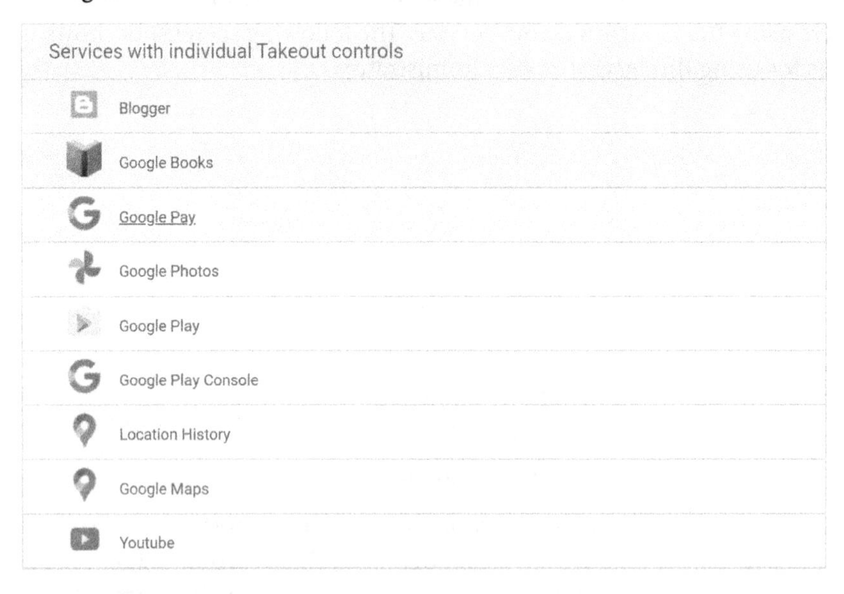


Figure 7.8 – Google services that support Takeout

The services that are available as part of Google Takeout will differ, based on Workspace licensing editions.

Among the list of services available for Google Takeout, administrators can pick and choose services to allow users to export their data.

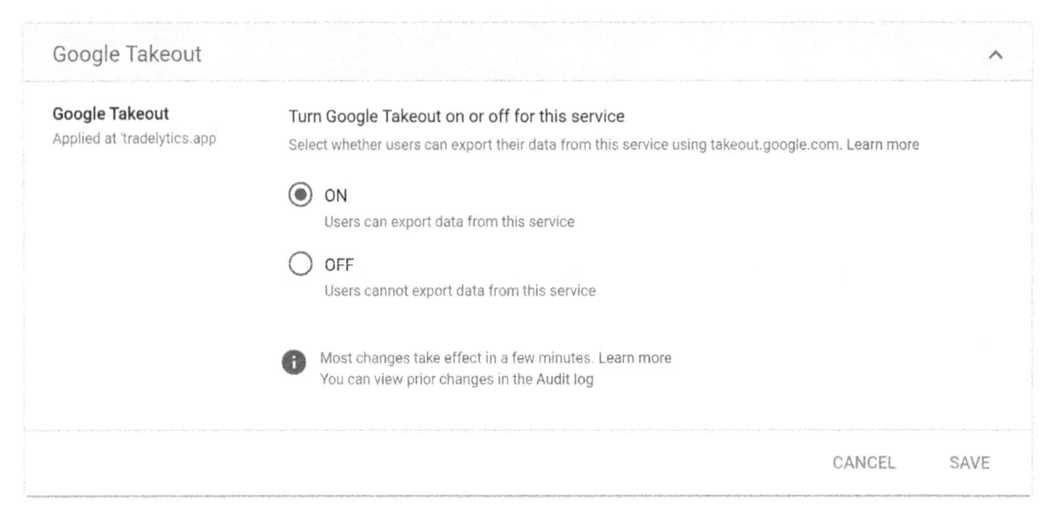


Figure 7.9 – Google Takeout enablement for specific services

Now that Google Takeout is configured for use by administrators, let's review the user side of this service.

## Using Google Takeout as a user

Users have the ability to pick and choose data to export from approximately 50 different Google services. They also have the option to select the data format that allows them to import this data to another service.

Users have to go to `takeout.google.com` and sign in using their Google Workspace account to see the options. The following screenshot shows the list of services available to a user:

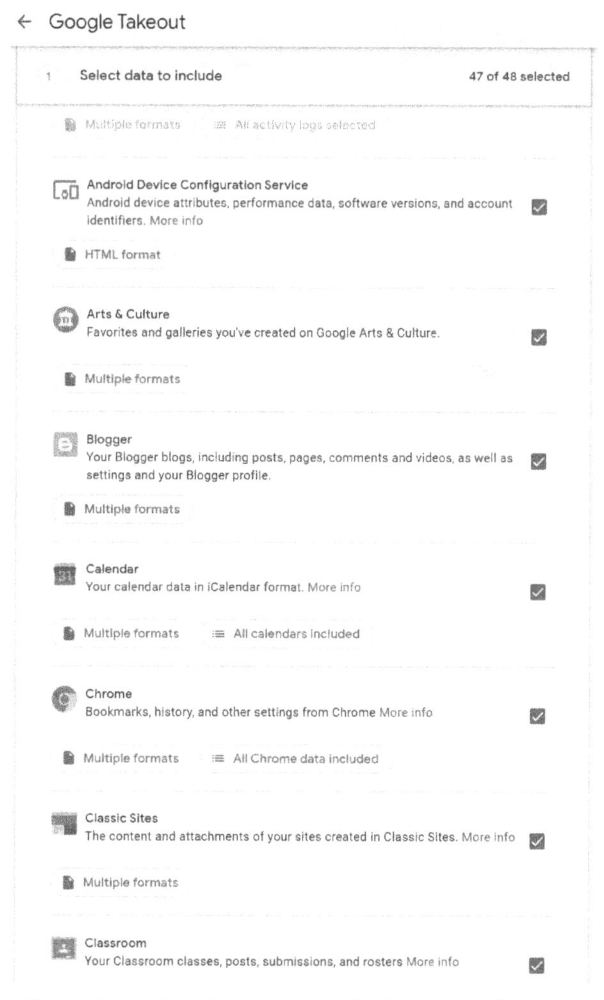


Figure 7.10 – Google services available as part of Takeout

Once the services are selected, **Delivery method** and **Frequency** can be selected:

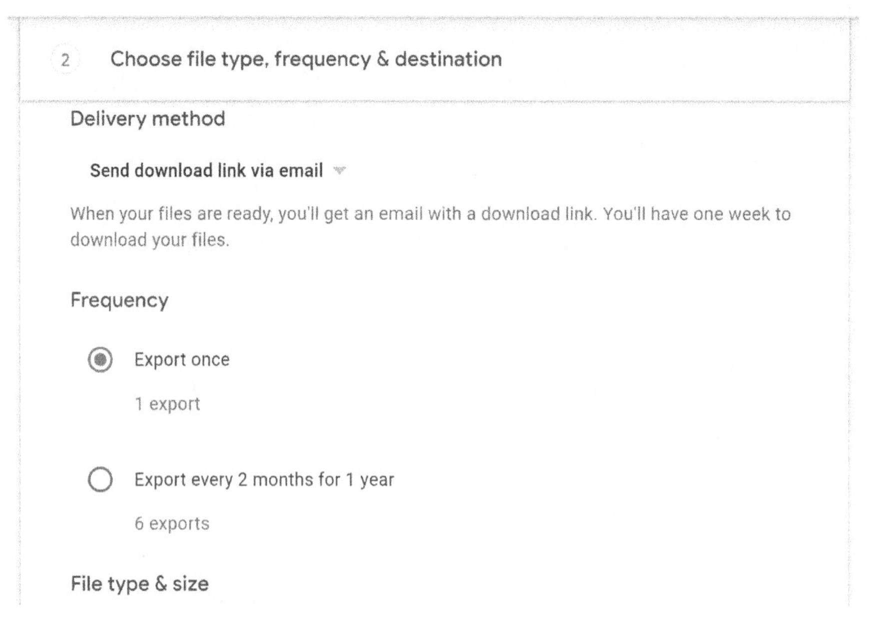


Figure 7.11 – Google Takeout Delivery and Frequency configurations

Once happy with the options selected, users can then hit the **Create** button to generate a downloadable version of their data. Once the **Create** button is clicked, the following screen will appear:

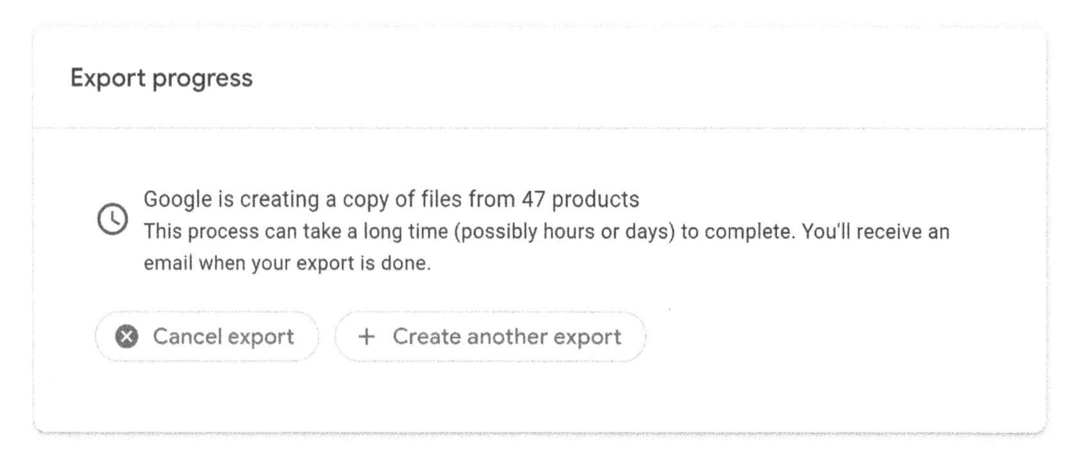


Figure 7.12 – The Google Takeout progress screen

Once the export is successful, Google Takeout shows a summary page with a link to download the data:

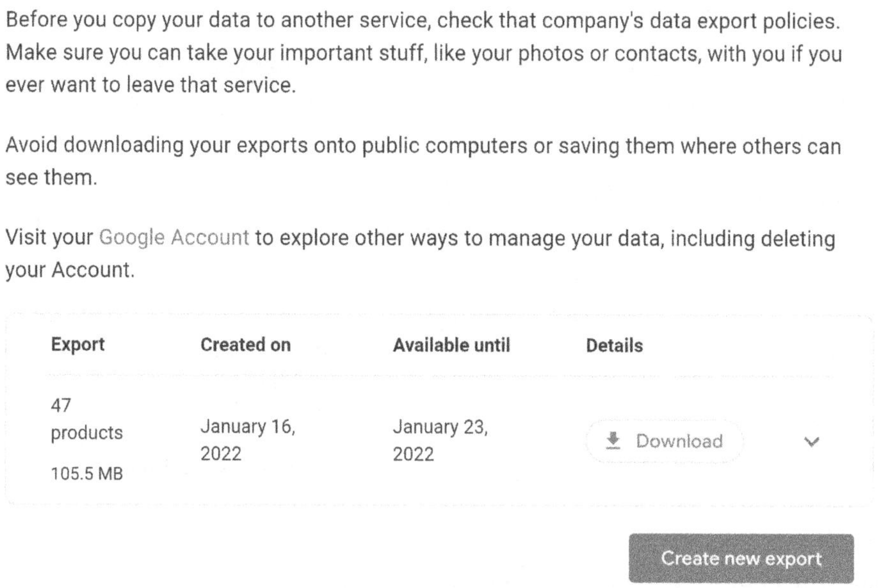

Before you copy your data to another service, check that company's data export policies. Make sure you can take your important stuff, like your photos or contacts, with you if you ever want to leave that service.

Avoid downloading your exports onto public computers or saving them where others can see them.

Visit your Google Account to explore other ways to manage your data, including deleting your Account.

| Export | Created on | Available until | Details |
|---|---|---|---|
| 47 products 105.5 MB | January 16, 2022 | January 23, 2022 | Download |

Create new export

Figure 7.13 – A Google Takeout report

If data could not be exported, this summary page will also show the errors and an option to retry.

**Important Note**

It must be noted that using the Google Takeout service to download data for users will not delete any data from Google servers.

This wraps up our discussion on tools and services that are available to either transfer or export data within Google Workspace. As you may have noted, we did not discuss migrating or transferring data from Gmail, and Google Calendar and Google Contacts data, as we need to learn about external data migration tools first.

Let's move on to focus on tools that are available when we want to interact with non-Google services.

## Data migration from external sources

In this section, we will look at the tools that are accessible to us to be able to successfully migrate data from a source external to Google Workspace.

As you can imagine, moving data from one platform to another will require detailed planning prior to, during, and after migration. A typical data migration would involve the following steps:

1. **Know the data**: You should know what type of data is going to be migrated, understand formats, limitations, quality of data, data governance, and a need for cleanup.
2. **Plan for migration**: What strategies are going to be adopted for data migration that a business would allow for? The key thing is to tailor the data migration strategy based on business needs, what the tolerance level is for customer impact and downtime, and so on.
3. **Flip the switch**: Once a plan is in place, migration can happen. During this phase, we will need to define what the source of truth is for data, as it may exist in multiple systems.
4. **Audit the migration**: Once the migration is complete, it is important to ascertain that all planned data has been migrated over and all systems are working as expected. If all goes well, it is time to disengage with the old system.
5. **Train the users**: Train users on the new platform so that they feel comfortable and the change goes well.

Google Workspace has a few services that can help us with data and user migration from other platforms. Proper migration planning will have to accompany these tools in order for the migration to be successful. Migration planners will also need to be mindful of the historical data they want to bring into the new Google Workspace environment.

*"How much data from the previous platform is required in Google Workspace? Is it 6 months' worth of data, 1 year, or 5 years?"* These are the important questions to ask, as this will dictate the migration strategy. There are a few migration tools that are available at our disposal, and the choice also depends on the number of users and the amount of data in the migration.

For fewer than 100 users, Google's **Data Migration Service** (**DMS**) works best. If your migration involves migrating data for more than 100 users, the following tools may come in handy:

- **Google Workspace Migration for Microsoft Exchange** (**GWMME**): This tool allows for data to be transferred from Microsoft Exchange, Novell, and other standard **Internet Message Access Protocol** (**IMAP**)-compliant servers.
- **Google Workspace Migration for Microsoft Outlook** (**GWMMO**): Using this tool, administrators can let users migrate their own mail and calendar events to Google Workspace. This tool works best when there are fewer than 20 users. We will not focus on this tool in this book. Administrators can get more details on GWMMO at the following link: `https://support.google.com/a/answer/176213?hl=en`.
- **Google Workspace Migrate** (**Beta**): This is a new and shiny service from Google, which is still in the beta phase. We will talk about this service briefly as we wrap up this section.

Let's first start talking about the DMS.

## Data migration service

The DMS tool is a service included in Google Workspace that easily imports data from various sources into Google Workspace. The data is copied over from source user account(s) to destination user account(s) with the flexibility of the source account continuing to have access to the data.

The DMS supports the following data sources:

- Gmail
- Office 365
- IMAP servers
- Microsoft Exchange Server 2006, 2010, and so on
- Only email supported for Microsoft Exchange Server 2003 or older

The DMS establishes connections to the source server to make copies of data to Google Workspace. The speed of the migration can be adjusted, based on the number of users being migrated.

Migrations can be paused and resumed if needed, and it shows the migration progress for easier tracking and monitoring. For example, if 10 users are being migrated, then the speed indicates the number of parallel requests being sent to the source server. Typically, the number of parallel connections established will be roughly equal to half the number of users. In order to avoid network saturation, this tool sacrifices scale for speed and, hence, is limited to fewer than 100 users.

In the upcoming sections, we will review some sample use cases of migrating data from different data sources, such as consumer Gmail accounts and Exchange, using the DMS tool.

## Transferring from personal Gmail and calendars to Google Workspace using the DMS

Users who own a personal email inbox through Google's consumer Gmail will have a lot of email and calendar data they have accrued over a period of time. In certain scenarios, when users have started using consumer Gmail, which has the `<@gmail.com>` domain, there could be a need to migrate the data for those users from Gmail inbox to Google Workspace.

A simple way to migrate is by using a mail client that uses the IMAP protocol to pull all emails locally, setting up a Google Workspace inbox in the same IMAP client, and then moving all emails from the personal account to the Workspace one.

At a high level, this is a three-step process:

1. Set up Gmail auto-forwarding for future incoming emails.
2. Migrate existing email data from the source inbox to the destination inbox.
3. Migrate calendar data from the source user account to the destination user account.

We will go through each of these steps in detail in the following subsections.

### Setting up Gmail auto-forwarding

Once you have decided to move to Google Workspace, all future emails to the personal Gmail account can be forwarded to the new Workspace email so that emails are not missed. This is done by setting up automatic forwarding of emails from the `@gmail.com` account to the destination Google Workspace inbox.

The following steps accomplish setting up Gmail auto-forwarding:

1. Navigate to the personal Gmail account.
2. Click on **Settings**.
3. Select **See All Settings**.
4. Click on the **Forwarding and POP/IMAP** tab.
5. Add the Google Workspace email address as **Forwarding Address**.
6. Click **OK** to save this change:

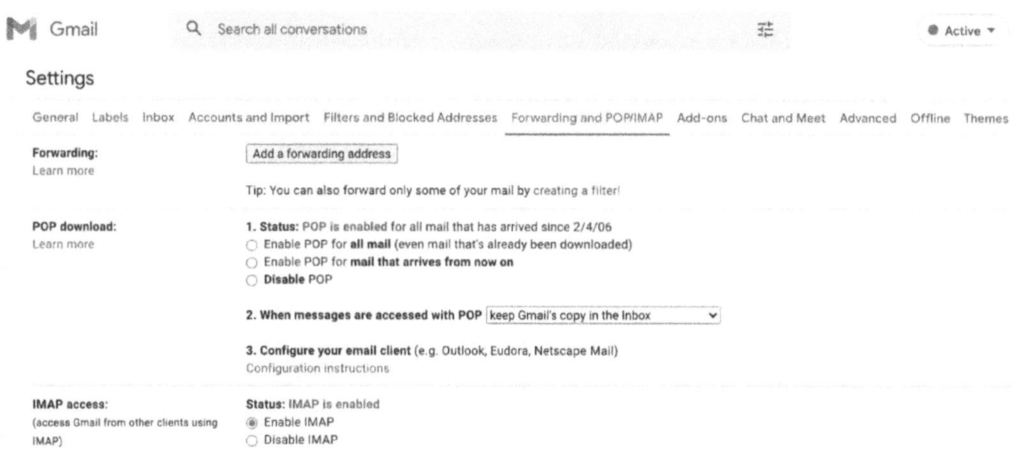


Figure 7.14 – The Gmail settings for email forwarding

This sends a verification email to the destination Google Workspace inbox. Once the verification is completed, all incoming emails to the `@gmail.com` inbox will be automatically forwarded to the Google Workspace inbox as well, along with a copy being retained in the personal Gmail account.

This step is important in order to maintain email sanity. All future emails will now be available in both inboxes. Now that the first step is complete, let's look at how to migrate existing emails from a personal inbox into Google Workspace using DMS.

## Importing Gmail data using DMS

With the need to migrate existing personal emails in Gmail to Workspace, let's put DMS to good use. The following steps detail how to get DMS to import data:

1. Log in to the Google **Admin** console.
2. From the home page, select **Data Migration service**. If it doesn't show up automatically, click on **Show more**. Once you do this, the following screen will appear:

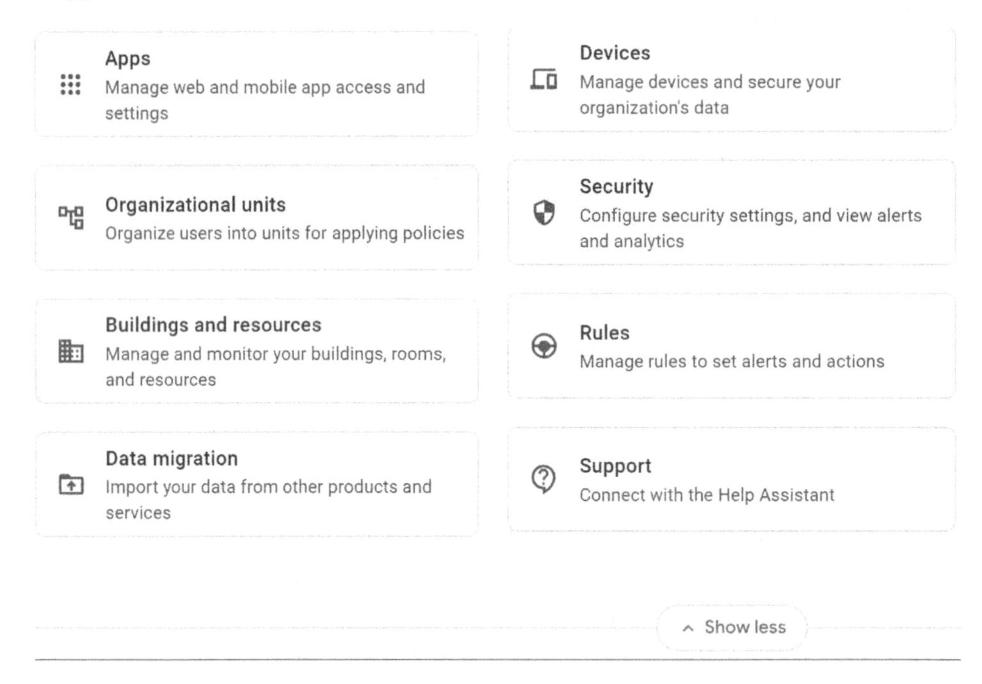


Figure 7.15 – DMS on the Google Workspace home page

3. Select **Data Migration** to start the migration setup process. Once selected, the following screen will pop up:

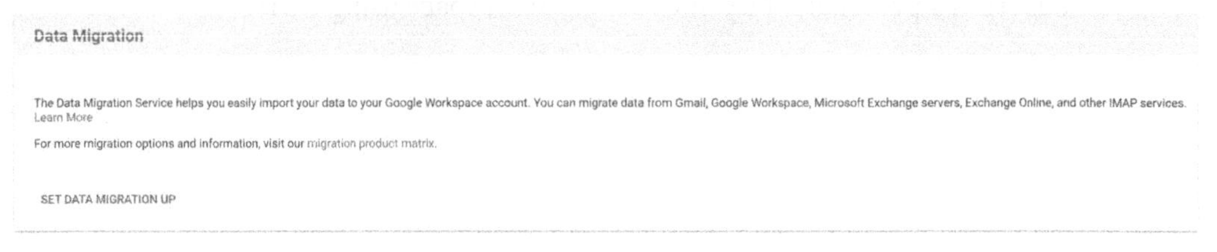


Figure 7.16 – DMS prerequisites

4. Click on **SET DATA MIGRATION UP**. This shows a selection page listing all the sources that the DMS can connect to.
5. Select **Gmail** from the list of sources:

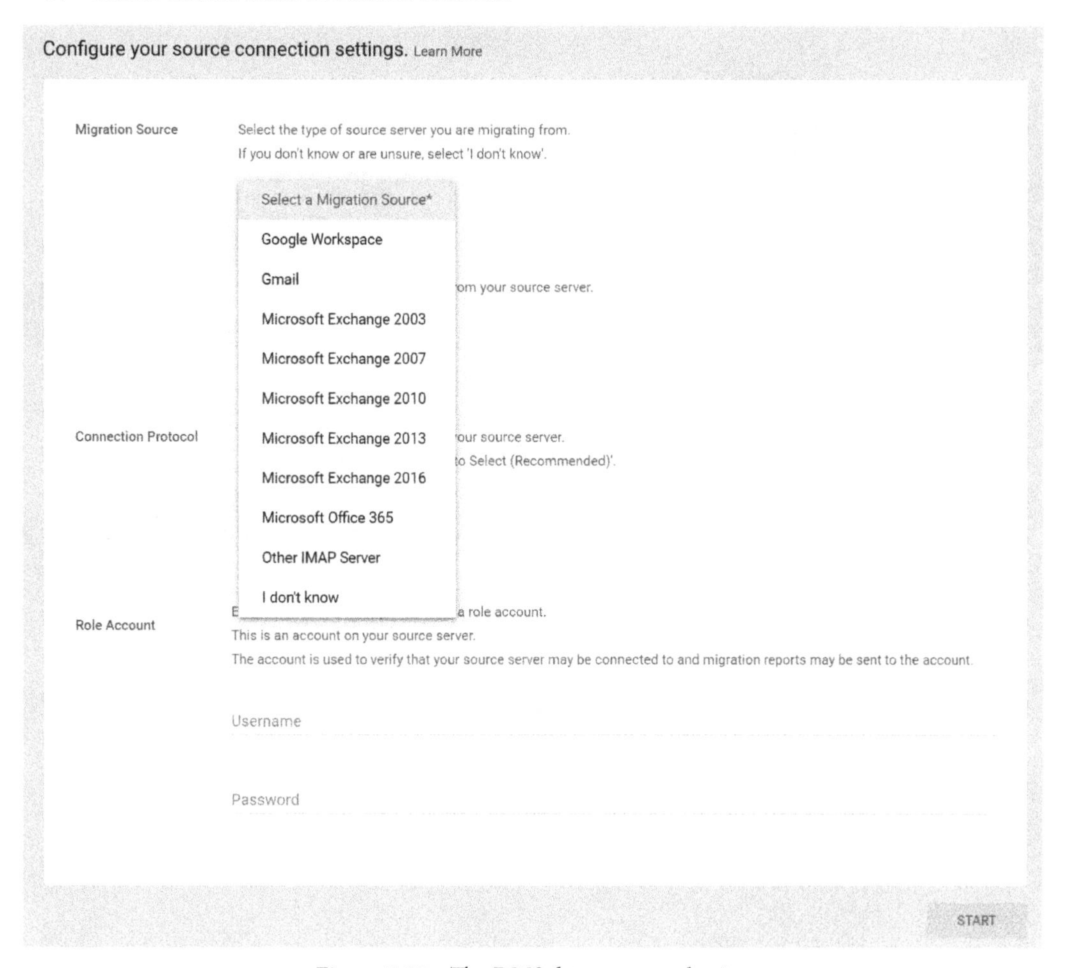


Figure 7.17 – The DMS data source selection

6. Clicking on the **START** button displays additional migration settings:

× Configure Data Migration Service

Source Connection Settings   2 Additional Migration Settings

Configure additional settings and add users.

Connection successful! You are almost finished.
In the next step you can select users* and migrate their data.

Migration Start Date   Select the start date for your migration. Your email will be migrated from that date to the most recent, starting with the most recent first.

Past 1 year

Migration Options   Choose migration options

- [ ] Migrate deleted mail.
- [ ] Migrate junk mail.
- [ ] Exclude the following folders from the migration (comma separated list)

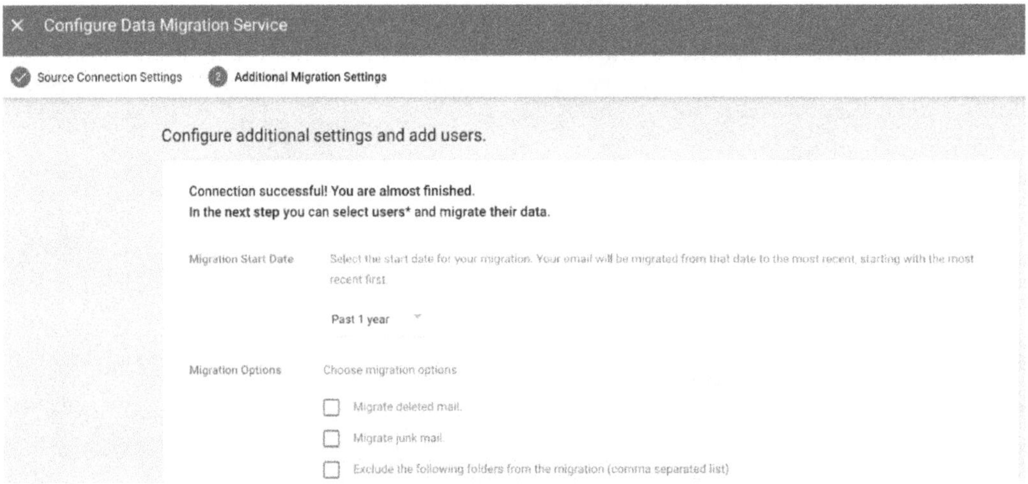

Figure 7.18 – Additional configurations for the DMS

These settings help in deciding the volume of content being migrated from the source to Google Workspace. The decisions made here are uniformly applied to all users who are being migrated from the source.

For example, do we want to import 1 year's worth of email from the source? Can we limit this duration to just 3 months?

Similarly, do we want to migrate junk mail or the messages that were previously deleted but waiting in the **Trash** folder?

7. Once these selections are made, click on the **SELECT USERS** button:

Migration Options   Choose migration options

- [ ] Migrate deleted mail.
- [ ] Migrate junk mail.
- [x] Exclude the following folders from the migration (comma separated list)

example,example2

Junk, unimportant

*By clicking the 'Select users' button, you authorize Google's Data Migration Service to fetch information from your server and upload it to your Google Workspace accounts. [If you go to Domain-wide Delegation during the migration, you'll see Google's Data Migration client in the authorized clients list for accessing pertinent information.]

BACK   SELECT USERS

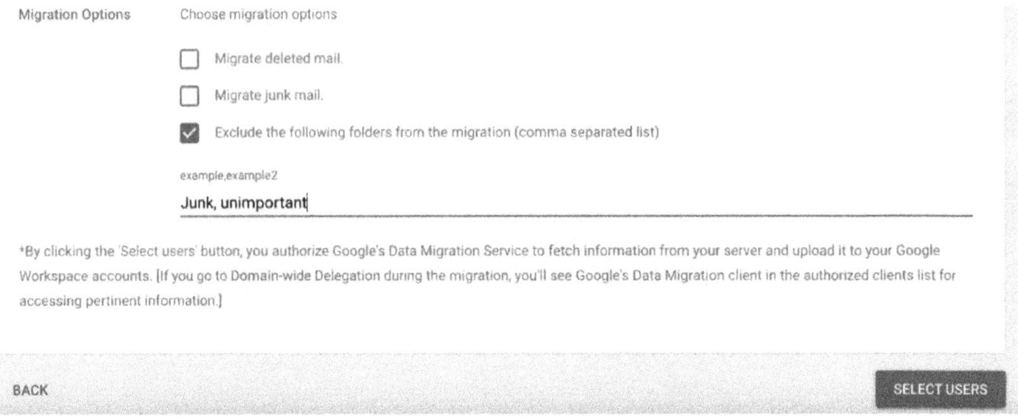

Figure 7.19 – More configuration options for the DMS

This will display a new screen where users can be added:

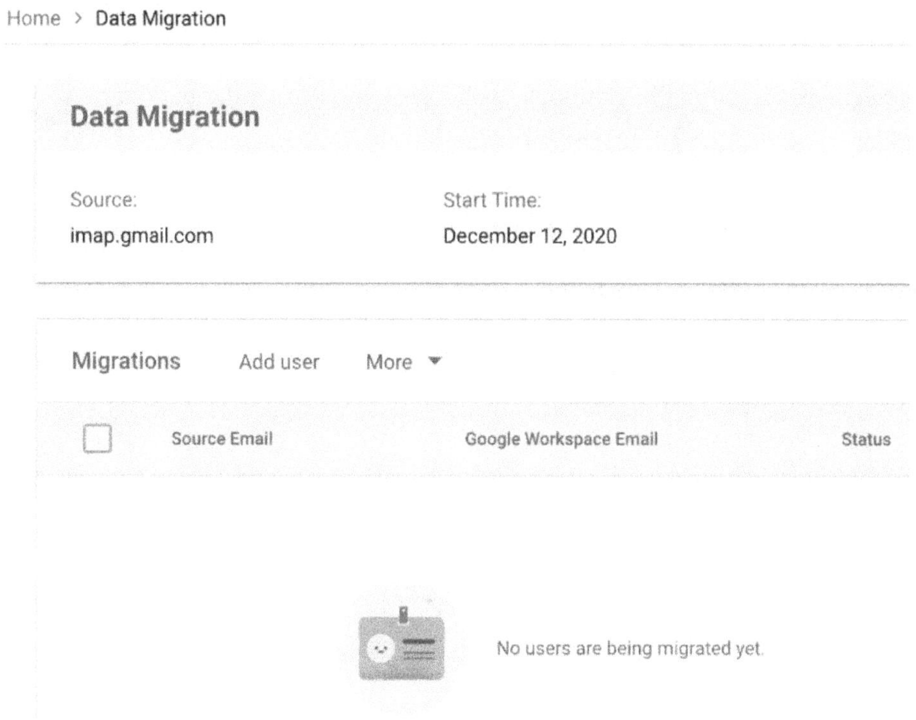

Figure 7.20 – User configuration options for the DMS

8. Click on **Add User** to add the Gmail user account you wish to migrate from.

   This will show an authorization page where user credentials of the source account will be entered. Google will display a consent page to receive authorization from the user for executing this migration.

   An authorization code will be sent to this address, which will need to be entered before the DMS can start its work.

This finishes the configuration, and the DMS will begin to copy all the data over to the destination account. At any point during the migration, administrators can track the progress, pause the migration, and resume the migration anytime.

Now that we have successfully learned how to migrate email data with DMS, let's focus on migrating calendar data to Google Workspace.

## Importing calendar data

Similar to emails, users can also import their calendar events from different sources to Google Workspace via the DMS.

For our calendar migration illustration, let's choose to move calendar data from Microsoft Exchange user accounts, since we already know how to work with personal Gmail accounts.

The steps for invoking the DMS are very similar to those in our email migration example. When the time comes to choose the source, we'll choose the right Exchange version from the list of sources and the right data type:

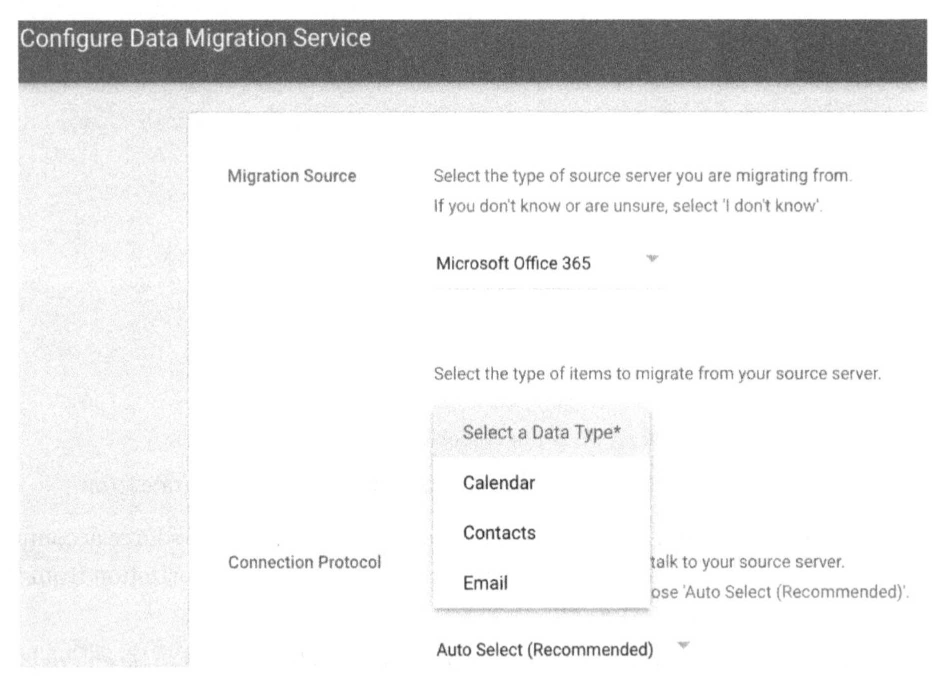


Figure 7.21 – Calendar data import configuration options for the DMS

Clicking on the **START** button displays additional migration settings.

Once the configuration for the source server is decided, we can move on to adding users. Similar to the process of migrating email content, the source user account is specified to receive an authorization code that needs to be keyed in. The destination user account will be the Google Workspace user account.

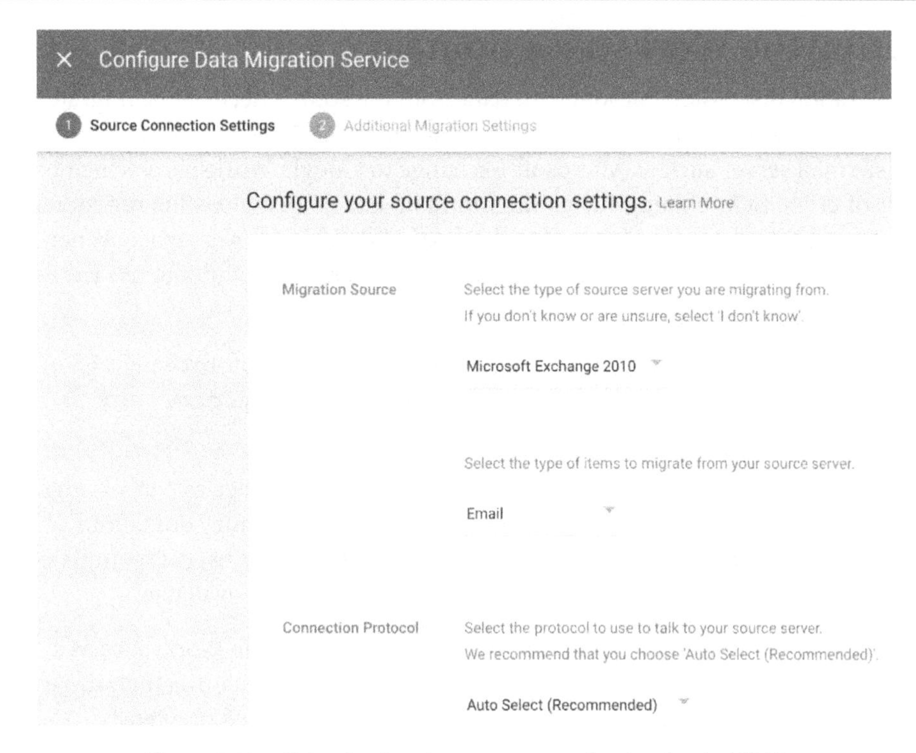


Figure 7.22 – Calendar data import source selection for the DMS

Once the migration is completed, a detailed migration report is emailed out. Similar to Gmail migration, this calendar migration can be paused and resumed if needed.

There is an option to bulk-upload a list of users through a CSV file that will be used for migrating the data.

The DMS is a nifty service that can come in handy when a small amount of a user's data needs to be migrated. For large user data, there are other tools available, which we will visit next.

# Migrating a large amount of user data

In the previous sections, we talked about data transfers between users in the same organization and the use of the DMS for small-scale transfers. However, when we are planning migration for a large number of users, the considerations differ. There is proper planning required in order for the migration to be successful. As indicated before, the Workspace migration tools that are available to us are just one part of the equation.

Any large-scale migration efforts in Workspace start by preparing your Workspace domain for the effort.

## Preparing the Workspace domain

For our migration discussion, although all data from the source needs to be migrated, for now, let's consider a big transfer of email, calendar, and contacts data from an existing on-premises mail server such as Microsoft Exchange to Google Workspace, which has thousands of users. Before doing such a migration of data from an existing functional mail infrastructure, it is important to set up the destination domain in Workspace. When one domain is active, the DNS servers do not allow another service provider to use the same domain name.

For example, if `myCompany.com` is my domain setup on Microsoft Exchange, all of the employees' emails would be annotated as `user1@mycompany.com`, `user2@mycompany.com`, and so on.

The same `mycompany.com` cannot be used with Google Workspace as part of migration, since it has already been claimed. This requires setting up a temporary domain in Workspace to carry out the migration. After the data migration for users is completed, delete the Microsoft Exchange instance, making the domain name available.

This `mycompany.com` domain name can then be added to Google Workspace as a secondary domain, and we can further upgrade the secondary domain as the primary domain, thereby swapping out the temporary domain name we used previously.

On a high level, this domain swapping from the source to the destination infrastructure is handled in a sequential manner. Irrespective of which migration tool is being used, the domain configuration process remains the same. The domain-switching dance will have to be performed to appease the migration gods.

Now that we have prepared the domain for the upcoming migration, let's look at a couple of large-scale migration methodologies.

# Google Workspace Migration for Microsoft Exchange

**Google Workspace Migration for Microsoft Exchange** (**GWMME**) allows for data formatted in the **Personal Storage Table** (**PST**) file format to be imported into Google Workspace. This tool also supports data being imported into inactive user accounts for legal data retention within Google Vault.

Let's review the migration prerequisites and the migration process with this tool.

## Prerequisites for GWMME

The following are the prerequisites for GWMME:

- Create a Google service account that can be used to authorize into the Google Workspace account for this migration. The service account can be created in a programmatic manner using Cloud Shell or manually through Google Cloud Console in **Google Cloud Platform** (**GCP**).

> **Cloud Shell**
>
> Cloud Shell is an interactive shell environment that runs from a web browser and makes it easy to interact and manage cloud resources within GCP.

- Grant domain-wide delegation rights to elevate the permissions granted for this service account. To grant these rights, follow these steps:

  I. Log in to the Google **Admin** console and select **Security**, followed by **Access and data control** in the left-hand panel.

  II. Select **API controls** and click on **MANAGE DOMAIN WIDE DELEGATION**:

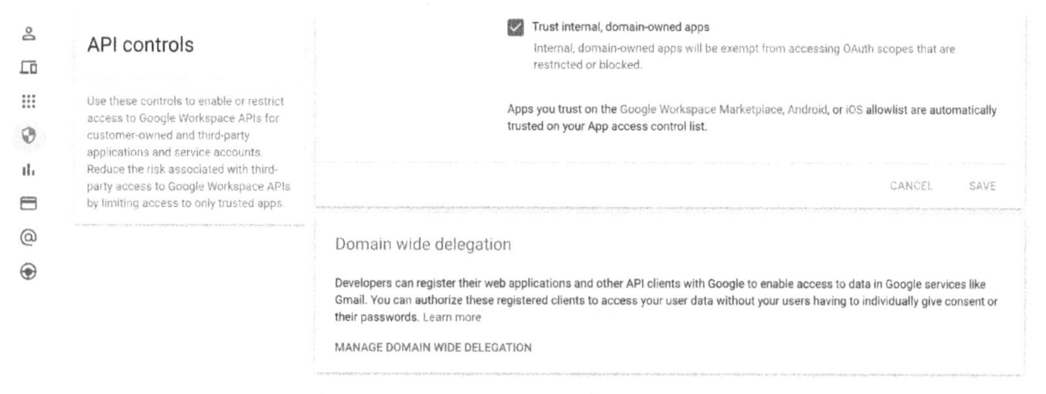


Figure 7.23 – Prerequisites for GWMME

  III. Add the service account user to this configuration.

- Source mail servers supported by GWMME are as follows:
  - Office 365
  - Exchange Server 2000, 2003, 2007, 2010, 2013, and 2016
  - Any **Request for Comments** (**RFC**)-compliant IMAP server such as Zimbra or Sunmail

- GWMME uses an administrative user account on the source mail server that has privileges to read content from each user's mailbox.
- It is a best practice to install GWMME in a separate client machine. The client machine is expected to have Windows versions 2008 or above and Outlook versions 2003 or above.

Once the required access accounts are configured and prerequisites are met, the tool can be installed from `https://tools.google.com/dlpage/gsmme`. With prerequisites sorted, let's dive into the actual migration procedures.

## Organizing and migrating data

With prerequisites taken care of and the tool downloaded, let's look at how to perform a migration with GWMME.

Several PST files that are planned for migration will need to be organized in the local client machine before the migration can begin. This ensures that user mapping from the source to the destination is accurate. It is a best practice to set up each user as a new folder and place the PST file within each folder for the sequential processing of data from those local folders to the respective user account in Google Workspace.

Set up a CSV file that maps the source users to the destination user's email address. For example, it could use different email naming conventions:

| **Source email** | **Destination email in Workspace** |
|---|---|
| `user1_lastname@mycompany.com` | `u1Lastname@myCompany.com` |
| `user2_formalname@mycompany.com` | `u2FormalName@myCompany.com` |

Now that the mapping file and data sources are organized, it's showtime! The following steps will walk us through the migration:

1. Open the downloaded GWMME tool and install the application on a Windows computer.
2. On a Windows computer, click on **Start** | **Google Workspace Migration** | **Google Workspace migration for Microsoft Exchange**.
3. Select the source PST file's root folder.
4. Click **Next** and enter the destination domain information. This is where the service account information is to be used.
5. Select the type of data to be migrated: **Email**, **Calendar**, or **Contacts**.
6. Use the prepared CSV file as the definitive mapping guide for the user migration.

Review the defined migration settings and click on **Start** to begin the migration. The following screenshot shows the start up screen for GWMME:

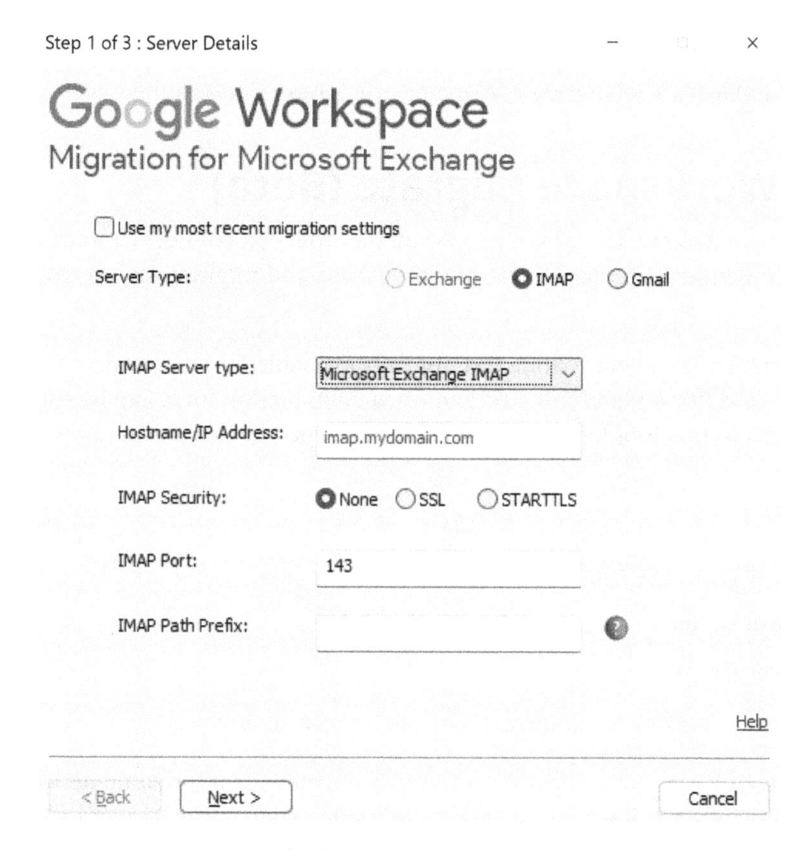


Figure 7.24 – The GWMME application start up screen

The GWMME data migration tool can also be used for migrating archived data into Google Vault for legal eDiscovery purposes.

GWMME can be used when the data sources are the following:

- PST files
- IMAP servers
- Exchange Server 2007
- Exchange Server versions 2010 or above for up to 1,000 users
- Office 365 for up to 1,000 users

> **Important Note**
> Please note that the GWMME tool works with 32-bit Exchange components and not 64-bit.

Let's move on and learn about Google Workspace Migrate (Beta) in the next section.

# Google Workspace Migrate (Beta)

Google Workspace Migrate (Beta) is a migration tool that can connect to sources such as Microsoft Exchange, Box, SharePoint, and OneDrive and migrate data to Google Workspace.

This tool is currently on a beta rollout and not fully available for all domains. If customers want to use this tool for an upcoming migration, an application form can be submitted, requesting access to this tool for migrating data into a specific destination domain.

## Prerequisites

This migration process requires four servers that can serve various purposes:

- A platform server
- A node server
- Two database servers for scanning data and migrating them

Ensure that these servers are compatible and can connect within the same network. These servers are Microsoft Windows-based and configured in such a way to avoid any random OS updates being triggered, interrupting an ongoing migration.

Similarly, port and IP address requirements for these servers are defined here:

`https://support.google.com/workspacemigrate/answer/9222864`

Once the migration servers are ready, let's get the migration user ready. Google admin roles have special privileges for migrations called **Manage Google Workspace Migrate deployments** and **Access Google Workspace Migrate deployments**.

Create a user and assign the appropriate admin role for executing this migration.

As a next step, enable the migration service by following these steps:

1. Log in to the Google **Admin** console.
2. Select **Apps** in the left-hand panel and click on **Additional Google Services**.
3. Select **Services** and then click on **Migrate**.

4. Select the correct OU in the left-hand panel.
5. Enable the **Migrate** setting and click **Save**.

Now that the infrastructure is set up and user access permissions are sorted out, it's time to perform the migration.

The Google Workspace DMS tool has the option to configure all migration settings, add the user mapping list, and run a scan to assess the volume of source data we are going to copy over. This is not a mandatory step; however, it gives you essential information about the amount of data we are processing, and any possible errors are identified ahead of time.

Depending on the source of data, the steps are well defined by Google in this article:

`https://support.google.com/workspacemigrate/answer/9223069?hl=en&ref_topic=9222928`

As you can see, migrating data from external sources can get complicated real fast, as migration typically deals with historical data, missing data, and different data formats. Also, there is a people component in any migration that cannot be forgotten. Employees who are well versed in the new Google Workspace product suite will not only be able to enjoy the benefits the platform provides, but also influence others within the team.

Training employees becomes a critical component that's often neglected.

Google has posted a nifty deployment guide to help organizations that are embarking on a migration journey to Workspace. The deployment guide can be found here:

`https://support.google.com/a/answer/9212586?hl=en`

# Summary

This chapter extensively talked about strategies, mechanisms, and tools for data migration between users within Google Workspace and also bringing data from other platforms over to Workspace.

We started the chapter by focusing on user life cycle changes and the considerations that bring about data a user holds. Suspending, deleting, and archiving users are a few considerations we talked about earlier in the chapter. We also saw how, as part of the Data Liberation Front, Google puts users' data in their hands with ease via its Takeout service. This self-serve option brings in a lot of transparency and paves way for an open, non-vendor lock-in ecosystem for the cloud.

We then moved on to talk about data migration tools for connecting with external sources and bringing in users from other platforms. GWMME and Google Workspace Migrate (Beta) are two fantastic services that can help you with the cause. And finally, we wrapped up the chapter by linking to Google's deployment planning guide for enterprises. Whatever platform you are on today, you cannot go wrong with migrating over to Google Workspace.

# Business Case Studies

With everything we have learned so far, it is apparent that Google Workspace is here to stay and can solve various problems for companies in this globally interconnected business environment. I would like to elucidate a couple of real-life business case studies that highlight how Google Workspace is helping businesses today.

The first case study will focus on how Google Workspace is helping companies move away from legacy technology and digitally transform how their employees collaborate. The second one will focus on how to reduce the **total cost of ownership** (**TCO**) that is required to maintain and run legacy environments.

For both of these case studies, we will look at a company named ACME with over 1,000 employees. They have been using legacy technology for their mail infrastructure for several years now. This company is looking to modernize its mail infrastructure to support growth across geographic locations internationally.

Let's look at how ACME could potentially approach this digital transformation.

## Case study #1

ACME is considering replacing its existing infrastructure setup with Google Workspace. With hybrid/remote work becoming prevelant, and with users accessing IT systems not just from corporate networks but also from public networks that could be vulnerable, the need to keep company data and systems secure is greater than ever. Toss in **bring your own device** (**BYOD**) policies, and the security landscape gets even more complicated.

There are several things for ACME to consider regarding digital transformation – and usually, this starts with understanding what employees do and want. This knowledge can be gained via a survey given to employees. The survey could tease out employees work preferences, the devices they intend to use, their appetite for going through systemic changes, any challenges they face with the existing system, and so on.

ACME could then map out its digital transformation strategy based on the responses of the employees. Typically, moving to a new system means not only a technical change, but a cultural change as well.

ACME's new technology of choice is Google Workspace and it is important that any current challenges with the legacy system are not amplified as the new technology is rolled out. The planning therefore needs to be meticulous and strategic. The more conversations with stakeholders that are had, the better.

Once ACME is ready to roll out the transformation, the migration strategy looks as follows:

1. Select the suitable Google Workspace SKU for ACME's needs.
2. Create user personas, a matrix to help plan which groups of users require which types of services.
3. Verify domain ownership and define an **Org Unit** (**OU**) structure for groups of users. Based on user personas, users are grouped into hierarchical Org Units.
4. Create a security deployment guide using the security checklist posted by Google at `https://support.google.com/a/answer/7587183?hl=en`.

    I. Every security setting can be configured for a specific Org Unit.

5. Create two sets of users for this deployment:

    A. **Core IT users**, the initial set of users starting to use Google Workspace and familiarizing themselves with the environment.

    B. **Early Adopter users**, the second set of users, who are important users representing their team or department and are eager to learn the new environment. These users will use Google Workspace for their daily business operations to confirm whether all their required tasks are possible on the new system, and whether there are any manual processes that need to be automated during this deployment.

    This step is also crucial because it helps the deployment team plan for other decision points such as mobile device management, the number of conference rooms required, and the number of support personnel required, among other things.

6. Based on the feedback from the two sets of users deployed so far, create change management resources including the following:

    - User training resources
    - Quick reference materials

- FAQ s
- A **Sites** page showing the project timeline and milestones
- Communication email templates for various stages of this deployment project
- A post-go-live support plan

7. Plan the data migration date and the final go-live when all the remaining users are added to Google Workspace.

Assuming the migration is successful and all users are fully deployed on the new system and are using Google Workspace, it is now time to think about the future. There are settings within the Google **Admin** console to enable new features as they are released. The **Scheduled Release** and **Rapid Release** tracks can help set the pace at which new features are rolled out for users.

When administrators choose the **Rapid Release** track for the account, users will be among the first to see new features when they are released. On the other hand, signing up for **Scheduled Release** means users get new features one week after they are released. The **Scheduled Release** track therefore helps organizations plan for upcoming changes.

The release track can be changed by going to **Account settings** and selecting **Preferences**.

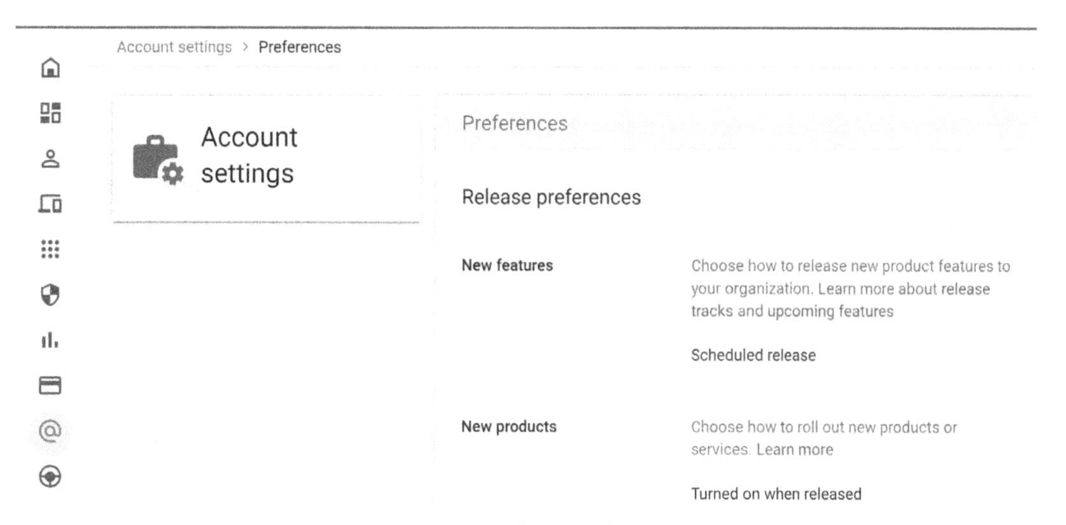


Figure 8.1 – Release preferences

Besides this, admins can stay ahead of upcoming features by subscribing to the blogs and Google Workspace release calendar.

Keeping users in mind through continued advocacy is valuable in efforts to keep adoption rates stable. There are templates available in Google Workspace Learning Center to help you create and run targeted transformation workshops to check how users are adapting to the new system and processes.

We will wrap up this case study by pointing to the excellent deployment guide that Google has put together to tackle migrations in large organizations. The deployment guide is available at the following URL:

```
https://support.google.com/a/answer/9212586?amp;ref_
topic=9212749&product_name=UnuFlow&hl=en&ref_
topic=9212749&visit_id=637797976936911775-2165288518&rd=1&src=
supportwidget0&hl=en
```

Let's now move on to the second case study.

# Case study #2

In this case study, we will look at how ACME can benefit from adopting Google Workspace in terms of cost savings over the years.

Typically, TCO is calculated as the sum of the purchase price for a product, plus the operating costs over the lifespan of that product. We will drill down into the operating costs for Google Workspace and how Workspace helps companies reduce costs in this case study.

There are certain hidden areas that won't be immediately apparent as the operating costs are computed. For instance, the following areas are some of those that are typically not visible:

- By letting employees collaborate better while working remotely, Google Workspace saves time and improves productivity for ACME.
- Google Workspace mitigates security risks for ACME by taking care of several compliance needs and generally being secure. For instance, its powerful anti-spam feature lets almost no spam emails in, which translates to users not wasting time reading those emails.
- ACME doesn't need to spend hundreds of thousands of dollars annually for server hosting and utility bills.

Also, with a wide array of services, Google Workspace allows ACME to consolidate the collaboration software vendors it relies on into just one. Prior to Workspace, ACME was using a few different vendors to satisfy its collaboration needs.

To expand on this further, ACME was previously using these tools and solutions for collaboration:

- Computers
- A network provider for internet connectivity
- Software for mail services
- A content management solution
- Web hosting software
- Telephony communication services
- A video conference meeting solution
- A messaging solution to communicate via text messages among employees
- A task management solution
- A whiteboarding solution
- Training tools for employees, both for annual training for existing users and for new employee onboarding
- A financial solution to track business performance numbers
- And to tie this all together, an authentication system with a **single sign-on** (**SSO**) user experience for employees.

With Google Workspace, a single license provides all these services, making tool consolidation a breeze. This not only helps by consolidating multiple vendors and reducing the costs associated with them, but also reduces the time spent on maintaining each of these services. Each of these solutions may also have required a knowledge expert for troubleshooting issues reported by users. This overhead is directly reduced by switching to the comprehensive platform provided by Workspace.

The time saved through this consolidation of resources can be put to better use in building innovative solutions that can improve ACME's overall core competency. For ACME's employees, Google Workspace turns out to be a one-stop solution they need to familiarize themselves with, instead of 50 other tools. The need to switch between multiple systems for each business operation is mitigated, and the steep learning involved in learning different systems is also eliminated.

The anxieties around new employee onboarding and having to constantly learn multiple systems are reduced, improving employee satisfaction ratings as the company set out to do. Eventually, these small changes also improve employee retention rates at ACME.

The business value generated by Google Workspace is immense, and I hope companies adopt Workspace to bring these tangible benefits to how they work.

# Index

## Symbols


2-step verification (2SV)
  about 60, 62
  key options 62


## A


absolute cell references
  versus relative cell references 166
Access Google Workspace Migrate deployments 224
administrator
  Google Takeout, using as 205, 206
admin roles 28
advanced email authentication methods
  DKIM 72
  DMARC 71
  Sender Policy Framework 71
Ajax 5
Alert Center
  about 112
  alert 114
  alerts, creating 113
  examples 114
  obtaining 113
  rules 113, 114
API controls 90
application programming interface (API) 147
applications
  configuring, in Workspace 47, 48
AppSheet
  about 186, 188
  app, building 188-193
  Core edition 186
  enabling 187
  Enterprise Plus edition 186
  Enterprise Standard edition 186
  Starter edition 186
  URL 188
Apps Script
  about 162
  adding, for Google Docs 180, 181
  code editor 165, 166
  custom menu item, creating 168-173
  Google Forms, using with 177-180
  Hello World! program 163-165
  macros 166
  macros, accessing 167, 168
  reference link 162
  security best practices 185

Sheets APIs, using with Gmail 173-177
web application, creating 182-184
Archived User (AU) 201
artificial intelligence/machine learning (AI/ML) feature 53
AU license 202
automated device management 121-123
automatic license assignment
enabling 46

## B

BeyondCorp model 58
Bring Your Own Device (BYOD) 28

## C

calendar data
importing 218, 219
Calendar VPAT
reference link 159
carbon-neutral data centers 8, 9
Clever
about 136
URL 136
commenter 72
Context-Aware Access
about 58
conceptual model 59
configuring 59, 60
with Cloud Identity 59
custom menu item
creating 168-173
Custom Retention policy 85

## D

data
transferring, any time 203, 204
transferring, during deletion of users 204
Data Liberation Front initiative
about 204
reference link 204
data loss prevention (DLP)
about 107
rule application, scope 110
rule templates 110, 111
usage scenarios 108
workflow 109
data migration
steps 210
Data Migration Service (DMS)
about 211
data sources 211
used, for transferring from personal Gmail and calendars to Google Workspace 212
data regions
editions 116
data regions policy
configuring 116, 117
data transfers
within Google Workspace 198
Default Retention policy 85
detector
creating, in DLP interface 108
device management
about 29
context-aware access 30
device approval/blocking 30
passcode enforcement 29

remote account wipe 30
remote sign-out 29
DLP detector
triggering, conditions 111
DMS
used, for importing Gmail 214-217
domain
about 20
verifying 22, 23
domain aliases
versus secondary domains 24-26
Domain-based Message Authentication, Reporting, and Conformance (DMARC) 53, 71
domain host
versus Google Workspace 20
DomainKeys Identified Mail (DKIM) 53, 72
Domain Name System (DNS)
about 21, 51
failures, reasons 21
DoubleClick 12
download your data service 204
Drive for Desktop 76
dynamic groups 30
Dynamic Host Configuration Protocol (DHCP) 21

## E

eDiscovery 86
editions, Cloud Identity
Free 31
Premium 31
reference link 31
editor 72
endpoint management 117
end-user security
2-step verification 62
about 60
password monitoring 61
Enom 24
Enterprise data regions 116

## F

Federal Information Security Management Act (FISMA) 6
files
transferring, in Google Drive 203, 204
Fundamental data regions 116

## G

General Data Protection Regulation (GDPR) 115
Gmail
about 5, 9, 68
auto-forwarding, setting up 212, 213
compliance 70
data, importing with DMS 214-217
default routing 69
enabling 51, 52, 68
end-user access 70
hosts 69
quarantines 70
references, for scopes 149
safety 70
user settings 69
Gmail VPAT
reference link 159
GoDaddy 24
Google
additional services 50, 51
Google+ 9

Google Analytics 26
Google App Engine 26
Google apps
  security 67
Google Apps for Business 6
Google Apps for Your Domain 6
Google Apps Manager (GAM) tool
  about 134
  reference link 134
Google Apps Premier Edition 6
Google Assistant, for Google Workspace
  about 152, 153
  Nest Hub 153
  Search and Assistant service,
    enabling 154, 155
Google Calendar
  about 9, 77, 78
  advanced settings 79
  general settings 78
  interoperability 80
  resources 79
  resources, sharing 53
  sharing settings 79
Google Chat
  about 10, 81
  ChatBots 82
  External Chat 82
  History for Chats 81
  History for Chat Spaces 82
  Smart Features 81
Google Chromebooks 14
Google Classroom
  about 12, 130, 131
  class settings 134-136
  enabling 131, 132
  grades 136
  Guardian access settings 134
  rosters 136
  settings, managing 132, 133
  student unenrollment 136, 137
  Teacher permissions settings 133, 134
  URL 132
  users 130
Google Cloud Directory Sync (GCDS)
  checklist 43, 44
  configurations 43
  download link 41
  of users 41, 42
  scheduled sync 44
  simulation mode 44
  using 40, 41
Google Cloud Identity
  about 28
  device management 29
  dynamic groups 30
  editions 31
  features 29
  groups 30
  multi-factor authentication (MFA) 29
  OUs, configuring 31-33
  single sign-on (SSO) 29
  users, adding 34
  users, configuring 33, 34
Google Cloud Platform (GCP) 30, 221
Google Cloud Search 10
Google Contacts 10
Google Currents 9
Google Docs
  about 5
  Apps Script, adding to 180, 181
Google Docs Editors 10
Google Drive
  about 6, 10, 72
  content, transferring 203
  files, transferring 203, 204

Google Drive and Docs, settings
  Add-ons 77
  Drive for Desktop 76
  Drive SDK API 77
  labels 76
  offline access 76
  Shared Drive Management 76
  Shared Drive settings 75
  sharing settings 75
  Smart Compose, within Documents 76
  templates 77
  transferring ownership 77
Google Drive File Stream 17
Google Education for Classroom Fundamentals 130
Google Forms
  about 10
  using, in Apps Script 177-180
Google for Work 6
Google Groups for Business 10
Google Jamboard 6, 11
Google Keep 9, 11
Google Marketplace apps
  about 137-140
  managing 140, 141
Google Meet
  about 10, 82
  interoperability 84
  live stream 83
  meeting safety 84
  Meet Quality Tool 84
  recording 83
  telephony 83
  virtual backgrounds 83
Google News 12
Google Scholar 12
Google Sheets 10
Google Sites
  about 11, 84
  custom URL 85
  sharing settings 84
  templates 85
Google Slides 10
Google Takeout
  about 203, 204
  using, as administrator 205, 206
  using, as user 207-209
Google Tasks 11
Google Vault
  about 11, 85
  rules 86, 87
Google Voice 11
Google Workspace
  applications, configuring 47, 48
  core services 49, 50
  data transfers 198
  domain, verifying 22, 23
  editions, selecting 19, 20
  evolution 4
  Google services 12
  licensing models 12
  portfolio 9
  reference link 7
  services 9-11
  users, accessibility 158, 159
  versus domain host 20
Google Workspace add-ons 11
Google Workspace Assured Controls 11
Google Workspace Business editions
  about 15
  Business Plus 15
  Business Standard 15
  Business Starter 15
  comparing 16
  features 15

Google Workspace editions
reports 99
Google Workspace Education editions
about 12
comparing 14
features 13
Fundamentals 12
Plus 13
Standard 12
Teaching and Learning Upgrade 12
Google Workspace Enterprise editions
about 16-19
comparing 18
features 17
security and compliance features 16
Google Workspace for Education
about 130
reference link 131
Google Workspace Migrate (Beta)
about 211, 224
prerequisites 224, 225
Google Workspace Migration for Microsoft Exchange (GWMME)
about 211, 220
data source, organizing 222, 223
prerequisites 221
Google Workspace Migration for Microsoft Outlook (GWMMO)
about 211
URL 211
Google Workspace Security Center
about 94
security services 95
Google Workspace services
add-ons 141-145
Google Workspace Sync for Microsoft Outlook (GWSMO)
download link 158
using 158
groups
reference link 30
G Suite 6, 7

## H

human resource information systems (HRIS) 40

## I

ICANN Lookup
URL 22
identity and access management (IAM) 30
identity management system (IMS) 28
identity providers (IdPs) 40, 63
Information Resource Management (IRM) 73
Internet Corporation for Assigned Names and Numbers (ICANN) 22
Internet Message Access Protocol (IMAP) 155, 211

## J

JavaScript 5

## L

labels 76
ldapsearch 67
LDAP server
user data, syncing with 35

licenses
  assigning, manually to users 47
  managing 45
low-code development platform 186
Luhn algorithm 108

## M

macros
  recording in Sheets 166-168
mail clients
  access, enabling 156, 157
mail exchange (MX) records 68
mail exchanger (MX) records 51
Manage Google Workspace
    Migrate deployments 224
Marketplace apps 88, 89
Microsoft Hotmail 5
Microsoft Word 10
mobile management
  advanced 118, 119
  basic 118, 119
  workflow 119-121
multi-factor authentication (MFA)
  about 29
  verification methods 29
My Drive
  about 72
  expiring access 73
  Information Resource
    Management (IRM) 73

## N

near-field communication (NFC) 62
Nest Hub 153

## O

one-time passcode (OTP) 29
OUs
  configuring, in Cloud Identity 31-33

## P

password monitoring
  about 61
  recommendations 61
password vaulted apps
  using 64-66
PDF 10
personally identifiable information
    (PII) 70, 107
Personal Storage Table (PST)
    file format 220
Post Office Protocol (POP) 155
power users 70
pre-integrated apps
  enabling, in domain 63, 64
productivity suite 4
Progressive Web App (PWA) 81

## R

rainbow table attacks 62
Record Macro feature 166
reports 123-125
resources
  sharing, via Calendar 53
Room Insights Dashboard 80

## S

SaaS 4
School Information Systems (SISes) 136
Search and Assistant service
  enabling 154, 155
secondary domains
  versus domain aliases 24-26
secure LDAP
  using 66, 67
Security Assertion Markup
    Language (SAML) 63, 138
security dashboard
  about 98
  customizing 100
Security Health page
  about 95
  security settings 96
security investigation tool
  about 101
  audit event type, searching 102
  options, for remediation 103, 104
  query building 102
  use case 101, 102
  using 104-106
Security Investigation Tool 73
Sender Policy Framework (SPF) 53, 71
Service Provider (SP) 63
Shared Drive
  about 73
  roles 75
Shared Drive, access roles for users
  commenter 74
  content manager 74
  contributor 74
  manager 74
  viewer 74
single sign-on (SSO) 29, 59, 63
Sync for Microsoft Outlook 6
Systems, Applications, and Products
    in Data Processing (SAP) 40

## T

third-party applications
  access control 145-152
  auth scope 148
third-party clients
  access, enabling for mail clients 156, 157
  Google Workspace Sync for Microsoft
    Outlook (GWSMO) 158
  using 155
top-level domain (TLD) 21

## U

user data
  large amount of user data, migrating 219
  syncing, with LDAP server 35
  transferring 203
user life cycle
  changes 198
users
  adding, in bulk 34
  adding, to Cloud Identity 34
  archiving 201, 202
  configuring, in Cloud Identity 33, 34
  creating, manually 34
  deleting 36-38
  Google Takeout, using as 207-209
  merging, with unmanaged
    Google Account 35, 36
  recovering 39
  suspending 199, 200

viewer 72
VirusTotal
  about 115
  reputation data 115
Voluntary Product Accessibility
    Template (VPAT) 159

Workspace domain
  preparing 220

YouTube 12

# Other Books You May Enjoy

If you enjoyed this book, you may be interested in these other books by Packt:

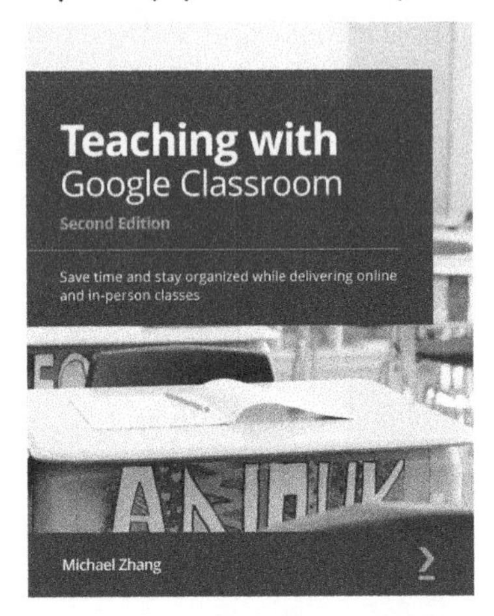


**Teaching with Google Classroom**

Michael Zhang

ISBN: 978-1-80056-592-0

Create a classroom and add customized information for each individual class.

- Send announcements and questions to students.
- Create, distribute, collect, and grade assignments through Google Classroom.
- Link student accounts to guardian emails for daily or weekly updates.
- Use Google Forms to create quizzes that automatically grade and return results to students

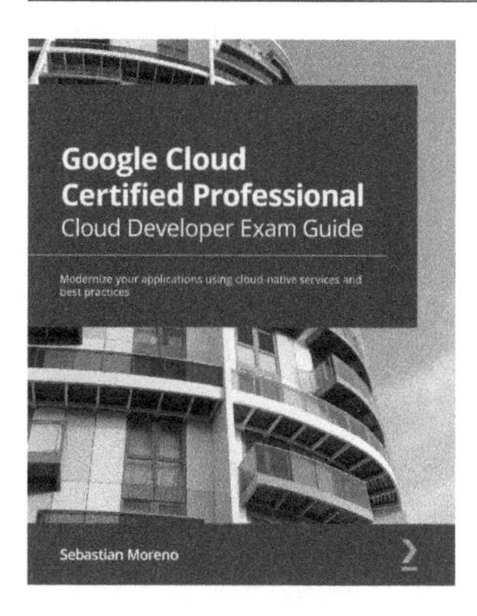


**Google Cloud Certified Professional Cloud Developer Exam Guide**

Sebastian Moreno

ISBN: 978-1-80056-099-4

- Get to grips with the fundamentals of Google Cloud Platform development.
- Discover security best practices for applications in the cloud.
- Find ways to create and modernize legacy applications.
- Understand how to manage data and databases in Google Cloud.
- Explore best practices for site reliability engineering, monitoring, logging, and debugging.

## Packt is searching for authors like you

If you're interested in becoming an author for Packt, please visit `authors.packtpub.com` and apply today. We have worked with thousands of developers and tech professionals, just like you, to help them share their insight with the global tech community. You can make a general application, apply for a specific hot topic that we are recruiting an author for, or submit your own idea.

Hi!

I am Balaji Iyer, author of *Google Workspace User Guide*. We really hope you enjoyed reading this book and found it useful for increasing your productivity and efficiency in Google Workspace.

It would really help us (and other potential readers!) if you could leave a review on Amazon sharing your thoughts on *Google Workspace User Guide*.

Go to the link below or scan the QR code to leave your review:

`https://packt.link/r/1801073007`

Your review will help me to understand what's worked well in this book, and what could be improved upon for future editions, so it really is appreciated.

Best Wishes,

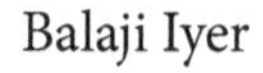

Balaji Iyer

CPSIA information can be obtained
at www.ICGtesting.com
Printed in the USA
LVHW061024140922
728359LV00009B/201

9 781801 073004